When Tengu Talk

When Tengu Talk

Hirata Atsutane's Ethnography
of the Other World

Wilburn Hansen

University of Hawai'i Press
Honolulu

Library of Congress Cataloging-in-Publication Data
Hansen, Wilburn.
  When tengu talk : Hirata Atsutane's ethnography
of the other world / Wilburn Hansen.
    p. cm.
  Includes bibliographical references and index.
  ISBN 978-0-8248-3209-4 (hard cover : alk. paper)
  1. Hirata, Atsutane, 1776–1843. 2. Hirata, Atsutane,
1776–1843. Senkyo hibun. 3. Japan—Religion. 4. Takayama,
Torakichi, b. 1806. 5. Mediums—Japan. 6. Kokugaku. I. Title.
  B5244.H474H36 2008
  181'.12—dc22
                          2008018603

FRONTIS ART: Tengu Boy Torakichi *(left)* and Hirata Atsutane *(right).*
Source: *Hirata Atsutane zenshu* (1911)

Designed by University of Hawai'i Press Production Department
Printed by The Maple-Vail Book Manufacturing Group

Contents

Acknowledgments

This book is the culmination of work first conceived in my master's program more than a decade ago at the University of Colorado. As such I need to start my acknowledgments by giving thanks to Edmund Gilday, who encouraged me then and continues to support my efforts. Because of that start I was able to continue my studies at Stanford University under the guidance of Professors Bernard Faure and Carl Bielefeldt, who both continue to inspire me to better my scholarship and become a teacher who motivates and inspires. I would also like to thank my fellow students at Stanford with whom I forged lifelong personal and professional bonds, especially those with whom I spent long hours in *samadhi* under the Bodhi Tree outside the Coho—you know who you are. I must also acknowledge the patience, persistence, and criticisms of my readers and editors at the University of Hawai'i Press, especially Patricia Crosby. She saw the value in this project from the beginning and forced me to make my work better than I thought it could be. If I appear articulate and somewhat literate that is where the credit lies. I also must thank my wife Kelly for making my work intelligible. She proofed, edited, and critiqued every line before anyone else, for which she did not always receive my highest words of praise. It is also clear to me that I could not have written this book without someone picking up the slack on the home and work front when I stayed home all day writing and cursing while living in our rabbit hutch those wonderful years in Yokohama. So double and triple thanks are due to Kelly. I would also like to remember and thank in print my departed parents Wilburn Nels Hansen Sr. and Mitsue Ishikawa. If you do not like what you read in the book then blame the Pacific War for bringing those two opposites together.

A New Medium for an Old Message

The (Dis) Enchanting New Medium and
the Importance of *Senkyō ibun*

The Japanese religious academician Hirata Atsutane (1776–1843) has been the subject of hundreds of scholarly studies undertaken by Japanese intellectuals of varying types beginning not long after his death and continuing into the twenty-first century. Atsutane's prodigious output of written text and transcribed lectures still leaves room for, in fact begs for, new discoveries and fresh analyses in this new century of scholarship on Japanese religion. Western scholars of the last century, most notably Donald Keene and Carmen Blacker,[1] have confirmed Atsutane's importance to the Western academy by their recognition and inclusion of his idiosyncratic writings and interests in their own academic publications. Yet within the virtual forest of writings Atsutane left us, there are still too many "shady" areas in need of illumination. These "shady" areas, in my opinion, call for an attempt to cast light on topics ignored in the previous century of Atsutane scholarship.

In the early nineteenth century this nativist[2] scholar proposed a vision for a new Japan, a vision inherited and refined from his intellectual inspiration, Motoori Norinaga (1730–1801), recognized then and now as the greatest of all nativist scholars. In this vision, Japan was second to none in all things and owed nothing except its shortcomings to the influence of foreign cultures. Atsutane writes:

> All the world's peoples refer to Japan as the Land of the Kami. In addition, they say that we are all noble descendants of the *kami*, and in fact, they are not wrong. Our noble country was born from *kami*, uniquely blessed by the Kami of Heaven.[3] There is a world of difference between Japan and all other countries; in fact, there is no comparison. Japan is surpassingly blessed and clearly is the Land of the Kami. Even the humblest man and woman in Japan is an actual descendant of the *kami*. Given this certain

> truth, I find it extremely regrettable that there are so many Japanese peo-
> ple who do not recognize the fundamental fact that this is the Land of the
> Kami, and that they are the descendants of the *kami*.[4]

In Atsutane's mind, the reason so many Japanese people did not recognize
this "fundamental fact" was that the proponents of Indian, Chinese, and
Western cultures stood in the way of their realization of this elemental
truth. He saw the common Japanese as guilty of championing these foreign cultures—in their guises of Buddhism, Chinese studies,[5] and Dutch
studies—in ways that flatly contradicted Atsutane's nativist vision. Furthermore, unlike Atsutane's nativist teachings, these other discourses were
supported by the traditional and authoritative weight of great masses of
historical, religious, and scientific text. Atsutane himself begrudgingly val-
idated these non-nativist sources in his own lectures and writings by often
quoting the Ming Buddhist canon, the Confucian and Neo-Confucian classics, and Western religious and scientific texts.

Atsutane was frustrated by this dependence on the very discourses he
despised, and he knew that his alternative vision could not be credibly supported by the same methods used by his competitors, so he embarked on a
lifelong project of discrediting, subverting, and even co-opting those "foreign" writings, claiming some of them to be of Japanese origin. But in the
middle of his career he developed a new strategy. Fate and his own cun-
ning delivered a new medium into his hands, an affirmative way to create
a new counterdiscourse that supported his new vision of Japan. Atsutane
himself chronicled the appearance of that new, carefully premeditated
strategy and its implementation in his often misunderstood work *Senkyō
ibun*, which Carmen Blacker translated in the 1960s as "Strange Tidings
from the Realm of Immortals."

Atsutane wrote *Senkyō ibun* in 1822. It is a voluminous work centered
upon his interviews with the so-called *tengu*[6] Kozō Torakichi. Deeply interested in supernatural[7] experiences, Atsutane was captivated by Torakichi's
claim that supernatural experiences were part of his everyday life for several years of his early youth. In *Senkyō ibun*, Atsutane records approximately eight months of interaction with the Tengu Boy, who was to live in
his house for the following several years.

Senkyō ibun has not been considered the most important or defini-
tive work in Hirata Atsutane's impressive corpus of writings. That distinction most often goes to *The August Pillar of the Soul* (*Tama no mihashira*).
Although this study focuses on *Senkyō ibun*, it is not an attempt to displace
The August Pillar of the Soul and claim that distinction for *Senkyō ibun*. My
more modest aim is to present a deeper, more nuanced understanding of

the *Senkyō ibun* text and hence a fuller view of Atsutane's religious convictions and aspirations. And even though *Senkyō ibun* may not displace *The August Pillar of the Soul,* there is no question in my mind that to undervalue *Senkyō ibun* is to completely misunderstand Hirata Atsutane.

From the genesis of Atsutane studies in nineteenth-century Japan, the undervaluing of this particular text because of its emphasis on the "superstitious" and "supernatural" helped enable scholars and students of Japanese religion to overlook Atsutane's historical link to twentieth-century *minzokugaku,*[8] Japanese folklore studies, as well as organized Japanese occult mysticism of the later nineteenth and twentieth centuries. For the longest time, Atsutane studies in Japan and the West were content to focus on his contribution to the construction of nationalist state religion in Japan. The unavoidable problem with that approach is that it shaped the conclusions of such studies by assuming a goal not yet imagined by Atsutane himself.

Any in-depth study of Atsutane's life will certainly reveal that he was completely absorbed with the task of building a reputation for his academy, his new school of *kokugaku,* along with his controversial new theories within the Japanese intellectual milieu of the 1820s and 1830s. His largest contribution to religion in his day lay in his investigations of what we might today call folk religion/superstition and the occult, not imperial restoration. The voluminous record of common nineteenth-century Japanese religious belief and practice, which makes up most of the content of *Senkyō ibun,* thus becomes the strongest reason why it among all of Atsutane's works deserves reconsideration and re-evaluation.

There was a time not so long ago when Atsutane was considered by scholars both Japanese and Western to be an unwanted detour on Japan's road to modernity, mainly because of his mystical and spiritual biases, which caused him to value irrational religious experience over rational thought. There was also a postwar tendency on the Japanese side of scholarship to avoid serious consideration of Atsutane's thought because of a prejudice in Western scholarship that aligned him with the forces of authoritarianism, militarism, and fascism. Atsutane was implicated after the fact in the reinstitution of premodern emperor worship[9] and the production of a fascist and nationalist ideology of Japanese superiority.

In the latter half of the twentieth century there was a re-evaluation of Atsutane's thought, a new wave of critical thinking about his work. Yet while Atsutane studies have been distanced from the Pacific War, Atsutane's work has come to be seen as a precursor to the process of Japan's modernization. To place Atsutane within the modernization process makes him a part of a master narrative that tends to ignore any historical particulars that do not support that narrative. As a result, Atsutane once again becomes known for his contribution to a historical context that had not yet come into existence, or merely existed as a barely recognizable prototype, in his time.

In other words, those master narrative studies have anachronistically defined Atsutane's role in history. For example, because Atsutane attempted to elevate the spiritual status of the Japanese common man and made a direct appeal to the Japanese peasant, he is credited with leading a movement for the democratization of religion. He is sometimes also credited as the creator of a set of beliefs that became the foundation for a Shinto-based folk religion focusing on guardian deities, a religion said to have resulted in reinforced feelings of community in the Japanese countryside. In addition, he is sometimes portrayed as an important force in the intellectual history of Japan who is thought to have helped develop a new model of Japanese identity required for effective adaptation to Japan's role in the modern world. Finally, he is sometimes seen as the first to study spiritualism in an attempt to form a purely Shinto understanding of the soul and the afterlife. In short, Hirata Atsutane, the man and his work, has been comprehensively packaged and explained in terms of how he helps complete the modern scholar's version of Japanese history.

In recent years in Japan, there has been scholarly work that once again reconsiders and re-evaluates Hirata Atsutane's work, but this time focusing on his contribution to Tokugawa religion. Since Western scholarship has yet to respond adequately to this development, it is incumbent upon us to move in this new direction. Atsutane is still best-known to Western academe for his radical racist, nationalist ideas, and also as the founder of the Hirata School of Shinto that helped engineer the persecution of Buddhism and the establishment of a State Shinto in the early days of the Meiji Restoration. The problem with that reputation is that Atsutane, who died in 1843, was nowhere near the scene of the crime. Viewed through the lens of the Pacific War and the Meiji Restoration, Atsutane's historical importance has been defined by those events. Unfortunately, those are definitions that not only distort his legacy but also divest it of its fascinating detail, diversity, and depth.

When Atsutane died in 1843, he had approximately 550 students registered in his academy, and many of his works had been printed, reprinted, and widely distributed. Within a generation after his death, the size of his academy had increased almost tenfold, as had the number of his publications. While he was alive, he was hired as an instructor of Shinto priests in both the Yoshida and Shirakawa shrine houses. He hobnobbed with many influential intellectuals and was patronized by wealthy and powerful men. He was influential and controversial enough to be censored and sent into exile by the Tokugawa government. There is enough of an impressive résumé here to warrant attention for his role in the development of Japanese religion.

The simple fact that a figure so active in the world of religion had written a significant book detailing human contact with ghosts, demons, spirits, monsters, and gods in the world of the afterlife would, one would think, have attracted much interest and study. Yet this religiously rich aspect of this work, *Senkyō ibun*, has received little attention in the West. The religion in the text has received only cursory questioning and has been summarily relegated to the genre of folklore and superstition, and as such is ignored by scholars of religion.

On top of that, and in some ways equally important, continuing to pigeonhole Atsutane as merely a nationalist, thus undervaluing and overlooking this particular text as the ravings of a fascist crackpot, deprives us all of an astonishing true story that describes in great detail the intellectual salon society of early nineteenth-century Edo. *Senkyō ibun* tells the story of an impoverished but imaginative and talented waif from the slums of old Edo whose claim to have been raised by supernatural beings in the mountains of Japan caused him to be paraded through the salons of the intellectual elite of Edo society by a superstitious and ambitious leader of a rising religious and political movement. Those circumstances alone make the story interesting enough to warrant attention.

Yet the first and last time this fascinating text was the focal point of any lengthy consideration in English was in 1967, when Carmen Blacker published an article that translated several passages from the work and provided an overall description and assessment.[10] Her coverage of the text took up the major part of her article, titled "Supernatural Abductions in Japanese Folklore." Blacker, however, admitted in her piece that *Senkyō ibun* was

> not an entirely representative example of our theme [supernatural abduction]. It lacks also something of the visionary, fantastical quality of the earlier tales. There is something curiously matter of fact about Torakichi's detailed description of the Other World on Mt. Iwama which will disappoint those accustomed to the enchantments of Celtic fairylands. . . . For this disenchantment we should blame Hirata, for whom the story in all its matter of factness was undoubtedly deeply satisfying. The very quality of familiarity, of closeness to the humans, was welcome to him as confirming his theory that the afterworld was not fraught with dark and fearful terrors, but a pleasant replica of our own.[11]

Blacker used the story of Tengu Boy Torakichi as an example of a folk-lore pattern of the supernatural abduction of children, examples of which she believed could be seen throughout the world. As the vehicle and a reason for *Senkyō ibun* to be brought to light in English, the folklorist's attention is welcome. However, this text has a more interesting story to tell if we background the folklore angle and feature the "disenchantment" that Blacker felt Hirata found so "deeply satisfying." Although many of the elements of Torakichi's stories are fantastic, they are his personal stories, not actually folk tales. Furthermore, although I agree with Blacker that Atsutane is to be blamed/credited for the disenchantment of the tales, his more serious offense was abducting Torakichi and his supernatural stories and using them not merely to confirm his theory of the pleasant afterworld, but, more importantly, to construct a supernatural identity for living Japanese people.

What Blacker seems to be disappointed in most is the "matter of fact-ness" and the "disenchantment," which she attributed to Atsutane's influence. We can see that she thought these characteristics, in particular, were actually what made the stories welcome and satisfying to Atsutane. Therefore, she has also recognized just that point of incongruity that further distances Torakichi's tales from any folklore paradigms and signals that Torakichi's stories have another story to tell.

Torakichi was the informant, the named source of *Senkyō ibun*, but Atsutane wrote the book. Atsutane asked the questions, edited the answers, and provided the commentary. Besides that, he supported and educated Tengu Boy Torakichi, the alleged narrator, for years before, during, and after the drafting of this work. If these fantastic stories seem disenchanted and matter-of-fact, and if this situation appeared to please the writer, editor, and publisher, Atsutane, might he not have participated in the production of these stories to influence their outcome? If that is the case, then for what purpose did he make such an effort? Torakichi's stories of personal involvement with *kami*, demons, spirits, and monsters are fascinating in and of themselves, but Atsutane's involvement in disenchanting and factualizing the fantastic is an equally fascinating tale—the tale that will be told at length in the following pages.

Torakichi and Atsutane: Leading Conclusions of Recent Japanese Scholarship

Kamata Tōji published the most recent in-depth treatment of Atsutane and Torakichi in Japanese in 2002.[12] In this work he envisioned Torakichi

and Atsutane's interactions and Atsutane's subsequent writings about Torakichi as evidence of the depth of Atsutane's spirituality. Kamata argued
that Atsutane saw in Torakichi the means of verifying his own romantic
and passionate belief in a pleasant afterlife, a motivation that was also
suggested by Blacker in the 1960s. Moreover, Atsutane clearly indicated in
the first pages of his most famous work, *The August Pillar of the Soul*, in
1812 that the establishment of a firm belief in a pleasant afterlife for the
Japanese people was the essential goal of that work. Due to that, Kamata's
and Blacker's answer has been a common and recurring theme in Atsutane studies for at least a hundred years.

Atsutane's predecessor, Motoori Norinaga, had posited that according
to the ancient Japanese histories, the afterlife was lived in an unpleasant
and defiled world. This was the subterranean afterlife seen in the ancient
stories of Izanagi's attempt to bring his dead wife Izanami back to the
world of the living. Norinaga insisted that as unpleasant as it was, it was the
only afterlife available for the Japanese people. Furthermore, his methods
of investigation into the nature of the world did not allow him to discover
or uncover any other afterlife. Atsutane was not similarly constrained. He
argued against his self-styled teacher,[13] Norinaga, that there was a pleasant
but usually unseen Other World,[14] where the soul went when one died. In
volumes of his published essays and lectures we can see Atsutane's vigor-
ous attempts to back up this opposing theory of the afterlife.

Kamata further argued that Atsutane had been searching for other
ways to prove that the Other World of the afterlife existed, and that he
especially wanted to make contact with that world. Kamata claimed that
Atsutane desired a pleasant afterlife because his own personal life was
filled with tragedy. As evidence, he gave Atsutane's own statements about
his childhood problems and insecurities, and he emphasized the devasta-
tion Atsutane displayed when he lost his beloved first wife and his only
two sons.[15] Kamata also analyzed the personal situation and even the personal appearance of Atsutane to produce a psychological profile of a person who needed to believe in a pleasant afterlife and therefore was particularly receptive to Torakichi's stories and other stories like them.[16]

Koyasu Nobukuni is the foremost living Atsutane scholar, and his latest contribution to the field that contains analysis and commentary on
Atsutane and Torakichi was published in 2001.[17] Koyasu also concluded
that Atsutane was searching for a way to prove his theory of the destination of the soul after death. Koyasu argued that Atsutane questioned Torakichi to study this Other World and that Atsutane and his followers were
only interested or convinced by Torakichi insofar as he told them what

they wanted to hear. Koyasu's conclusion was that Atsutane met Torakichi while in the midst of creating a new worldview for late Tokugawa society, and his mystical or spiritual research was one means to that end.

Both of these recent analyses of *Senkyō ibun* agree that Atsutane was involved in a project that involved establishing a new cosmology, which would have an afterlife that provided comfort to all Japanese. Koyasu's focus was on the discourse on the Other World and how Atsutane's efforts took a theological and spiritual turn away from previous *kokugaku* philological endeavors. Kamata's study also followed Atsutane's spiritual developments, but Kamata's interest lay in an attempt to reach a phenomenological understanding of that new discourse.

The difference in their approaches is that Koyasu was interested in the overall trajectory of Atsutane's new discourse, the move to spiritual studies or theology, in which, according to Koyasu, lay the difference and therefore the importance of Atsutane's textual compositions. Kamata was concerned with smaller spiritual elements of Atsutane's text and, as a result, was inclined to devote greater effort to the description of the ascetic and spiritual exercises of Atsutane's exalted occupant of the Other World, the *sanjin*, about whom much more will be written later. In addition, Kamata was also interested in understanding Torakichi's spiritual experiences.

Koyasu's reading of *Senkyō ibun* as a new discourse focusing on spiritual studies or a new theology for later religious developments provides a good start, but his approach leaves a wealth of interesting material unmined. Kamata started to flesh out the description of Torakichi and the *sanjin*, but he seemed only interested in what could be seen as spiritual qualities or exercises. Although much detail given in *Senkyō ibun* describes the ritual practices and ascetic ordeals of the *sanjin*, most of the detail is not intended as an explicitly spiritual or religious explanation.

Examining the discourse and ignoring the thick description of *sanjin* overlooks the multiple and important roles and functions Atsutane played in the development of new nativist discourse. He teased out the *sanjin* in his questions to Torakichi because the *sanjin* helped to fill in a hole in his cosmology. The *sanjin* was meant to help Atsutane's discourse successfully compete with those discourses challenging his version of the truth about Japan. Examining the *sanjin* and focusing only on his spirituality depletes the many meanings Atsutane had infused in him. What is to be desired in the present scholarship and what is offered in this study is a thick description of the *sanjin*, arranged in a manner which will show off Atsutane's new multifaceted religious hero as a Shinto holy man armed to the teeth with miraculous power, knowledge, and weaponry to defeat all of Japan's enemies.

In addition, and related to the discovery of the ideological *sanjin*, this study contends that the results of Atsutane's supernatural inquiries should be characterized as a pseudo-ethnographic account of Atsutane's, rather than Torakichi's, imagined world of the supernatural. Atsutane's ethnography needs to be scrutinized to examine the implications of his method and to produce a better understanding of his motivations and intentions. Some Japanese scholars have suggested that Torakichi may have bewitched Atsutane with the promise of providing evidence of something in which Atsutane passionately believed. Others have suggested that Torakichi and Atsutane had areas of shared belief and that Atsutane exploited those areas by having his mystical medium speak for him on those points, and by having him do so, Torakichi gave credence and a kind of divine authority to Atsutane's teachings.

What has been neglected is that there is enough evidence to strongly suggest that Atsutane used Torakichi as a medium to spread his own message. This study will show that Atsutane himself spirited away, coerced, and seduced Tengu Boy Torakichi. Torakichi, though, soon learned his role and participated actively[18] in the joint creation of a public spectacle in Edo society that was to give birth, at least in Atsutane's imagination, to the new Japanese superman and culture hero, the *sanjin*.

Overview of Atsutane Studies in the West

There have been a number of studies of Hirata Atsutane undertaken in the West in the 150 years or so since his death. Ernest Satow was first in 1875 when he came out with a study of the *kokugaku* scholars, with Atsutane getting the bulk of the attention.[19] However, in 1905 William Aston, in his work entitled *Shinto*, commented that "the writings of the eighteenth and nineteenth century scholars amount to a voluminous literature, no part of which has been, or is likely to be translated."[20] One hundred years later, Aston's prediction remains nearly accurate in Atsutane's case.[21]

The Pacific War put an additional damper on any hope for Atsutane studies for a long time. In the 1950s, Donald Keene wrote about Atsutane and Western learning,[22] and in the ensuing fifty years,[23] Atsutane studies in the English language have been haphazard and erratic. The earlier studies, besides filling in biographical data, focused on his nationalistic teachings and his ethnocentric theory of Japanese superiority, and they even uncovered his "hypocritical appropriation" of Western sources.[24] Later studies managed to find new directions and eventually leveled their focus on the development of his academy and the social milieu of late Edo Japan from whence he sprang and on which he had an undeniable influence.[25]

Recently, an American scholar of Atsutane devoted several pages to the story of Torakichi and Atsutane's *Senkyō ibun* in two separate publications. They are not the focus of either publication, but in an academic drought such as this, they are an oasis of scholarship and only serve to emphasize the need for more work in this field, an assertion that this study intends to justify.[26] In 1998, this scholar, Mark McNally, came out with a convincing dissertation on Atsutane and nativism that explains how Atsutane achieved his position and later reputation within the *kokugaku* movement.[27] In his book *Proving the Way, Conflict and Practice in the History of Japanese Nativism*,[28] published in 2005, McNally includes a short section devoted to Torakichi and *Senkyō ibun* in the chapter called "Forsaking Textualism: Ancient History and the Supernatural." Torakichi is also briefly discussed in McNally's chapter titled "The Proof Is Out There: Hirata Atsutane, Evidential Learning, and the Afterlife," in *Practicing the Afterlife: Perspectives from Japan*, published in 2004.[29]

In otherwise informative and enlightening studies of Atsutane, McNally gives too little attention to the *Senkyō ibun* text and, like the great Atsutane scholar Koyasu Nobukuni before him, overlooks the implications of the *tengu/sanjin* controversy, which is not overlooked by other Japanese scholars and which I contend is central to an understanding of *Senkyō ibun*. In fact, McNally avoids even using the term *sanjin*, which is used frequently in the actual *Senkyō ibun* text, and instead identifies Torakichi's mountain master as "not a true *tengu*, but a member of a special group of mortals who had access to the spirit realm." As a result, I believe McNally is predisposed to underestimate some important implications of the relationship between Torakichi and Atsutane,[30] but on the positive side he generously left it up to this study to mine the long, tedious, and often repetitive *Senkyō ibun* text for the rich analyses and new insights to be presented in the following chapters. In fairness to McNally, his work was not devoted to the story of Torakichi and Atsutane, as this one is, thus the time needed to render what I consider justice to *Senkyō ibun* would not have been warranted for the purposes of his study.

Summary of Chapters

This book is composed of seven chapters. Chapter 1 locates Atsutane in the milieu of 1820s Edo Japan. A rough sketch of the complicated history of ideas and Atsutane's position within that history provides the backdrop against which the drama of *Senkyō ibun* unfolds. Atsutane's stance and attitude toward three powerful "enemy" discourses are articulated and put in context. These discourses originate from within Japan, but each of them concerns what Atsutane conceived as a foreign culture and a threat to the furtherance of his own ideological end. Atsutane's ideological end is shown to be the construction of a unique Japanese cultural identity, one that was clearly separate, independent, and superior to those offered by the three foreign cultures. Atsutane's technique is recognized as being in defiance of the accepted practice of history in his day, and his methodological move beyond the history and philology of his time is characterized as a move toward anthropology and ethnography.

Using examples from Western anthropology as well as East Asian trends that encouraged attempts at scientific explanation, Atsutane's work is explained as an attempt at nineteenth-century armchair, or *zabuton*, ethnography. We may think that the world of the afterlife Atsutane wrote of is imaginary, but we must assume that he did not. The study of a new world and culture required Atsutane to make a methodological move toward ethnographic writing. Therefore, in chapter 1, recent critiques of ethnographic writing are used to analyze the writing of ethnographic narrative. The conclusion is that such writings actually begin to resemble fiction more than they resemble scientific observation. This line of argument is pursued to explain a reading and analysis of *Senkyō ibun* as a work of ethnographic fiction. The goal of the study is to clarify exactly what Atsutane has constructed in these pages, behind the veneer of ethnography, and just how his fiction was masked by what Blacker has called his attempts at "disenchantment" and his "matter of fact" style of storytelling.

Chapter 2 explains the relationship between the implied author and outside narrator: Atsutane the believer in the Ancient Way, and Tengu Boy Torakichi the informant and inside narrator. Their relationship as shown in the text is described, and Atsutane's projections onto his inside narrator are scrutinized. One recurring theme is the portrayal of Torakichi as a believable and reliable narrator and a true witness and participant in fantastic events. One point of intense scrutiny is the meeting between the two main characters, which is portrayed in the book as both fated and fateful for Atsutane and the world. There is also an examination of the setting of the acts of narration and an analysis of how the setting of the action is intended to verify the action. Attention is also paid to Atsutane's recognition of public doubts concerning the boy. These scenes add drama and pathos and ultimately are designed to direct the reader to an appreciation of the faith and courage exhibited by Atsutane when he championed the boy at such high social risk to himself.

Besides establishing the portrayal of the special quality and intimacy of the relationship between Atsutane and Torakichi, another issue of prime importance in this chapter is the questioning of Torakichi's independence

as a narrator of the fantastic tales. The close relationship between the
author and the narrator, or the ethnographer and the informant, gives rise
to the question of whether and to what extent Atsutane has altered Torakichi's stories. Torakichi's dependency on Atsutane and Atsutane's strong
and unbending stance on most issues are enough to raise these doubts, if
not to prove them. However, close analysis of the text concerning important issues of religious and political dogma for Atsutane will reveal manipulation of the informant by the ethnographer. Although manipulation can
be shown at several junctures, this evidence is not meant to suggest that
Atsutane merely employed a religious charlatan or that the two of them
conspired to deceive educated Edo salon society. All evidence points to
Atsutane's believing, or at least wanting or even perhaps needing to believe,
in the Other World, but his personality and his own convictions and intelligence would never allow Torakichi's imagination to exert control over his
own vision of that Other World.

Chapter 3 starts with a rough sketch of the Other World Atsutane
helped Torakichi describe. That world was supposed to be in Japan, yet
inaccessible to most people. A special medium was needed to penetrate
it and bring back descriptions of it. In many ways the Other World was
supposed to be the same as the revealed world, but it was important that
Torakichi also showed it to be qualitatively different. The plants and animals of that world were mostly the same as this world, but on occasion
certain fantastic examples were introduced. The most important aspect
to report about the Other World was the intelligent life that inhabited it.
Kami who inhabited that world were immediately placed beyond the pale;
they were not the objects of Atsutane's research. The quest for intelligent
life in that world first came to focus on the *tengu* who resided there. However, the ultimate goal of the ethnography was to discover the practitioners
of Atsutane's Ancient Way who also resided there. The *tengu* mask these
practitioners had previously hidden behind was taken away to introduce
the new culture hero. The process by which Atsutane discovered the *sanjin*
hiding among the *tengu* is a prime example of how an eager ethnographer
can manipulate a willing native informant into telling him exactly what he
wants to hear.

Chapter 4 shows how Atsutane's nativist discourse concerning the
newly discovered *sanjin* and his independent and superior Japanese cultural identity responded to the challenges from Chinese culture. Norinaga's legacy of hatred for things Chinese and for Japanese sinophiles had
been passed on to Atsutane, and the construction of the figure of the *sanjin* bore traces of that legacy. This chapter samples Atsutane's pre–*Senkyō
ibun*, anti-China arguments and shows the new moves that a Tengu Boy

medium and ethnographic fiction allowed him to make in his struggle to establish a believable independent Japanese culture, even one that boasted its own writing script, free from Chinese characters. At the same time, chapter 4 points out Atsutane's and the *sanjin*'s own deep and continuing debt to Chinese culture.

Chapter 5 details Atsutane and Torakichi's attitudes toward Buddhism. It starts by showing Atsutane's disdain for the Buddhist religion and his genetic and environmentally deterministic beliefs about Japanese superiority to all other cultures and peoples of the world. This is followed by the description of a religious *sanjin* whose abilities and practices were defined in comparison and contrast with the abilities and practices of Buddhist heroes. The chapter contends that the *sanjin* described by Torakichi and recorded by Atsutane was in part defined by supernatural abilities similar to the traditional ones attributed to the Buddhist bodhisattva. A further contention is that while Buddhist practices were evaluated and usually found wanting, comparable *sanjin* practices proved effective and superior. The salvific role of the *sanjin* was established in a system that emphasized the ultimate importance of the native *kami*, and, likewise, the role of the bodhisattva was described as either ineffective or corrupt and the Buddha was labeled a charlatan. Nevertheless, as negative as Atsutane's discourse on Buddhism was, he clearly relied on Buddhist models to create his *sanjin* culture hero and develop his own religious practices.

Chapter 6 contains the description of the *sanjin* as holders of secret and powerful technologies previously thought to have come from or to have been perfected in the West. Atsutane recognized the importance of Western knowledge in fields such as geography, astronomy, and military technology, but he denied its Western provenance. He attempted to de-emphasize the impact of Western technology by claiming it had come from Japan's Other World. To further this end, he encouraged the medium, Torakichi, to testify to the everyday use of Western technology in the Other World.

This chapter shows in detail how Atsutane used Torakichi to make the claim that the West had nothing good to offer whose origin could not ultimately be traced back to Japan's Other World. However, it also shows Atsutane continuing to encourage the adoption of Western scientific theory, a stance consistent with Atsutane's earlier cosmological writings. Finally, chapter 6 reveals that Atsutane recognized a military threat from the West, but offered comfort to the Japanese people by claiming that the supernatural beings who inhabited Japan's Other World were ready, willing, and able to adequately repel all invaders, no matter how destructive and powerful Western military technology was feared to be.

The conclusion makes clear that Atsutane, a would-be ethnographer of the imaginary, endeavored to craft a description of the supernatural inhabitants of the unseen Other World consistent with his pre-existing Ancient Way cosmology. The role of *Senkyō ibun* was to establish that those beings truly did exist and that they possessed wondrous abilities and performed special functions. If Atsutane's stated goal of *The August Pillar of the Soul* was to provide comfort and confidence for the people of Japan in a pleasant afterlife, then the goal of *Senkyō ibun* was equally important. In *Senkyō ibun* he sought to establish a religious hero whose primary reason for existence was to render comfort, assistance, and protection to the people of Japan until they reached that Other World. Atsutane was not satisfied in having his followers and fellow believers in the Ancient Way longing for the good life in the next world; he also attempted to empower them with ways to ask the *kami* for wealth, health, and security in this world.

The development of the *sanjin* was a failed attempt to bring the Other World closer to the seen or revealed world. Had it succeeded, it would have brought the need for religious attention, mediation, and practice concerning that Other World into greater perspective. That is to say, the discovery of the religious importance of the *sanjin* was also meant to make Atsutane more important in his time. The *sanjin* was a theological development that would make the world a better place for believers in the Ancient Way, and it also had the potential of making the world a better place for Atsutane in particular.

In addition, this final chapter assesses the relationship between the ethnographer and the informant to assign liability for the content of the stories, and it evaluates the extent to which Atsutane and Torakichi believed in the truth of the narrated events. The conclusion finalizes the assessment of how and to what extent Atsutane manipulated the narrative.

Finally, the conclusion addresses Atsutane's contribution to the construction of Japanese identity in the modern period. By Atsutane's time, intellectuals uncomfortable with continued cultural dependence on China had grown vocal. In addition, the supporters of Neo-Confucian[31] and Ancient Learning[32] movements based on Chinese scholarship were at odds with one another and found themselves in competition politically, socially, and economically. The Buddhist establishment was under fire from positivistic historiographers that had begun to question the many contradictions found in Buddhist texts. While those traditional discourses were in increasing disarray, the Western discourse of science and technology was gaining public acceptance. The nativist Japanese cultural consciousness was finally in a situation where it was confident enough to challenge the more powerful "enemy" discourses.

In the midst of this intellectual upheaval, Atsutane started an appeal to a wide cross-section of people. For a variety of reasons, class did not limit Atsutane's economic and social dealings, and as a result, his teachings did not place great importance on social class boundaries. He called for an ideological unity of all strata of society based on their common identity as Japanese people. Atsutane addressed international and universal issues, and he claimed to be frustrated by those who used foreign ideas for personal gain at the expense of their fellow Japanese, although this charge could well be leveled at him. The conclusion questions whether Atsutane's xenophobia might be recognized as a unifying force or as a more democratic re-evaluation of the common Japanese folk. Previous Buddhist- or Chinese-inspired discourses had supported certain privileged classes. Atsutane's rhetoric attempted to unite the people of Japan into appreciating all members of the society as equally special because all were able to become *kami*. The foreigners, Indians, Chinese, and Westerners were the real bogeymen of *Senkyō ibun;* the demons and spirits of the Other World were the natural and welcome inhabitants of Atsutane's vision of Japan.

In addition, his endless comparisons and the twisted analyses, which found in favor of Japanese superiority, revealed strained feelings of inferiority. For example, although Atsutane ostensibly denied the later development of Japanese culture, claiming Japan to be the first land created and the birthplace of the world's culture, he also defended and praised late development when forced to admit to some examples of slow Japanese growth. He used biological examples, citing the intellectual superiority of late-developing primates over instantly self-reliant insects. He cited Lao zi, writing, "The Great Vessel is the last to be formed,"[33] meaning of course that the Japanese were the great vessel, which would logically place them last.

In the end, Atsutane himself could be charged with attempting to orientalize the Japanese ethnic polity before any modern Western scholar had seriously begun to shoulder that grave undertaking. Part of the legacy of Atsutane's teachings was the notion that the best inherent Japanese trait was an intellectual and spiritual ability to appropriate and customize material culture originally not its own and to somehow improve it by infusing it with Japanese spirit. Since it was his subconscious feeling that he had to excuse Japan for not having the material evidence to show its superiority over all others, in order to feel worthy he advocated that Japanese people be understood as mystical spiritual anomalies—an inscrutable people, yes, but incapable of individual creativity, an unfortunate but lasting label.[34]

CHAPTER 1

Constructing Japanese Identity
Senkyō ibun

Ethnography of the Afterlife

Carmen Blacker's translation of *Senkyō ibun* is "Strange Tidings from the Realm of Immortals." The word "immortals" is one standard translation for the Chinese character sen commonly found in combination in Japanese as *sennin*.[1] The tradition of the so-called immortal comes from classical Daoism. In its most general sense, it refers to a man who may or may not leave civilization for the mountains, but who performs special ascetic and/or ritual practices for the purpose of attaining a transcendent state of being. Atsutane's text will extensively refine that definition into a specific class of humanity, and that refinement will be discussed in detail in later chapters. For now it will suffice to identify the immortals of the title as a small class of Japanese males with religious aspirations. Atsutane's realm of immortals is an actual physical space, the sparsely populated mountains of Japan. Specific mountains are named in the text, many of which are still centers of ascetic or cultic activity. This realm also consists of spiritual space, but to reach the spiritual space the physical space must first be traversed.

The "strange tidings" of the title comes from the fact that the book is Atsutane's retelling of approximately eight months of interviews with a Japanese boy who claimed to have been spirited away to the mountains by one of their immortal inhabitants. The descriptions of that world given by the boy Torakichi and recorded and commented upon by Atsutane were not all fantastic; many of them were quite ordinary. Many of his other stories about that world were not new but rather were "customized" retellings of legends from past ages. The novelty of Torakichi's strange tales, what made them truly different, was that they were supposedly firsthand reports from a living person who was willing to submit to questioning about them.

There has been a tendency to think of this work as a collection of ghost stories or folk tales, but that is mistaken. The reader who seeks to find only weird or traditional tales will come away disappointed, as Carmen Blacker can verify. This is not to say that these stories do not contain ghosts, demons, monsters, and magic; they do, and in healthy portions. Nevertheless, these are not stories meant to entertain the village folk, the neighbors, or even the nuclear family on a dark and stormy night. These stories have been collected by Atsutane as part of a scholarly endeavor to educate and inform other scholars and students about a new source of vital information concerning the true nature of Japan.

Therefore, Torakichi is not to be likened to some precocious child storyteller and entertainer; his situation is more akin to that of the sole survivor of a shipwreck washed up on the isolated shores of nineteenth-century Japan. His culture seemed to be alien to the Japanese people because he claimed to be from a land little known to the common citizen. Atsutane asked Torakichi about subjects we would certainly deem to be supernatural, but just as often he asked him about the food, clothing, lodging, entertainment, and education in his land. For example, one strange tale from the realm of the immortals included instructions for hemorrhoid relief remedies in their world.

Atsutane had long suspected, believed in, and theorized about the existence of this Other World. H. D. Harootunian writes about this as follows:

> Atsutane posited that there was another world within the tangible and visible world in which humans normally lived. His faith in the verity of certain stories from the most ancient Japanese texts suggested to him that such a world did exist.
>
> For Hirata [Atsutane], *kamigoto* [affairs of the *kami*] represented an unseen reality. An invisible domain where the gods carried out their affairs, it concerned the creation of heaven and earth as well as the sacred affairs of the world of darkness and concealment. Elevation of this realm to equivalence with the world of the living provided authority to his argument concerning consolation. "It is difficult to accept the old explanations that dead spirits migrate to the land of *yomi*. But where do the spirits of people who have died in this country go?" If this question were not clarified there would be no chance for achieving genuine happiness. The question was rhetorical, since Hirata had already established the coexistence of a realm that remained unseen and hidden to all but the departed spirits and a visible world inhabited by the living.[2]

In Torakichi, Atsutane felt for the first time that he had gained access to a witness to the daily happenings in the Other World. But, since he had already been writing about this Other World before he met Torakichi, he clearly had preconceived notions about what it should look like. When these notions were not supported by Torakichi's reports, Atsutane made extra efforts to browbeat the "correct" answers out of him. This aspect of the relationship between Atsutane and Torakichi will be discussed in detail in chapter 3, which examines what contributions Atsutane might have made to Torakichi's record of the Other World.

Atsutane had an agenda to follow during his interaction with Torakichi. One of his lifelong projects had been ethnographic description of other cultures. Within this study, Atsutane's earlier characterizations of foreign peoples and foreign countries will also be recounted as they pertain to his questioning of Torakichi. It is clear that he considered himself to be an expert in geography and ethnology.[3] His study of the Other World in Japan was undertaken as a similar scholarly endeavor. That is to say, he would have the readers of *Senkyō ibun* believe that he had discovered another culture and people within Japan, one significantly different than the Japanese culture known and practiced in his time.

In *Senkyō ibun*, Atsutane embarked on a project of defining differences between the Japanese he knew and a long-sought-after and revered Japanese "other," or alter ego, who he claimed inhabited the mountains. The reason for this discovery/reconstruction of the ideal Japanese was to use it to critique the existent "flawed" Japanese. In *Senkyō ibun*, he created a Japanese "other" in order to define the Japanese "self," a phenomenon not unknown or uncommon in the practice of anthropology today. James Clifford in his collection of anthropological essays, *Writing Culture*, writes, "It has become clear that every version of an 'other,' wherever found, is also the construction of a 'self,' and the making of ethnographic texts . . . has always involved a process of self-fashioning."[4]

Not to diminish Atsutane's inventiveness, but his use of ethnography to critique his own society is not as unusual as it might first sound. Montaigne's "Of Cannibals"[5] and Montesquieu's "Persian Letters"[6] did something similar earlier in the West. However, the Japanese "other" Atsutane discovered enjoys a clear superiority over the society he critiqued in all ways, more so than the hypothetical or fictional "others" of those predecessors. Also in modern anthropological practice, there is a growing trend to send ethnographic researchers into their own communities.[7] In other words, in *Senkyō ibun*, Atsutane was using a tried-and-true anthropological method of ethnography to find the "other" within, a technique that is continuing to display its popularity in modern Western anthropological studies. However, his was an attempt to deconstruct the Japanese "self," which he despised, and replace it with an imaginative new alter ego he had discovered/constructed in the mountains.

To get a better idea of the Japanese "self" Atsutane was critiquing and the Japanese "self" he wished to create, it is necessary to put him in his historical context. Not only was this a time of internal instability and dissatisfaction with the domestic state of affairs on many fronts, but there was also a sense of crisis from outside, a growing shadow of a threat and impending crisis caused by new Western knowledge and technology with unknown potential. It was a mere thirty years before Commodore Perry's black ships opened Japan with the threat of force.

Atsutane in Context—Three "Foreign" Discourses

When Atsutane wrote *Senkyō ibun* in the 1820s, Chinese language and learning dominated the fields of scholarship and written communication. It went without saying that in Japan in the early nineteenth century, the language of scholarship and most written discourse was a Japanese style of Chinese. The script was from China and the grammar and syntax, completely different from that of spoken Japanese, was based on Chinese grammar and syntax. Confucianism may not have been the set of categories through which people saw their world during the Tokugawa period,[8] and the Tokugawa orthodoxy may not have been based on Neo-Confucianism in the way it is often facilely packaged,[9] but Chinese language and Chinese learning made up the building blocks of Tokugawa ideology. Private academies based on the teachings of Zhu Xi (1130–1200) and Wang Yangming (1472–1528), among others, filled the cities. The field was referred to as *kangaku, rigaku,* or *sōgaku.*[10]

Marius Jansen aptly describes the situation: "All educated men had a good knowledge of the Chinese classical tradition, for that was the medium in which scholarly literacy was transmitted."[11] There was little written scholarly discourse in Japan in this era that did not take place in Chinese. Chinese language, in some form, was the dominant medium of the written discourse whether that discourse concerned Chinese learning or even Buddhist and Western learning. Atsutane, on this point, stood out as a glaring exception. He chose a more classical Japanese as his written medium of expression. The reasons for this choice were both ideological and practical, and will be examined later.

However, it was not just that Chinese was the dominant language of discourse that Atsutane found unacceptable; he also found the sinified state of the so-called native tradition of Shinto unbearable. Even before the Tokugawa period, Yoshida Kanetomo (1435–1511) had established his new brand of *yuiitsu,* or Yoshida Shinto, which intentionally incorporated Neo-Confucian metaphysics while also claiming a superior status for Shinto over Confucianism and Buddhism. This set the stage for Neo-Confucian Shinto, which during the Tokugawa period was to become even more prevalent than Buddhist-influenced Ryōbu Shinto.

In addition, Watarai Nobuyoshi (1616–1690) converted the Ryōbu Shinto of the Outer Shrine of Ise to another Neo-Confucian blend. While he did not root out the Buddhist elements, he downplayed the formerly all-important Esoteric aspects. He too made Neo-Confucian philosophy, along with Daoism and Yin Yang theory, central to the theology of his new Neo-Confucian Shinto hybrid. Yamazaki Ansai (1616–1682) started and popularized his own school of Neo-Confucian Shinto whose teachings reached and influenced those in the highest levels of power in the Tokugawa establishment even long after his death. One of his assertions was that original Shinto, an imagined Shinto without any Buddhist influence, would look exactly like the Chinese Way of the Sages, or Confucianism.

On top of this, another trend in Tokugawa scholarship, based on ancient Chinese thought and perhaps even inspired by nearly contemporaneous Chinese thought, was growing in power and popularity. This was the school of *kogaku*, or Ancient Learning (often referred to as *kangaku* or Han Learning), championed by Itō Jinsai (1627–1705) and Ogyū Sorai (1666–1728). Chinese scholars in the Ming and Qing dynasties had shown dissatisfaction with Song dynasty learning, that is, the Neo-Confucianism associated with Zhu Xi. These Chinese scholars advocated a return to the study of the five classics instead of the four books, which had been the cornerstone of Song dynasty learning. This movement required close and thoughtful readings of ancient texts and eschewed any reliance on secret traditions or commentarial literature, which had often been used to support assertions not found in the actual texts. This new movement also insisted on a strict philological methodology, and the more ancient the text, the more credible it was. Of course, the subject of study was still Chinese, not Japanese, classics.

This movement also had an effect on Shinto. One of Ogyū Sorai's students, Dazai Shundai (1680–1747), wrote a work called *Writing Explaining the Way* (*Bendōsho*) that sent shock waves through the Shinto establishment. *Writing Explaining the Way* charges that Shinto is not a well-formed tradition in the manner of Buddhism and Confucianism and in fact, without the Buddhist and Confucian additions, it is little more than a set of primitive rituals. Furthermore, it says that Shinto's claim to be the ancient way of Japan is false; it was actually started based on Chinese sources that Dazai documented. He further asserts that the ancient Chinese had used the ideas that became Japanese Shinto merely as a political tool to better govern the populace. Therefore, Dazai concludes, the present Tokugawa forms of Neo-Confucian Shinto are deluded misunderstandings of the proper political purposes of Shinto. *Kami* and spirits important to Shinto exist, but they are not soteriologically important. The rituals may be politically important, but the Neo-Confucian–influenced speculation on metaphysics is useless and meaningless.

In Atsutane's time, Buddhism still maintained the hegemonic position in religion it had first gained in the Nara period. Nevertheless, it was not monolithic, and the Tokugawa period exhibited a wide variety of Buddhisms. But even though it was not the only religion in Tokugawa Japan, Buddhist doctrine, deities, and material culture had been introduced and adopted liberally into all the alternatives. Movements to purge Shinto of Buddhism had been active since the late medieval period, but these movements were not intended to eradicate Buddhism and in effect simply urged that Shinto should be practiced independently of, not to the exclusion of, Buddhism. On top of this, by Atsutane's time, Buddhism had been officially linked to the Tokugawa government for two centuries through the *terauke* system,[12] which required that each member of the Japanese populace be registered at the local Buddhist temple.

In the 1820s when Hirata Atsutane wrote *Senkyō ibun*, Western discourse had already started to transform the field of science in Japan.[13] However, two centuries earlier, a change had started slowly within the Japanese public. In her recent work, Mary Elizabeth Berry writes of a quiet revolution of knowledge that started in Japan in the seventeenth century.[14] Inquisitive Japanese took it upon themselves to begin to collect and give order to information of all sorts, recording it in maps, surveys, manuals, and encyclopedic works.[15] Some of this information was imported from Western sources, but much of it was native information or information from the Asian continent.[16] This new native Japanese epistemic change would create new requirements for cultural literacy, some of which would indeed rely on information imported from the West.

One certain influence of Western culture on Japanese knowledge in Atsutane's time was the immediate inclination to grant credibility to any new source that even pretended to have an aura of science and objectivity. Tables and taxonomies of the imaginary and the supernatural, much like an ethnographic record of the Other World, became more believable simply because the form of presentation was considered believable.[17] In other words, information that was considered well-ordered was thought to have a better chance of being factual, and such well-ordered Western models of science were coming into vogue.

In the 1720s, one hundred years before Atsutane wrote *Senkyō ibun,* the Shogun Yoshimune[18] (1684–1751) relaxed the restrictions on the importation of certain books on Western learning. As a result, *Rangaku,* or Dutch studies, continued to pick up momentum throughout the eighteenth century. Two landmarks events were the publications of Japanese translations of a Dutch anatomy text, *New Book of Anatomy* (*Kaitai shinsho*), and a Dutch astronomy text, *Directions for the Use of the Two Charts of the Heavens and Earth* (*Tenchi nikyū yōhō*), in 1774. The first provided the earliest accurate and detailed Western scientific description of the human body inside and out, and the second marked the introduction of the round earth and Copernican theory to Japan. However, the 1774 astronomy text was not circulated except among Tokugawa officials in their state-sponsored astronomy apartment. Shiba Kōkan (1747–1818), renowned artist of the Tokugawa period, published his own version of the theory based on this translated text. This text was circulated widely and is a more popular example of the spread of Copernican theory, which was coming to be publicly known in Japan in the late eighteenth century. Another important artist and all-around force for cultural creativity, Hiraga Gennai (1728–1780), was also impacted by Western knowledge. Hiraga, who was blessed with a naturally inventive and creative spirit, invented his own electricity generator after viewing a Dutch model.

Despite the shortcomings of the translations of books on Western learning and the shortcomings of the state of science itself in those days, the practical applications of the knowledge were proving attractive to the Japanese of that time. Books on Western science—for example, botany, zoology, and physics—developed a popular following. The most avidly pursued topics besides medicine were astronomy and geography. Christian books piqued the interest of relatively few. Atsutane, however, was one of those few.

Knowledge of the novelty and power of Western science was not limited to private, educated elites. As mentioned earlier, the Tokugawa government had some control, although certainly not absolute control, over what information could be imported into Japan. The government set up its own bureaus to study the new sciences of astronomy and geography because they were both impressed and frightened by them. In 1803 the Tokugawa government established its own official translation office for Dutch texts in the Bureau of Astronomy, which had already conducted calendar revisions based on the new Western learning. Linguists who studied other European languages were employed by the translation office, and eventually even Western military science came to be studied there.

Russia had been making advances into the Kuriles from the beginning of the nineteenth century. A Russian trading mission landed in Naga-saki in 1804 and waited for permission to trade, which it did not receive. This refusal resulted in raids on Japanese settlements in Sakhalin and the Kuriles in 1806 and 1807. The Japanese later managed to capture the cap-tain of a Russian survey vessel, and these conflicts soon led to govern-ment efforts to strengthen the northern defenses. In 1808, a British ship sailed into Nagasaki and raided the Dutch trading station. At this time the Tokugawa government also began learning of the Napoleonic Wars and the French and American revolutions and feared that the destabilization of Europe and the Americas would eventually have an impact upon Japa-nese shores.

Due to the actual conflicts with Europeans and fueled by alarming news about Europe and the Americas in discord, in 1825, just about the same time as Atsutane's *Senkyō ibun*, the Tokugawa government issued an order to fire on all Western ships in Japanese waters and capture and incarcerate all Western foreigners who dared to come ashore. Even if the ships happened to belong to the Dutch, who were allowed into Nagasaki, it was deemed better to shoot first and ask questions later.[19] The official response of the Tokugawa government to actual human contact with West-erners was to refuse it. However, it was also official policy to import West-ern scientific knowledge, learn from it, and use it to strengthen Japan. Thus, Western discourse at the time of Atsutane's *Senkyō ibun* was present and powerful in Japan. For Atsutane, it created the third challenger to his teachings supporting Japanese superiority, and as such required a firm response.

Kokugaku

Kokugaku[20] is usually seen as having started in the seventeenth century both as an outgrowth and a response to historical developments. The choice of certain Ming and Qing scholars to return to the ancient texts to find their real original unmediated meanings, an attempt to bypass Zhu Xi by those dissatisfied with the domination of that school, became known in Japan and sparked similar activities. However, perhaps piqued by Chinese ethnocentric tendencies in historiography, and certainly partly because of Japanese ethnocentric proclivities, the idea of going back to the first classics, the principle that the original form is the true form, inspired an interest in Japanese studies, or *kokugaku*. This new school would be a Japanese nativist response to the Ancient Learning school, which focused on Chinese classics, that is, a type of Ancient Learning whose object was not China, but Japan.

Two historical figures are usually designated as starting this movement. One of these is Keichū (1640–1701) a Shingon priest who was involved in a project to decipher the *Manyōshū*, the ancient Japanese poetry collection that had become almost impenetrable to Japanese scholars in the nearly thousand-year interval since its composition in the Nara period. Keichū practiced a philological method using known writings from the same period to help gloss the obscure poetry. His method is often associated with that of the Ancient Learning movement, which was gaining momentum in the same period.

Although Keichū's method and subject of study were the same as those of later *kokugaku* scholars, his ideology was not. Keichū remained a Buddhist priest throughout his studies. His purpose may have been to locate just what was originally Japanese, but he did not consider that to be a quality that made his subject matter superior to writings of India or China. The first historical figure credited with a nativist commitment to the belief in the superiority of Japanese compositions was Kada no Azumamaro (1669–1736). His claim to the position of first *kokugaku* scholar is due to a famous petition he submitted to the Shogun Tsunayoshi (1646–1709) in 1705 that was supposedly the first document to use the word *kokugaku*. It was contained in Azumamaro's request for support in the establishment of an academy dedicated to the study of Japanese learning.[21]

Kamo no Mabuchi (1697–1769) is the next important figure in the succession of Tokugawa *kokugaku*. He was the first to put methodological technique, inspired scholarship, and pro-Japanese ideology together in one package. Mabuchi claimed there was an indigenous Japanese Way of the Kami, Shinto, in response to Dazai's claim to the contrary. He claimed that since *kami* are qualitatively better than sages, who after all are only human, the Japanese Way was independent of and even superior to the Chinese Way of the Sages. Mabuchi also produced the idea that the power of the *kami* was imbedded in native Japanese words, that is, *kotodama*. He claimed that Japanese words originally had a mystical unity of word and meaning, of signifier and signified. Therefore, the use of Chinese symbols to represent Japanese words destroyed that unity and changed that sacred meaning, bringing into serious question whether Chinese graphs could be an appropriate medium for expressing Japanese ideas. However, Mabuchi was not anti-Chinese in all things. He was certainly anti–Neo-Confucian, but not completely critical of Han or Ancient Learning.

The next important figure in the historical development of *kokugaku* was Motoori Norinaga (1730–1801), a physician who had more interest in his hobby, the study of ancient Japanese texts, than in his profession. As time went on, he turned his unofficial pastime, which started as a gathering of friends on the second floor of his house, into a nativist academy. He was a capable scholar and had enough of a reputation to be granted a meeting with the then famous Mabuchi, with whom, after that successful audience, he corresponded for the last few years of Mabuchi's life.

Norinaga used sophisticated philological methods to analyze Japanese literature and history. He is famous in the field of literary criticism for his writings on *Genji monogatari* and his refinement of the literary aesthetic term *mono no aware*.[22] His particular contributions to *kokugaku* were a clear and firm stance against Chinese culture and an overall xenophobic stance toward the rest of the world. He posited a true Japanese way of understanding, *magokoro*, which was superior and in opposition to the Chinese way of understanding, *karagokoro*. He also provided arguments for Japanese superiority over all other nations and support for worship of the divine Japanese emperor. He steadfastly affirmed the existence of an ancient *Kami no michi*, a Way of the Kami that was an image of a Shinto religion devoid of all foreign influence. His method emphasized a precise investigation of text much like that of the Ancient Learning scholars. Although he believed in the superiority of Japan to all other lands, he was harshest toward China and was somewhat accepting of Buddhism and Dutch studies.

Atsutane's Career in Context

Atsutane was a prolific writer with scores of works of varying length still in existence. A short look at some of the works leading up to *Senkyō ibun* should provide a clear picture of what his major concerns were, whom he considered his enemies, and just how he characterized them. The topics are wide-ranging but are arranged to show his attempt to disparage ideas of Chinese, Buddhist, or Western superiority and to ridicule any Japanese who would dare believe those ideas. However, a closer look at these works shows Atsutane's willingness to adopt foreign ideas by labeling them Japanese in origin.

In 1803, Atsutane wrote his first work, A *Criticism of Deceitful Writings* (*Kamōsho*). In it he first criticized Dazai Shundai, the student of Ogyū Sorai who in *Writing Explaining the Way* devalued Shinto and elevated ancient Chinese Confucianism, which the Ancient Learning school made their object of study. Dazai's work had been critical of Neo-Confucians, claiming that they too misunderstood the role of Shinto. Atsutane also was critical of Neo-Confucians for the same reason, but differed from Dazai by criticizing anyone who showed any fondness for a teaching of Chinese origin. Atsutane continued his anti-Confucian posturing in the 1805 work *A New Discussion on Gods and Demons* (*Shinkishinron*).[23] In 1811 he produced *The Essence of Confucianism* (*Judō taii*), which was an expansion of two other works, *The Essence of Chinese Studies* (*Kangaku taii*) and *An Indignant Discussion of Chinese Writings* (*Seiseki* [*Saijaku*] *gairon*). The title of the latter indicates the overall tone of these works, which consist of strong and spirited criticisms of Chinese studies.

In 1811 Atsutane also wrote *The Essence of Popular Shinto* (*Zoku shinto taii*), which was again highly critical of the Neo-Confucian Shinto practiced at the time. For Atsutane, Shinto as it existed at that time in Japan had been overcome by Chinese influences; it was not the Way of the Kami of which Norinaga wrote, and it was not the *kodō* or the Ancient Way he was interested in uncovering and propagating. Atsutane wrote another work, *The Sacred Letters of Japanese Traditional Script* (*Kanna hifumiden*), in 1821 specifically to combat ideas of Chinese cultural superiority. This work showcased Atsutane's conviction that Japan had a native script that had originated there and was in use before the Japanese imported Chinese characters. He believed that this native script was used by the Japanese in the ancient Age of the Kami before being lost.

In 1811 Atsutane penned *The Essence of Buddhism* (*Butsudō taii*), which also came in a version with the derogatory title *Laughing Discourse after Emerging from Meditation* (*Shutsujō Shōgo*). This was an all-out attack on Buddhism, the people who practiced it, and the country from which it came.[24] Expanding on the method he learned from Tominaga Nakamoto (1715–1746), he examined Buddhist histories and pointed out their many errors and contradictions with vicious but easy to substantiate historiographic arguments.[25] He cast aspersions on India and the nature of the Indian people. Atsutane's style was not merely to point out flaws; he preferred also to poke fun at his enemies, and name calling was an important part of his arsenal. For example, another work from 1811 critical of Buddhism was titled *A Dissertation on Enlightenment* (*Godōben*), but it also went by the satirical title *The Asshole's Tale* (*Shirikuchi monogatari*).

In 1806 Atsutane wrote a work titled *Outer Chapters of Our Doctrine* (*Honkyō gaihen*). In this work Atsutane revealed that he had read three different Christian works that had been banned by the shogunate.[26] The works were *The True Meaning of Christianity* (1603), *Ten Chapters of an Eccentric* (1608) by Matteo Ricci (1552–1610), and *Seven Conquests* (1614) by Didacus de Pantoja (1571–1618).[27] Some scholars have argued that Atsutane's theology was modeled after the ideas from Christianity he learned in these books.[28]

In 1807 Atsutane wrote *White Waves of the Kuriles: Maps Appended* (*Chishima shiranami fuchizu*) in response to raids on Japanese settlements on Hokkaido and Sakhalin led by Russian naval officers Khostov and Davidoff. The Russian czar had sent an emissary to Japan in hopes of opening some kind of trade relations, but the emissary had been rebuffed. The Russian raids were in retaliation for the rejection, and even more were threatened but did not materialize. In this work Atsutane made recommendations for defending against barbarian invasions as well as suggestions about future Japanese conquest. In short, Atsutane, similar to the Tokugawa bakufu, welcomed Western knowledge that worked for Japan while rejecting actual friendly contact with Westerners.

Atsutane wrote *Essence of the Ancient Way* (*Kodō taii*) in 1811. This text, which summarizes the principles of his teachings, includes passages that show a clear dependence as well as acceptance of Western astronomy and geography. He upheld the idea of a heliocentric universe with eight planets (not the traditional seven from Chinese cosmology) because he could rationalize the centrality of the sun by equating it with Amaterasu, the sun *kami* of ancient Japanese mythology. In addition in this text, Atsutane used Western geographic data to support his claim that Japan's longitude and latitude gave it the optimum climate and protection from other lands, which suggested Japan's favored status in comparison with those other lands. Still, Atsutane did not praise Western science for these advances in knowledge. Even though he used the knowledge, he claimed it was ultimately petty and not on par with the knowledge one acquired from studies of Japanese antiquity.[29]

As Atsutane entered the 1820s, his writings began to focus on supernatural phenomena. In 1820 he wrote *New Discussion on Gods and Demons* (*Kishin shinron*), which affirmed his belief in the existence of all sorts of supernatural spirit beings. In 1821 he wrote *Thoughts on Supernatural Beings of Past and Present* (*Kokon yōmikō*). In the same year he wrote an introduction to a ghost story called *Record of the Haunting of Master Inō* (*Inō mononokeroku*), which had been circulating and which he claimed to be true. In 1822 he recorded *Senkyō ibun*. Later supplements to this subject matter written by his students are also extant.[30] That year he also wrote *A Recorded Account of Katsugorō's Rebirth* (*Katsugorō saisei kibun*), which was another example of Atsutane's seeking out and interviewing people who claimed to have visited the Other World.

The *kokugaku* movement, from Keichū to Norinaga, had always been characterized by its reliance and emphasis on philological method, no doubt due to the powerful influence of the Ancient Learning scholars.

However, Atsutane had made metaphysical claims that were difficult if not impossible to prove using that methodology. The textual evidence for much of his new speculation was sparse. Since he was a *kokugaku* scholar, the Japanese mythology found in most ancient Japanese histories, poems, and gazetteers should have been an important source for his teachings. But for Atsutane, because these sources were tainted by the fact they were either written in Chinese or in a Japanese script that had been created using Chinese as a foundation, they were always considered suspect. On top of that, Atsutane is usually not considered to be one of the better philologists of the Tokugawa period. Perhaps all those factors explain Atsutane's methodological change; still, for whatever reason, he felt compelled to find another source and method for his Japan-centered metaphysical cosmological theories. It was his search for an alternative and superior source and method that led him to create *Senkyō ibun*, which should be understood as an attempt to change the course of Japan studies by verifying a new medium and new method for establishing Atsutane's ethnocentric teachings as rooted in a new source of world knowledge.

The Methodological Move to Ethnography

Once again, the word *ibun* can be translated as "strange tidings" or "strange stories." *Senkyō* is the realm of mountain men or the so-called "immortals" of the Daoist tradition. However, for Atsutane, the *sen* refers to the mysterious men in the mountains of Japan whom he named *sanjin*, or mountain men. In other words, Atsutane intended *Senkyō ibun* to be understood as a large reserve of privileged information, normally only available to *sanjin*, certainly unknown to Japanese society in general, and not available to Chinese, Buddhist, or Western scholars. It was to serve as a source of power for Atsutane and the starting point for a discourse that would verify the superiority of Japan as well as the superiority of Atsutane's teachings.

Of course, for this strategy to work, one would have to believe that information held by homeless vagabonds living in the wild was more valuable than information held by priests and scholars, and Atsutane certainly held that belief. He railed against scholars whose knowledge came only from books. He claimed to scorn commonly accepted knowledge and the modes of learning which brought forth that knowledge. He sided with the knowledge more generally associated with the common Japanese, the peasant, and which came from everyday experience. In defense of this anti-intellectual stance he called on Norinaga's argument that thinking too much was characteristic of *karagokoro*, or Chinese Mind. This argument claimed that the ancient Japanese did not have to think, analyze, and study to know, but knew things naturally and intuitively. Norinaga called this phenomenon *magokoro*, or True Mind.

In *The August Pillar of the Soul*, where Atsutane introduced his new creation story and cosmology clearly influenced by Western science, he also relied on a story from the ancient classic histories. When the earth *kami* Ōkuninushi relinquished the land of Japan to the *kami* from heaven, in return he was promised sovereignty over an invisible world. Atsutane used this as the foundation of his assertion that Japan was bifurcated into a visible world and an invisible world. The visible world was the one inhabited by normal humans, and the invisible world was the Other World inhabited by supernatural beings. This became his pre-Durkheimian division between the sacred and the profane, with the invisible Other World being the sacred.

Accordingly, the invisible was pure, true, and real. The visible world was depraved, false, and artificial. Therefore knowledge about things and events in the visible world was second-class knowledge, the kind held by Chinese, Buddhist, and Western scholars. Although it might be temporarily useful, it was ultimately meaningless. In addition, one could not study books and learn about the Other World; one had to experience it or find someone who had.

The Other World occupied the same space as the visible world, but normally could not be visited or experienced by the average human being. Although the two worlds were thought to overlap so that the visible and the Other World were juxtaposed at every point, there seemed to be places that offered better opportunities for passage between the worlds, and special people who were capable of making that passage. The places that seemed to allow passage into the Other World were not in civilized areas, but rather in the mountains, which had a long history of being considered sacred space in Japan.[31]

Some of the inhabitants of this Other World were of course the Japanese *kami*, so it was natural that it was also thought that shrines, especially shrines in mountainous regions, were places that allowed occasional nexus. The few people who inhabited these regions, called *sanjin* by Atsutane, had a mysterious reputation that often included stories of special abilities or unnatural skills. Furthermore, there had long been a practice of going into the mountains for religious or spiritual purposes in Japan, a tradition that had been affected by similar practices from other parts of Asia. In short, the connection between the mountains and numinous power was not difficult to make and was done long before Atsutane wrote *Senkyō ibun*.

The remaining work for Atsutane was to find the medium that could make the trip or become the bridge between the visible world and the Other World, between the world of the humans and the world of the *kami*. *Kami* cults had long had mediums, and the ancient histories document activities of these mediums. However, Atsutane did not make those classical *miko* his medium of choice; in fact, he even worked to discredit them.[32] He found a new medium, one that was more than a portal or bridge between worlds. His medium was a powerful hero with a commission from the *kami*.

The main function of *Senkyō ibun* was to find and describe for the first time the true Japanese religious virtuoso. Buddhism had popular and powerful bodhisattvas that started out as human beings but became so spiritually developed that they came to serve as mediums between ordinary humans and their spiritual goals. These bodhisattvas also protected and offered comfort along with ultimate salvation to their worshipers. Confucianism had its *junzi*, the ethically perfected gentlemen, the absolute expression of the way of humanity. Neo-Confucianism had its *shengren*, completely in harmony with the cosmic Dao. Christianity had its saints and martyrs. Shugendō had the spiritually charged *yamabushi*, emulating the miraculous legendary founder En no gyōja.[33] Daoism had many heroes, among them the *xianren* (*sennin*), or the immortal, which not coincidentally was the established religious model most like Atsutane's refigured *sanjin*.

Defending the reality of this heretofore unknown religious hero, Atsutane wrote:

> The term *sanjin* is the Japanese word for *sen*. It was read that way in the ancient sacred poems and in the *Manyōshū*. I hear that Torakichi's master refers to himself as *sanjin*. It is a remnant of the ancient language. The notion that immortals exist only in China and not in this country is held only by people of limited experience. The fact that there have been numerous inhabitants of a sacred realm of immortals living in Japan from ancient times can be found in innumerable places in the ancient texts.[34]

Tokugawa Shinto was not completely bereft of religious heroes, but none of them were suitable for Atsutane's purposes. Shinto's heroes had been combined with heroes from India and China, and many of them were also important in Japanese Buddhism, which of course made them completely unacceptable to Atsutane. In fact, Atsutane expended a great deal of time and effort denouncing the state of nineteenth-century Shinto.[35] Atsutane should not be thought of as an orthodox member of the Shinto establishment, even though he held official appointments as an instructor to Shinto priests.[36] Atsutane was not a champion of Tokugawa Shinto; instead, his project was the recovery of the "true" Ancient Way, or *Kodō*, which he considered to be the true religion of Japan.

Atsutane's cosmology had a dual structure and was in need of a medium, thus the *sanjin*. His teachings also needed a hero and role model that could compete with those of the other more popular and powerful religions, thus the *sanjin*'s supernatural capabilities. The peculiar fantastic nature of that *sanjin* medium will be studied in detail in the following chapters. Those details will also show how Atsutane was making a bid for power by creating a discourse on the *sanjin* and his Other World. These strange new truths were cast in a light that was supposed to trump the established knowledge touted in Chinese, Buddhist, and Western discourses. The supernatural powers of Atsutane's medium were to be turned on his intellectual rivals within Japan who championed foreign discourses.

Philology and historiography depend on written histories, but Atsutane was not interested in reproducing the standard ancient histories. He was interested in explaining what happened before there was any "foreign-influenced" history, and, by doing so, creating a new history. Moreover, despite Atsutane's claim that there was a form of Japanese writing in the Age of the Kami, he did not claim that there were extant copies of a history using that writing. Atsutane came to the conclusion that since there was no extant history he considered true, either he was going to have to find another source, which explains his interest in Torakichi, or else find alternative methods of creating his own "true" version of history.

One of Atsutane's methods of deciding what was "true" history was decidedly different from Norinaga's. While Norinaga relied on a single text, *Kojiki*, to produce his history titled *Kojikiden*, Atsutane relied on several different texts and took parts from each of them to construct what he believed was the one true account remaining within them. Atsutane called his new history *Reconstituted Ancient History* (*Koshi seibun*). Despite all the time and effort he put into historiography and philology, though, he recognized that even this new creative method had its limits. The ancient world described in his history had seemingly disappeared, and no philological method could recover it. However, Atsutane at some point came up with the inspired claim that what was once real had disappeared, not into oblivion, but into the Other World located in the mountains of Japan. This meant that the real ancient Japan still existed somewhere in the Other World, and thus his pursuit of history led him to make contact with that Other World.

Atsutane's belief in a cosmology that could only be weakly supported by philological techniques required that he change either his belief or change his methods. Clearly Atsutane chose the second option, which led him to adopt an ethnographic method that called for interviews with informants from that Other World. Torakichi was not the only informant used by Atsutane, but he is the best and most interesting example.

Our first thought might be to liken Atsutane to people today who feel they can contact the dead, or to those who hold some strong belief in alternative planes of existence. However, Atsutane can be more fruitfully compared to Western anthropologists who once speculated about ancient human societies existing somewhere in the yet unexplored world. Some of these romantic adventurers approached primitive peoples with the thought that they might be living reminders of the progenitors of the human race untarnished by civilization. Others, who might not readily have admitted it, seem to have been searching for Adam and Eve in the jungles of South America or in the islands of the South Pacific.

There also may be some profit in thinking about Atsutane's work in the light of a more recent Western anthropological endeavor, namely the work of Carlos Castaneda for which he received a doctorate in anthropology from UCLA in 1970.[37] Castaneda's ethnographic records of the Native American sorcerer Don Juan have long been under great suspicion, and there are credible reports that Castaneda himself admitted to the deception.[38] Yet there are also those who still say that the stories of his confession are just more slander by those who spurned Castaneda's spiritual message. Whatever the case may be, the popular reception received by Castaneda's books show that this kind of phenomenon has occurred recently and could occur again, and that postmodern Western society has not grown too savvy for Other Worldly ethnography. Clearly, it is worthy of closer attention.

Methodology: Critical Reading of Ethnographic Fiction

Questioning and examining the text of *Senkyō ibun* should lead to some interesting discoveries related to the nature of Atsutane's ethnographic enterprise. Past studies that have examined some of the ways that nineteenth- and twentieth-century ethnographies and ethnographic studies have been conducted have taught us how those encounters with other cultures have been used to define and redefine the identities of the anthropologist self and the informant other. In the case of *Senkyō ibun*, Atsutane's ethnographic writing proves to be an exercise of the imagination as it posits the culture of the anthropologist self as corrupt and the culture of the

informant other as ideal. The text essentially becomes a central pillar in
the construction of a new version of a Japanese cultural identity capable
of satisfying a changing world context.

Placing Atsutane and Torakichi in the roles of anthropologist and
informant also serves to highlight the incongruities in the text. The anthropological backdrop makes the two of them seem like actors performing in
a pseudo-scientific attempt at positivistic science. However, the idea that
there should be a clear line between art and science in anthropology was,
no doubt, not one of Atsutane's pressing concerns; still, the lack of just
such a clear line is central to the creative power of ethnographic writing,
and as such was once a pressing concern in the modern Western understanding of the anthropological profession. Noted anthropologist James
Clifford voiced his doubts about those who felt they could mix the two
when he said, "Indeed, the very notion of a 'literary' approach to a disci-
pline, 'anthropology,' is seriously misleading."[39]

The fact is that ethnographic writing has long been suspect as an objective scientific method. Herodotus and Montesquieu are revered in Western
universities, but they inhabit the humanities departments and their writings are taught in literature classes. Of course, those writers came before
the scientific revolution changed the expectations for scholarly studies of
foreign cultures, but the fact remains that the problem with ethnographic
writing lies not within any particular recorder but rather in the limitations
of ethnography itself. Simply put, writing about a culture is expressly for
the purpose of communicating the meaning of a culture, but that very act
is part of the process of constructing that meaning. In short, the medium
is not transparent.

Furthermore, ethnography's identification with literature is not solely
limited to our classical icons, who languished in the ignorance and bliss of
prescientific thought.

> "Literary" approaches have recently enjoyed some popularity in the human
> sciences. In anthropology influential writers such as Clifford Geertz, Victor
> Turner, Mary Douglas, Claude Lévi-Strauss, Jean Duvignaud, and Edmund
> Leach, to mention only a few, have shown an interest in literary theory and
> practice. In their different ways they have blurred the boundary separat-
> ing art from science. Nor is theirs a new attraction. Malinowski's authorial
> identifications (Conrad, Frazer) are well known. Margaret Mead, Edward
> Sapir, and Ruth Benedict saw themselves as both anthropologists and lit-
> erary artists. In Paris surrealism and professional ethnography regularly
> exchanged both ideas and personnel.[40]

Some might think Atsutane's name has been added to the ranks of too distinguished a company, but his study of the afterlife should at least locate him squarely in this ancestry as the ethnographer of the surreal.[41]

Mistaken as any of us might consider Atsutane to be about the reality of his Other World, there is little doubt that he really believed in its existence and no doubt that he intended his description of that world to be taken as the truth. Therefore *Senkyō ibun* was meant to be understood as a work of ethnography. However, as shown earlier, there is a strong trend among anthropologists themselves to recognize ethnography as a type of fiction. To again quote James Clifford on this point,

> To call ethnographies fictions may raise empiricist hackles. But the word as commonly used in recent textual theory has lost its connotation of falsehood, of something merely opposed to truth. It suggests the partiality of cultural and historical truths, the ways they are systematic and exclusive. Ethnographic writings can properly be called fictions in the sense of "something made or fashioned," the principal burden of the word's Latin root, *fingere*. But it is important to preserve the meaning not merely of making, but also of making up, of inventing things not actually real. (*Fingere*, in some of its uses, implied a degree of falsehood.)[42]

In the case of *Senkyō ibun*, calling it a work of ethnographic fiction means it has been crafted based on the skills and dispositions of its author, while recognizing that he believed it to be, for the most part, the truth as he understood it. For example, the text was made up of specific questions selected by Atsutane followed by Torakichi's answers to those questions, all recorded by Atsutane. Besides that, there are other formats of presentation of the ethnographic evidence, such as the short narrative anecdote by Atsutane or Torakichi. Sometimes the book contains a longer anecdotal tale, sometimes told by a third party, and sometimes the contents consist of lists. There are also times when Atsutane injected commentary and notes between questions. There are other times when Atsutane remarked that something strange required later scrutiny, which he sometimes failed to provide. Clearly among all this variety there has been preselection, and certainly, merely by the appearance of notes and references, this text has undergone editing. As haphazard as the text may sometimes appear, there is order and there is a mind that crafted it.

It might be easier for some to call *Senkyō ibun* fiction if the work was explained as stories of Tengu Boys who fly to places such as the Island of Women, or escape dragons, or purposely avoid stepping in the dung of thunder beasts, all of which happen in the text. Yet it is not only the nature of the informant Torakichi's information that makes us doubt the supposed scientific and objective quality of this ethnography. The real problem with credibility and objectivity results from overwhelming evidence that shows that the stories are being told from the ethnographer's biased point of view.

Anthropologist Vincent Crapanzano writes of the problems inherent in three ethnographic accounts by George Catlin, Johann Wolfgang von Goethe, and Clifford Geertz.[43] The source of the inaccuracies, or inconsistencies between the ethnographer's story and the real events, is the ethnographers' attempts to make their stories interesting and convincing. In Crapanzano's words,

> In all three instances the events described are subverted by the transcending stories in which they are cast. They are sacrificed to their rhetorical function in a literary discourse that is far removed from the indigenous discourse of their occurrence. The sacrifice, the subversion of the event described, is in the final analysis masked . . . by the authority of the author, who, at least in much ethnography, stands above and behind those whose experience he purports to describe.[44]

The opening passage of *Senkyō ibun* reveals the "transcending story" along with its explicit expression of the ethnographer's intent. A look at the passage will also reveal a subtle announcement that a narrative is unfolding, one whose ending can be predicted. The "author" of the story uses the literary device of foreshadowing, providing a solid clue that we readers are not just watching a natural scene unfold; rather, we are watching a sequence of events laid out for us, not by chance nor even in accord with some scientific protocol, but by a writer of fiction.

> It was about four o'clock in the late afternoon as the day was coming to a close on the first day of the tenth month of Bunsei three [1820]. Old master Yashiro Rinchi[45] came by with a very welcome invitation. He said, "You are probably aware, I think, that the boy, who was reputedly abducted into the longtime service of a tengu, is now staying with Yamazaki Yoshishige,[46] and he has been telling us about his various experiences there in the Other World. When I heard some of the things he said, I noticed that there were many things in common with ideas you have set down in the past. I am going over to Yoshishige's house now and I thought that you might like to meet the boy. How about it, won't you come along with me?"

I [Atsutane] said that I had wanted to meet someone like that for a long time and I had a lot of questions for him. I was so happy; it was a godsend. Ban Nobutomo[47] had just come over, but I told him to wait and I would be right back in little while, and I set out with old master Yashiro to Yoshishige's house.

On the way there, I said to old master Yashiro, "When people who have been spirited away talk, their stories are usually vague and rambling, and especially where it concerns the Other World they speak unclearly and secretively. Is this boy like that?"

Yashiro reassured me saying, "Most people we hear have been spirited away are like that, but it seems like this child speaks without hiding anything. Yoshishige said that recently when they went to Ninagawa's house, the boy said that he had visited the pure lands in the far west and that there he had seen the Kalavinka bird and even imitated the bird's cry.[48] I also heard others who had recently been invited to see him say that he speaks without holding anything back. So many things that had not previously been allowed to leak from that world into this world have recently been revealed. Ask all sorts of questions and write it all down so as not to forget."

As I was listening and nodding I thought that the world we know had been undergoing quite a bit of change lately. Now so many things were becoming public knowledge. There were many texts, events, and objects, which had been completely secret, but which were now matters of public knowledge. Even the smallest details of the previously unknown ways of the world of the *kami* had been coming to light one after the other. In addition, facts about foreign countries and even many of their gadgets were being made known to the public more and more every year. I believe all of this to be the will of the *kami*. Certainly, having this kind of opportunity present itself, especially the possibility of learning about the Other World, is definitely owing to them. As I was walking along thinking about those kinds of things, in no time at all we arrived at Yoshishige's house.[49]

Before Torakichi even says a word, the reader is being told that he is going to receive clear and accurate information of the Other World. He is assured that this information has the authority and the sanction of the *kami*. He also is told that what Torakichi will say is going to match what Atsutane had previously been theorizing about the Other World. The reader is informed that the time has come for great change to occur in the world, and in fact is already occurring. That change is characterized as an increase in public knowledge. Furthermore, new information has come in from Western sources and tools and gadgets have arrived with it. Yet even here, Atsutane was quick to point out that any new knowledge being brought into Japan purportedly from the West could be attributed to the will of the *kami*.

Another interesting point in the introduction above is that the ethnographic method of recording all that was said in the question-and-answer session was suggested by Atsutane's friend Yashiro. He recommended it so Atsutane would not forget exactly what was said. However, the record of this exchange also serves to reassure the readers that Atsutane did his best to accurately represent Torakichi's answers. Another possible reason to credit a third party for the ethnographic method was to protect Atsutane from the charge of having planned this new method to foist his ideas upon an unsuspecting audience. In addition, the record of his conversation with Yashiro guarantees that the reader is told from the start that the similarity between Atsutane's previous theories concerning the Other World and Torakichi's stories of his direct knowledge of that world can be verified by a third party. This all looks very much like an attempt to establish that the ethnographic record of the conversations with Torakichi was not part of a premeditated and calculated plan by Atsutane. However, it is doubtful if there is any reader of this introduction now or then who would conclude that Atsutane believed he was going to meet anything other than a credible source with a detailed story. The readers are being led to believe in Atsutane's foregone conclusion.

As Wallace Martin stated in his *Recent Theories of Narrative:*

> Once freed of the notion that they should study only stories that are untrue and highly respected (the domain of traditional literature), critics realize that the anthropologist, folklorist, historian, and even the psychoanalyst and theologian are all concerned with narrative in one way or another.[50]

Moreover, reading Atsutane's ethnographic narrative as a work of fiction, as in the way I have just demonstrated, has already shown promising possibilities. Performing a fuller analysis of *Senkyō ibun* and treating it as if it were a fictional narrative—that is to say, specifically looking for evidence of authorial manipulation—can help locate and flesh out what Crapanzano called the many "transcending stories in which they [Torakichi's accounts of the events of the Other World] are cast." To deepen the analysis and enrich the context, I have also read and analyzed many of Atsutane's cosmological, metaphysical, and political texts written prior to or during the same period as *Senkyō ibun*. These writings help to clarify Atsutane's pre-established beliefs and convictions that have produced the "transcending stories" that guided the way he put together the ethnographic fiction of the Japanese Other World in *Senkyō ibun*.

Starting with the premise that *Senkyō ibun* can be understood as a work of ethnographic fiction; that is, attempting to study it as a work of narrative literature, does not make the critic's job any easier. For example, the difference between such theoretical entities as historical author, implied author, narrator(s), and levels of narration should be given some consideration throughout the process to be certain we are clear who is saying what or who is being characterized as saying what. There are a number of different voices in this text, but often they seem to share the same identity; they are all in some way Atsutane's voice taking on different guises. In other words, to be clear on the importance and validity of certain statements we must pay attention to whom Atsutane is attributing them.

Senkyō ibun starts out as a narrative explaining the "fateful" meeting and subsequent interaction between Atsutane and Torakichi. The narrative brings the characters to several junctures where guests have gathered in salons to hear the boy's answers to a wide range of questions pertaining to life in the Other World in which he had been raised. At these junctures the narrative turns into dialogues between various interlocutors and the supernatural informant, Torakichi. Important to note here is that at these points the text closely resembles the structure of Ge Hong's (283–343) *Inner Chapters* of the *Baopuzi*, a text that profoundly influenced Atsutane.[51] In both cases the interlocutor sets up the spokesperson for the immortals with questions that allow him to clarify the superiority of his practice and lifestyle. The situation is clearly contrived to exalt the wise and supposedly independent proponent of *shinsen,* or Japanese immortal practices.

One narrator with actual firsthand experience, Torakichi, often has his stories supplemented by another narrator, Atsutane or an interlocutor invited by him, who tells stories he has heard only secondhand. More often than not the secondhand narration is verified by the firsthand narration. In that way, even ghost stories heard third- or fourthhand by Atsutane come to share the authority of Torakichi's life experiences.

The opposite dynamic is also in action where Atsutane would narrate Torakichi's stories and then add his own commentary to explain and verify the accuracy of the information, as strange as it might appear to be. This further shows that the narrator had an interest and a stake in the "hero" of his tale and could not keep himself, or would not have thought of keeping himself, from inserting his opinion and assessments into the story.

The author, Atsutane, had an affective and also an intellectual relationship with his main character. Of this type of narrative relationship Gérard Genette[52] writes:

> We have here something which could be called *testimonial function* or function of *attestation* [Genette's italics]. But the narrator's interventions, direct or indirect, with regard to the story can also take the more didactic form of an authorized commentary on the action. This is an assertion of what could be called the narrator's *ideological function.*[53]

In essence, the narrative attempt is to have the reader believe that the "hero" can legitimate the narrator's point of view with just as much authority as the narrator can validate his own "hero's." The question of objective authority is begged with perfectly circular logic. Moreover, as John Winkler points out in his study of narratology, when an outside narrator claims to exist in the same world as his inside narrator, it becomes inevitable that the outside narrator's secondhand information should naturally require another level of questioning than the supposed firsthand knowledge of the inside narrator.[54]

In the following chapters I have separated and arranged the entire *Senkyō ibun* text into thematic units. Atsutane's text was often repetitive as Torakichi went over the same ground in different interviews. This thematic regrouping of Atsutane's stories allows for the recognition of subtle but important changes in Torakichi's stories. The regrouping also shows that Atsutane the anthropologist asked to hear the same story at different times on fishing expeditions for different answers, ignoring in some instances crucial changes clearly made to accommodate the listener, himself.

The point of reading this ethnography of the imaginary as fiction, then, is not merely to tease out new meanings or to turn the book on its head to see what new meaning might drop out. The main purpose of this enterprise is to determine the contribution of the ethnographer, Atsutane, to the raw material provided by the informant. Atsutane felt it relevant to comment that this question-and-answer performance, which turned into *Senkyō ibun,* was often subjected to severe criticism in which he himself was accused of manipulating Torakichi's testimony.

Certainly we will never know if the vast medical knowledge recorded as Torakichi's was actually only Torakichi's, or if his knowledge of ancient writing and modern Western technology was really something he learned only in the woods. We will not know to what exact extent the tirades against Buddhism and Chinese philosophy are actually Torakichi's own ideas and to what extent they are the standard rhetoric and ideological stances of

Atsutane. Nevertheless, the close reading and the thematic arrangement can show what methods of questioning brought what answers. It can also show what kinds of questions were asked and what kinds of answers were rewarded. In these ways we can see more of the intent and interest of the questioner, Atsutane, and the requirements of his "transcending story."

As we know from the examples of ethnographic method practiced by modern anthropologists, there are many potential problems in this kind of intellectual endeavor, not the least of which is the underlying self-interest of the ethnographer. We shall see how skillfully Atsutane used this method in his interviews with Torakichi. If we are careful, we might even come to see if and how the ethnographic method was manipulated to achieve Atsutane's desired results.

CHAPTER 2

The Medium Finds a Promoter
Torakichi and Atsutane

The Medium

A Visitor from the Other World

Although Atsutane placed himself in a genealogy of nativist scholars whose scholarship depended on philological method, he claimed to dislike learning that focused on the organized study of classics. Clearly, by his choice of method in *Senkyō ibun,* Atsutane had begun to experiment with an alternative he hoped would be a superior means of acquiring knowledge and, not coincidentally, was the very way he acquired his in-depth knowledge of the *sanjin.* This brings us to the tale, strange in itself, of how Atsutane came to befriend the so-called Tengu Boy whom Atsutane usually referred to as Torakichi. Torakichi was to play a major role in Atsutane's attempt to consolidate his new discourse on the Other World and fill in some holes in his cosmological speculations. He was to serve as Atsutane's informant concerning the world of the *sanjin* and as a living example of a semisupernatural medium whose very existence was supposed to substantiate Atsutane's new discourse on Japanese religious and cultural identity.

In 1820, Edo academic salon society[1] was filled with rumors concerning the appearance of a boy who claimed to have been raised and trained by *tengu* in the mountains. The boy's name was Torakichi, and he was the second son of a poor Edo family. His father was a cart puller[2] who lived in Edo, not far from Atsutane's house.[3] That year, Torakichi had been taken in by Yamazaki Yoshishige, a young merchant/literatus who had studied at various Edo academies and at one time had been a student in Atsutane's academy. Rumors about the Tengu Boy reached Atsutane's ears through his friend and fellow academician Yashiro Hirokata.

That this wonder boy was called Tengu Boy Torakichi added to his celebrity. At this time in Edo the designation of *tengu* was not necessarily a cause for derision, nor would it have caused most eyebrows to rise in disbelief. A clear example of the popularity of the belief in *tengu* during the Tokugawa period can be seen in the writings of the famous and prestigious Hayashi Razan (1583–1657). Razan was a Confucian scholar and government official employed by the Tokugawa bakufu for fifty-two years, serving four successive shoguns. He was taught Neo-Confucianism by the famous scholar Fujiwara Seika (1561–1619), and it was Razan who persuaded the bakufu to grant the land to open a Confucian college. Razan wrote a work titled *A Study of Shrines in Our Land* (*Honchō jinjakō*), the purpose of which was to call for a Shinto purified of Buddhist influence. However, in the middle of this work, he expended great effort to examine in detail the supernatural creature called the *tengu*. The work was not dismissive of the creature; on the contrary, it affirmed its existence. Two centuries later this work inspired Atsutane's own work about the supernatural, including the *tengu*, titled *Thoughts on Supernatural Beings of Past and Present* (*Kokon yomikō*).

The Atsutane scholar Haga Noboru writes of Atsutane's debt to Razan in *Thoughts on Supernatural Beings of Past and Present* and also of the commonality of the belief in *tengu* during the Tokugawa period:

> This work was strongly influenced by Hayashi Razan's *Jinjakō*, and there are also more than a few instances of Atsutane parroting those earlier ideas; however, the fact is that he had a stronger belief in the existence of *tengu* than Razan. Yet, Atsutane's belief in *tengu* was not very different from that of the common person of his day.

By most accounts, it seems that the majority of people believed in *tengu* in Atsutane's day; that is, belief ranged from the man on the street to the scholar who advised the shogun. Therefore, it seems only natural that Atsutane and his friends should be excited at the chance of interviewing one.

As told in chapter 1, Yashiro came to Atsutane's house one day with the news that he was going over to Yoshishige's house for a chance to interview this boy, and he invited Atsutane along. Atsutane wrote of his delight at this opportunity, for he too had heard rumors about the boy, particularly that he spoke plainly and clearly about occurrences in the Other World. After they met, he wrote that he had been immediately impressed by the boy. Torakichi had looked at Atsutane and called him a *kami*, and then Torakichi asked if it were not true that Atsutane studied and believed in the Way of the Kami. Atsutane writes with surprise, and with no little naivete, feigned or otherwise, that he could not understand how Torakichi could have known such a thing. Atsutane's record of the first meeting with Torakichi was also his first attempt to exalt this boy's supernatural abilities in order to impress his readers. He writes:

Torakichi was deliberately staring at my face and smiling when a thought came to him, and he repeated three times, "You're a *kami*." When I did not respond due to the strangeness of his remark, he asked, "Don't you study and practice the Way of the Kami?" Yoshishige said, "This is the teacher Hirata, a gentleman who is a scholar of Ancient Learning and the Way of the Kami." Torakichi smiled and said, "I knew I was right." That was my [Atsutane's] first shock as I wondered how he could have known that. When I asked him whether he thought the study of the Way of the Kami was good or bad, he answered, "It just popped into my mind that you were a gentleman who believed in the *kami,* and belief in the *kami* is a very good thing for there is nothing I revere more than the Way of the Kami."[5]

We readers should recognize that Torakichi might have been using this first meeting to flatter this stranger, gain his favor, and, at the least, gain the approval of his benefactor Yoshishige by impressing his guest. It is also a distinct possibility that Atsutane used the story of the first meeting to introduce how much the Tengu Boy revered the *kami* and respected those who studied the Way of the Kami. We also should not forget, as Atsutane seemed to have, that Yoshishige might have mentioned something to Torakichi in advance about his expected guests. This would also have been in Yoshishige's interests at this point, as he was writing his own book about Torakichi, *Heiji daitō,*[6] and he too had motivation for having the boy thought to be in possession of special knowledge and power. Atsutane could have responded to this suspicion by pointing out that according to him, he had been invited by Yashiro, not by Yoshishige, and his arrival was supposed to be understood as unexpected. However, my point is that clairvoyance would not necessarily be everyone's first assumption upon hearing Torakichi connect Atsutane with the *kami,* no matter how anxious Atsutane was to have his readers make that their first assumption.

From the beginning of Atsutane's association with Torakichi, he portrayed him as something special and apart from the normal human being. Atsutane attempted to make Torakichi's special adventures and exotic experiences appear to be his destiny. First of all, we learn from Atsutane that Torakichi was born at approximately four o'clock in the morning on the thirtieth day of the twelfth month in 1806. Since that was the year, day, and hour of the horary sign of the tiger, he was named Torakichi, a two-character compound consisting of "tiger" and "auspicious." Therefore, those who believed in Japanese/Chinese astrology would consider this convergence of tiger influences not coincidence, but fate. This astrological fact was probably included by Atsutane to add fuel to the current popular rumor that this boy was something very special, or at least something very different.

Atsutane first met Torakichi when the boy was nearly fourteen years old, and at that meeting he asked him how he first came to be lured away to the mountains. Torakichi said that when he was six years old[7] he had been fascinated by a street fortune-teller who had set up shop in his neighborhood. The itinerant fortune-teller practiced a form of yin yang divination and Torakichi asked him to teach it to him, but the fortune-teller did not take the little boy seriously and instead pulled a trick on him.[8] This man dismissed Torakichi, but this encounter can be seen to foreshadow what would later come to pass.

Later in that same year, Torakichi was playing near a temple when he saw a strange-looking man selling pills on a reed mat he had spread by the back gate. The man kept his pills in a four-inch-diameter pot. When he decided to quit for the day, he packed his belongings into the pot and then stepped into it himself. This impossible feat was followed by another, as the too-small pot then rose into the air and flew away.[9]

Torakichi was impressed and went to watch this man every day. He worked up the courage to speak with him and was relieved when he turned out to be friendly. The stranger offered to give Torakichi a ride in the pot, but Torakichi was wary of him. Then he bought Torakichi some sweets and, learning of Torakichi's desire to learn yin yang divination, promised Torakichi he would teach him if he got in and took a ride with him. Torakichi agreed to get in, and that was the start of the next eight years of continual interaction with his *tengu/sanjin* master.[10]

It could be argued that Torakichi made a choice concerning his future career; at least he was not forcibly carried off by a stranger against his wishes. However, as a six-year-old with an interest in fortune-telling equipment, bribed by sweets, and fascinated by strange occurrences, it would have been hard for him to have said no. Perhaps the power of persuasion evident in Torakichi's master's techniques of seduction coupled with Torakichi's own desires and propensities made it easy for Atsutane to insist that it was fate that brought Torakichi into a relationship with his supernatural master.

In actuality, Torakichi's background made him susceptible to this kind of seduction/abduction. He came from a poor family living in an Edo slum, and his parents did not have the time or the inclination to watch over him during the day, so he was free to spend his days however and wherever chance might lead him. He was given no education to speak of and was too young or not yet competent to take on any family or work responsibilities. So for years he could go on visiting his *sanjin* master and except for one occasion,[11] his parents and elder brother never suspected a thing. When he reached his early teens his mother and elder brother twice sent him to apprentice at Buddhist temples, where for different reasons he was not allowed to stay very long.

Atsutane wanted his readers to believe that the *sanjin* lifestyle was a kind of calling and not for the common man. His description of Torakichi was intended to make him out to be a rare type of spiritually empowered person, subject to spirit possession. At their first meeting, Atsutane, who had studied medicine and been employed as a physician, gave Torakichi a cursory examination to start his investigations and perhaps to determine whether or not he was indeed human. To fill out Torakichi's medical history, Atsutane questioned Torakichi's mother about his childhood problems and proclivities, which also helped to fill out his supernatural profile.

According to Atsutane's observations, Torakichi had large eyes that seemed to give off light, which gave his face an overall odd appearance. His stomach was small but strong and his pulse was thready, more like the pulse of a six- or seven-year-old. Torakichi said he was fourteen, but judging by his size and appearance, Atsutane said he would have taken him for twelve. He could be excessively childish and wild on occasion, and having no social graces, had to be scolded before he would pay proper respect or display courtesy to others.

His mother said that when Torakichi was a child he was prone to stomach aches, and as he grew older he was often pale, colicky, and prone to bedwetting. She said that she and her husband often feared he would not be strong enough to make it to adulthood, but by the time he reached the age of thirteen he seemed to have gained strength. Sometimes he would become nervous and greatly agitated, and at other times this would lead to an all-out fit. Supposedly associated with these sensitive traits, it seems that from an early age he had the ability to see the future.

Once as a child, he climbed up on the roof of his family's house, looked over at the main street, and claimed he saw a large fire raging there. This alarmed his family and the neighbors, and they excitedly came over to take a look, but no one else could see a thing because there was no fire. However, the next day a fire broke out just where Torakichi said it had been.

On another occasion, he suddenly announced to his father that a thief would sneak into their house that night. He was ignored, the burglary occurred, and Torakichi's strange reputation grew. He was also ignored when he accurately predicted that his father would be injured on a certain day. When he made predictions, he explained that first he heard a noise in his ears. The noise then became a voice saying words that ended up coming out of his own mouth. His mother also added that he had often demonstrated the ability to remember events from his infancy, even from the time before he could walk.

Torakichi told a story of his own prognostication abilities that ended up forcing him to leave his position as an initiate at a Buddhist temple.[12] It seems that on one occasion he managed to divine the location of a temple patron's lost item, and because of that, other patrons started asking him to make predictions concerning lottery numbers. Torakichi was not 100 percent accurate in his predictions, but he claimed to be correct a large majority of the time, and he could explain the inaccuracies as the fault of his questioners. According to Torakichi, the lottery predictions eventually led to scandal, which he claimed he had always tried to avoid, but the abbot still felt compelled to dismiss him for the good of the temple's reputation.

There was one more thing in Atsutane's writings that served to add to Torakichi's status and secure his position as a true *tengu,* or at least a novice *tengu* who would despite his youth serve as a reliable medium between the visible and the Other World. Torakichi told Atsutane of an initiation ritual meant to test his ability, desire, and fitness to live in the Other World. He claimed to have passed the initiation and won the recognition of his peers and, later it seems, Atsutane himself. The *tengu* initiation ceremony was a torturous survival test.[13] Torakichi claimed to have been tied to a tree to enforce a fast of one hundred days. Certainly no ordinary human could have survived such an ordeal. Torakichi's survival should have suggested, to those who would believe it, that he was more than human.

When one first starts on the *tengu* path there is the fast of the first hundred days. It is painful and nearly impossible to endure. When I [Torakichi] did it, after four or five days I was so hungry and so weak-willed that I couldn't take it, so I secretly took a rice ball from somewhere and was severely scolded, and even thrown down the mountain several times. Finally, they tied me to a tree on the mountain and I was forced to try it again. After awhile, I couldn't tell if it was day or night, and I was always so hungry I just couldn't stand it. A chestnut fell right in front of me and I wanted to eat it so much that sweat poured off of my forehead, but I was tied up. They just told me I had to stand it. The time passed but it was horrendous. Eventually I felt like I had died. Suddenly I opened my eyes and just like that the hundred days were over. To me it only felt like it had been seven days. Even now when I think of how quickly the hundred-day fast was over, I still can't believe it. Another strange thing was that before the fast began, the master made me swear an oath to do my best and not be weak, and then he took my hand and tore the nail off my little finger to give me an example of the pain so that I could imagine what I would be in for.[14]

It would lend credence to Atsutane's discourse on the *sanjin* if the reader were to believe that Torakichi was a special kind of human being with a supernatural calling. His informant had to be considered an authority to be believable. With the rejection of a philological source of knowledge, which had been the classical method of *kokugaku* scholars, Atsutane's adoption of this new methodology was riding on the reputation (and imagination) of one uncultured, undisciplined, and uneducated boy from the slums of Edo.

If that strange little boy could gain credibility as a medium by Atsutane's recounting of and emphasis on his supernatural credentials, which linked him to traditionally recognized creatures accepted as supernatural mediums, then his tales of the *sanjin* master might be accepted as fact. These then would be seen as new facts discovered by Atsutane, and firmly within his control. Furthermore, the stranger and more marvelous the stories about Torakichi's *sanjin* master were, the greater the chance for increasing the status and power of his student, Torakichi, and the student's new mentor, Atsutane.

In *Senkyō ibun*, Torakichi is shown to have become the center of attention of a group of educated academic elites in Edo. This meant that Atsutane also became a center of attention for his patronage of this boy. However, that success only occurred after Torakichi left Yoshishige's house and came to stay with Atsutane. Before Torakichi's impact on Edo society can be analyzed, the story of how Torakichi came to stay with Atsutane must be told. We will see that Atsutane wanted a new medium for his supernatural research bad enough to steal Torakichi away from his own former student and colleague.

Torakichi's Abduction

After Atsutane's initial meeting with Torakichi, he invited both the Tengu Boy and his current temporary master Yoshishige over for a large reception followed by a question-and-answer session. Despite Yoshishige's initial acceptance of the invitation, he had grown less inclined to share his *tengu* child with others who had their own scholarly purposes to fulfill. On the agreed upon afternoon, Yoshishige and the child failed to show up at Atsutane's salon gathering, much to the disappointment of his many guests and members of his academy. Yoshishige sent an excuse by messenger, but this only served to anger Atsutane and his supporters all the more.

The next day his angry students and household were determined to go over to Yoshishige's house to demand at least an apology and at best an audience with the *tengu* child. Atsutane claims that he did not instigate this mass action, but that he could not dissuade them, so he decided to go along just to keep things under control. When they arrived at Yoshishige's place, Yoshishige's mother greeted them and said she regretted to inform them that her son was out and that Torakichi had also left to visit his own mother. Torakichi later confirmed that this was a lie. He said he had been standing just inside listening to the uproar and had been told to keep quiet. Atsutane's crowd was not satisfied with this answer, but had no other course of action except to go find Torakichi at his mother's house.

When they arrived at Torakichi's family home, actually just a one-room hovel, they found that Torakichi was not in. In fact, his mother said she had not seen him in the months since she had placed him as a servant with another family. Unbeknownst to her, that family had found him stupid and useless and had turned him out. Fortunately for Torakichi, Yoshishige, who found his stories of the mountains quite intriguing, discovered him, befriended him, and took him in. His mother said she knew nothing of Torakichi's current whereabouts. It was at this time that Atsutane and his followers heard the amazing stories from Torakichi's childhood, which only fueled their desire to question him further. Unfortunately for them, there was nothing more they could do that day and so they went home.

Atsutane sent presents and his friend Yashiro to plead for another audience with the Tengu Boy, and Yoshishige agreed once more to bring him over. Atsutane again filled his salon full of friends and students all excited to hear this visitor from the Other World. They seemed to have found that first evening very informative and entertaining, and were loath to let the Tengu Boy slip away. However, before it grew too late, Yoshishige took his discovery home with him.

For days after Torakichi left, Atsutane was despondent. He had exacted a promise from Yoshishige that they would be allowed to meet again before the next month, when Torakichi said he was due to return to the mountains for the ascetic winter practices of the twelfth month. Atsutane sent a student to Yoshishige's house to thank them for coming and ask when the boy would be available to show him how to make a certain flute Torakichi said the *sanjin* used in the mountains. The student was met by Yoshishige's mother, who tried to put him off by saying that Torakichi was in such demand that he and Yoshishige had gone out and she did not know when he would again be available. Unfortunately for her, Torakichi overheard the talk of the flute, revealed himself, and volunteered to go immediately, embarrassing Yoshishige's mother.

Torakichi left with the student and went to Atsutane's house, where Atsutane and his circle were allowed to spend another full day with him. Atsutane recorded that they engaged Torakichi in an extended question-and-answer session, performed certain *kami* rituals, and held games and activities designed specifically to entertain the boy. Much too soon for Atsutane's liking, Yoshishige sent a messenger saying it was urgent that Torakichi return immediately. Atsutane tried to find a way around it but in the end had no choice but to return the boy. Yoshishige was clearly still jealously restricting access to Torakichi.

Once again Atsutane became despondent, and he and his students talked about nothing but Torakichi. Atsutane was disappointed because the flute designed in the Other World had still not been made for him, but more than that he lamented the fact that the evidence of the existence of the Other World was slipping away. He wrote that he believed that with Torakichi's help, he could get the proof and shed light on all the darkest nooks and crannies of the Other World. However, it was now clear that Yoshishige intended to keep the Tengu Boy away from Atsutane.

Atsutane's students received the import of their master's lament loud and clear. The next morning as Atsutane was moping despondently on his grounds, his handyman spotted Torakichi running desperately past the gates. Two of Atsutane's students were chasing after him and soon they caught up with the boy, grabbed his arms, and dragged him into Atsutane's yard. Atsutane told Torakichi he would have to remain there until he got the flute. Meanwhile, he sent for all his friends. Once again there were questions and answers followed by games, and delicious treats provided to please the boy. Torakichi got whatever he wanted and was promised more of the same the next day.[15]

Torakichi's abduction went as follows. Atsutane's students had reasoned that since Torakichi's mother or elder brother, who was eighteen and trying to take care of the household, did not know he had been staying at Yoshishige's, then Yoshishige could not be Torakichi's rightful master. They decided to speak with Torakichi's brother to have him persuade Torakichi into coming to Atsutane's household. How they persuaded him is left to our imaginations. Torakichi's brother went to Yoshishige's house and talked to Torakichi, who then ran away, and the students finally caught him as Atsutane was watching.

During this encounter Torakichi was wary of Atsutane, as Atsutane initially dealt with him more like a captive than a guest. Torakichi was agitated and begged Atsutane not to use his magic to restrict him from returning to the mountains. Atsutane softened and told Torakichi that someone had been filling his mind with slanderous stories, then offered him a rare stone flute along with more of the same kind of entertainment Torakichi had enjoyed so much during the previous visit. Torakichi's attitude toward Atsutane softened and, in response to Atsutane's kindness, he made a special flute for Atsutane the following day.

After making the flute, Torakichi was returned to Yoshishige's house along with an apology for detaining his servant. But later that day Torakichi again appeared at Atsutane's home with a travel bundle and the story that Yoshishige had told him to leave immediately for the mountains and his old master. Torakichi said he had stopped by just to let Atsutane know. However, this sudden appearance is suspicious, and it seems likely that Torakichi was harboring another motive for this hasty departure from Yoshishige's place.

Whatever Torakichi's intent may have been, Atsutane did not feel inclined to tell us. He wanted his reader to believe that he himself just took advantage of this opportunity but did nothing underhanded to create it. He readily offered Torakichi more of his hospitality and made it clear that he wanted to use this as an opportunity to establish a relationship with a powerful force in the Other World. He asked Torakichi to take a letter to his *tengu/sanjin* master and present his own master work *The August Pillar of the Soul* and another of his books, most likely a version of the one later known as *The Sacred Letters of Japanese Traditional Script* (*Kanna hifumiden*), which contained the theory of an original Japanese writing from the Age of the Kami. In this letter Atsutane asked for more information about the Other World and in return promised to include Torakichi's master among the *kami* he regularly worshiped.[16] He also asked if Torakichi's master would take a look at his books and tell him how to correct them.

Along with the books he gave to Torakichi to take to the mountains, Atsutane wrote some poetry for the occasion. He also wrote a formal letter of introduction to be delivered to Torakichi's master, whom we learn was to be addressed as Sugiyama Sanjin. The letter detailed Atsutane's interests and hopes for contact with such an esteemed member of the Other World. One of the farewell poems to Torakichi reads:

When Torakichi enters the mountains,
Whom shall I ask about the unknowable,
Ways of the Other World.[17]

The other parting poems praise the tradition of the *sanjin* and the Way of the Kami, ask for the teachings from Torakichi, and also tell of a monthly worship service for the mountain practitioners.

The text of the formal letter is as follows:

Recently, I met this servant boy of your august mountain and heard a brief account of your honorable abode. This cleared up many questions that have troubled me for years, and I gratefully regard our acquaintance as a once in a lifetime event. I hope you can overlook the impropriety of using Torakichi's return to the mountain to send you this letter. First of all I pray for the ever-increasing prosperity and diligent works of your servants. Because the seen and the unseen have been separated from each other since the Age of the Kami, the matters of the Other World are difficult to apprehend from the seen realm. You, on the other hand, seem to have a detailed knowledge of the affairs of the visible realm and must be very familiar with them. My sincere desire is to learn about the Ancient Way of the Kami of Heaven and Earth, and to spread this Way throughout the world. Although I am without talent, I have labored diligently for many years to carry the mantle of my master Motoori Norinaga and to study his teachings. However, as an ordinary inhabitant of the seen realm, it has been very difficult for me to glean any understanding of the Other World, and so there are still many things I am trying hard to figure out. In the future I would be grateful if I could make these inquiries of you and receive your august instructions about your realm in order to answer these questions. I wonder if you might not be able to grace me on those occasions with your teachings? If possible, I humbly request that you send me your answer when this servant boy descends from the mountain. If this request should be permitted, every month for the rest of my life I shall perform ritual worship for you. Also, please glance at the text *Tama no mihashira* that I have drafted previously. This work discusses the true principles of heaven and earth; although it is incomplete, it is based on the traditions from the Age of the Kami, and also concerns matters of the Other World. Because it depends on the weak understanding of the common man, if it were to be glanced at by someone of that noble realm I have great fear that there would be many flaws discovered in the theories. If you could take a look and I could receive your instructions concerning the flaws, this would be a great source of happiness in this seen world, and an overabundance of good fortune for me in my serious studies and also the unsurpassable fulfillment of a lifelong dream, so I earnestly request that it be kindly received by you the august master. Because it is from the sincere heart of a common man who in faith wholeheartedly studies the Ancient Way, but who does not understand even the simple rules of that noble realm, I humbly request your forgiveness for any offense committed and any disrespect in offering up this letter.

Sincerely yours,

Tenth month seventeenth day

To: The *sanjin* attendants of Mount Sōgaku in the Iwama mountains in Hitachi Province.

Hirata Daikaku

Taira no Atsutane[18]

The painfully humble contents of the letter attest to Atsutane's sincere and almost desperate belief in Torakichi's story, especially at this early stage in their relationship. It is truly as if Atsutane had been waiting for someone like this, as he wrote, to fulfill his lifelong dream. His promise to include Torakichi's master in his worship rituals also was kept. Kamata Tōji showed that starting from the fourth month of the following year, 1822, Atsutane performed monthly rituals for Sugiyama Sanjin, giving him the alias Master Takane.[19] In addition, Atsutane even altered his daily prayers to include this Master Takane as one of the attendants of the *kami* of Mt. Asama, Iwanaga-hime no kami. By these indicators, his own personal commitment, it would seem that Atsutane was not attempting to perpetrate a fraud in promoting the *sanjin*.

Torakichi's objective for the winter practices was the Tsukuba Mountains in Hitachi Province, presently considered not so very far from Edo. Unfortunately, Torakichi claimed he did not know the way, since when he had gone there previously he had always flown with his master. Atsutane, anxious to make his new supernatural contact, asked two of his students to guide Torakichi to the mountains. Soon after they arrived in the mountains, Torakichi claimed that he heard his former companions[20] calling him from afar and abruptly parted company with his guides. One student was immediately sent back to Edo to tell Atsutane that the mission had been accomplished, and he arrived back and informed Atsutane ten days after their departure date from Edo. Later that night Torakichi also returned suddenly to Atsutane's home. Torakichi said he had first tried to go to Yoshishige's house but that no one would open the door to him.

Atsutane was happy to see Torakichi and welcomed him in, asking why he had returned so quickly. Torakichi explained that he had met with his master and his small band of followers. His master had then informed him that he had to go to Sanuki (Shikoku) that winter to be a representative at the very important winter practices there; therefore the winter practices for the lesser students, Torakichi included, had been called off and Torakichi was told to return. Atsutane asked him if he had shown his books to his master and if so what had been his master's reaction to them. Torakichi said he had showed them and while reading the books his master had been nodding his head in approval. He added that his master did make a couple of corrections on some of the Age of the Kami letters and in the ritual dance steps Atsutane had written about, but other than that Torakichi did not seem to have specific responses to report.

Atsutane allowed Torakichi to stay with him from that time on, and for the rest of the *Senkyō ibun* narrative he was more like a member of the family than a servant or even a student. On just one occasion after that, Yoshishige asked Torakichi to come to his house for an evening to speak with a visitor who had asked about him. Torakichi went but returned to Atsutane's the next day. He was never again called to Yoshishige's home nor did he ever again claim to be called back to the mountains. He continued to be used as a resource at Atsutane's house, and his stories and the question-and-answer sessions there came to constitute the bulk of *Senkyō ibun*.

After his return, Torakichi told Atsutane various things he said he felt he could not have told him before. Torakichi claimed that while he was staying with Yoshishige, Yoshishige was constantly forcing Buddhist teachings upon him, urging him to become a Buddhist priest while at the same time slandering the *kami*. Torakichi resisted, he said, because he and his master Sugiyama Sanjin were devoted followers of the *kami*. Torakichi went on to add that while he was at Yoshishige's, before Atsutane's first visit, he had been secretly approached by one of his mountain companions, who brought a message from Sugiyama Sanjin ordering him to attend the winter practices, but also informing him that soon he would meet someone who would help him. Torakichi said that he knew the moment he saw Atsutane that he was the person his master had predicted would help him.

Here we have more evidence that Atsutane would have us believe that his meeting with Torakichi and their close relationship was fated. Torakichi, the medium who could see the future, verified that he had known this from the first meeting. The fact that he was dragged kicking and screaming from Yoshishige's house by Atsutane's students, and had at first attempted to return to Yoshishige's house but was subsequently denied entry, had been conveniently forgotten. Although Atsutane was compelled to record Torakichi's initial reluctance to stay with him, there seemed to be an attempt to cancel out this embarrassing fact by this belated revelation of a prophecy come true.

A little sympathy for the true-life figure of Torakichi is in order. He had twice been either lured or snatched away from his home, and both times he had returned to find himself unwanted. Perhaps his victimization had soiled him in the eyes of his family and maybe even in Yoshishige's eyes. If this were so, then this would be all the more reason to expect that

Torakichi would be sensitive and responsive to the demands of his abductors/masters and especially malleable to Atsutane's will.

To Trust a Tengu

In Torakichi's brief absence during the time he was traveling to the mountains and back, Atsutane wrote that he started to hear some distressing rumors. People had started to come forward saying they did not believe Torakichi's stories. Some of these nonbelievers were Atsutane's own students. Some of them even refused to return to the academy for the duration of the scandal. Seeds of doubt were planted in Atsutane's mind, but he continued to hold onto his faith in Torakichi.

Regardless of Atsutane's conviction that Torakichi was telling the truth, there are many things in Atsutane's own record of their interaction that call Torakichi's honesty into question. First of all, there is his self-serving prophecy about their fated meeting. Secondly, Torakichi's secret confessions to Atsutane seem too conveniently advantageous for both of them. In addition, certain statements seem to suggest that Torakichi would have been happier staying with Yoshishige.

Many of the events concerning Torakichi's "fated" involvement with Atsutane are suspicious. For example, in the incident when Atsutane's students decided to abduct Torakichi, Atsutane recorded that Torakichi himself declared that he ran from them because he did not want to go to Atsutane's house. Furthermore, the night following Torakichi's abduction, after Atsutane had sent him back with an apology, Yoshishige immediately sent the boy packing to the mountains. In addition, Torakichi's own story about his earlier employment experiences admits that he was found too stupid and too incompetent to hold a position in a household. On top of that, Atsutane's record makes it clear to the reader that Torakichi's stories had started to favor Shinto listeners in front of Atsutane and his crowd but clearly had been biased in favor of Buddhism before he met Atsutane.

All these circumstances seem to suggest what I believe Atsutane could never admit or recognize. That is, while initially jealous of Torakichi's interactions with Atsutane, at a certain point Yoshishige no longer valued the Tengu Boy's presence. In fact, Yoshishige was finished with Torakichi. He already had his material for his book that was circulated among the standard readership.[21] Furthermore, Torakichi's stories and reputation were becoming more and more disagreeable to Yoshishige, and therefore, after his overnight defection to Atsutane's salon, Yoshishige likely handed the boy his things and dared him to follow up on his claim to join the winter practices in the mountains.

In any case, Yoshishige made no further efforts to keep Torakichi with him. On the day Torakichi was forcibly detained at Atsutane's, after they had won him over with sweets and games, Yashiro expressed his concern that Torakichi should be returned to Yoshishige's as soon as possible and that keeping him at Atsutane's would be inappropriate. At that point Torakichi claimed he was not a servant in Yoshishige's house and that Yoshishige himself had said he could do as he pleased. If we can believe Torakichi at this juncture, this would mean that not only did Torakichi not want to go home just yet, having been treated so royally to make up for the abduction, Yoshishige actually may have made it clear to Torakichi that they had no obligations to each other. This seems even more likely when we remember that when Torakichi did return, Yoshishige had him leave, and when Torakichi tried again upon returning from the mountains, the door remained closed to him.

There was never any talk of Torakichi's leaving anything behind at Yoshishige's place, and he never had to return there for anything, nor was there any story of a complaint from Yoshishige when Atsutane sent a message telling him Torakichi was staying with him after his return from the mountains. When Torakichi did return from the mountains, he admitted to Atsutane that his first stop was Yoshishige's place but that the doors were not open to him. Why should we believe that Torakichi truly felt his meeting with Atsutane was fated when the record shows that if Torakichi could have chosen, he would have stayed with Yoshishige and continued to tell stories about Buddhism in the mountains?

Another suspicious aspect to Torakichi's story is the speed with which he returned to Edo from the Tsukuba Mountains. Atsutane arranged for an escort with food and lodging on the way to the mountains for Torakichi. The report given to Atsutane by his student escort only suggested that Torakichi must have gone into the mountains, but no one accompanied him to the foot of the mountains and no one saw him even walking toward them. At the last stop before the mountains when they were staying at a friend's place, Torakichi reported hearing the voice of a mountain comrade and left mysteriously. That was the last they saw of him. That day Atsutane's student set out on the return trip to Edo.

Torakichi claimed that he went up into the mountains and talked to his master there at some length. He also claimed that his master took the time to read the books and make some cursory comments about written character variants and dance steps. Torakichi also said that the master told him to assist Atsutane and tell him anything he wanted to know. Then Torakichi said he was escorted back to Edo by two of the senior students from the mountains.

Given the time constraints, it is much more likely that Torakichi got rid of Atsutane's books and secretly followed Atsutane's student back to Edo. Upon Torakichi's arrival at Atsutane's place, the household staff remarked that he looked as if he had hardly been traveling at all. This would be consistent with not having entered the mountains. Unless he could have flown back with his master, Torakichi could not have gone to the mountains for even that short consultation. For one who has doubts about a Japanese mountain practitioner's ability to fly, Torakichi's story about entering the mountains and consulting with his master about Atsutane's scholarship is preposterous.

Atsutane by his own admission was acutely aware of the opinions of many people in the Edo salons who thought this uneducated child was duping him. They saw the evidence of the situation as suggesting that Torakichi was just a strange child with many quasi-religious experiences who lied to curry favor. However, Atsutane sometimes considered the evidence provided by his own eyes and ears to be fallible. He was predisposed to believe that supernatural verification was the only verification that mattered, and that predisposition was supported by his deep faith in the *kami*.

Therefore, ultimately, Atsutane's faith in Torakichi was provisional. That is, Atsutane put faith in Torakichi only when he asserted something Atsutane already believed in. He corrected or apologized for Torakichi when he thought Torakichi was wrong. Thus for Atsutane, it was not really a matter of being duped by Torakichi or even a question of faith or trust in Torakichi; he already knew what he considered to be the truth.

After Torakichi returned from the mountains, Atsutane recorded several occasions when important officials would interview Torakichi. On some occasions these were local officials; on other occasions they were daimyō. At times, Torakichi would talk to physicians and other professional learned men. On a few occasions he was even questioned by Buddhist priests. According to Atsutane's descriptions of these occasions, those who doubted Torakichi interrogated him quite harshly, but those people were usually described by Atsutane as having Buddhist biases and prejudices, so the reader was to understand the fundamental evil of their starting point. Some of these interviews were recorded as being quite heated, ending with one party or the other storming out.

Some of Torakichi's interlocutors claimed to have tricked him into revealing that he had been lying or pretending to have knowledge he did not have. Even assuming bias in his accounts of these episodes, Atsutane was at least making it clear that he was no fool and that he was aware that there was much opposition to the boy's assertions and widespread doubt as to his abilities. Atsutane did not just record events that made Torakichi look like a genius; he recorded several occasions where Torakichi's behavior was childish, selfish, violent, and even what we might now call schizophrenic. There are also fascinating and strange descriptions of Torakichi's being possessed by demons. While these scenes do little to establish the stability and reliability of this supernatural informant, they do serve to display his spiritual abilities and his connection with the Other World.

Many people of the twenty-first century, with their scientific predispositions, would find the stories of Torakichi, as told by Atsutane, hard to believe. There is evidence within *Senkyō ibun* itself that many people of the early nineteenth century, even without scientific dispositions, also found them hard to believe. However, Atsutane was not merely intent upon recording only those things that made Torakichi easy to believe, he also recorded several examples of Torakichi's defensive statements given when he was accused of lying or of being inconsistent and contradictory in his storytelling. In my opinion, Torakichi's explanations often fail miserably to strengthen his case, and choosing to record these defenses or excuses clearly highlights the suspicion directed toward Torakichi's stories, of which Atsutane should have been well aware. Although this could have been a conscious effort on Atsutane's part to give his ethnographic record some greater degree of objectivity and integrity, I am inclined to believe instead that Atsutane included these incidents to allow Torakichi's voice to respond to existing criticism of him, and also because he believed Torakichi's shaky excuses and wanted his readers to do the same.

When Torakichi was accused of being inconsistent in his storytelling, he claimed that it was either because he could not trust certain audiences with the truth, or that on certain occasions he had purposely lied to expose the lies of another. That is, Torakichi admitted that on occasion he told false stories, which usually meant he affirmed Buddhist doctrines or practices, and when that particular interlocutor agreed with him, Torakichi would say that he had succeeded in exposing a crypto-Buddhist. (Later we may come to the conclusion that the real crypto-Buddhist was Torakichi himself.) When Torakichi was accused of claiming knowledge learned in this world, specifically at previous salon gatherings, to be knowledge learned in the Other World, he said that Buddhist sympathizers were just trying to disparage him. When it was said that on several occasions he had proudly expounded at length on his mountain master's study and practice of Buddhism and/or Shugendō, he claimed that those were all lies told by people, for example Yoshishige, who believed in Buddhism and wanted him to convert.

Even if Atsutane was not completely convinced by Torakichi's excuses for the inconsistencies in his stories, he had found in Torakichi something that made him indispensable to Atsutane's new brand of nativist discourse on Japan's place in the world. Therefore, although *Senkyō ibun* is supposed to be an accurate record replete with stories told by Torakichi to Atsutane, we should realize that there might have been many more stories that did not make the editorial cut. On the other hand, among the stories recorded by Atsutane that he included in this text, we should not immediately conclude that Atsutane always had to edit Torakichi's stories so they would support his nativist arguments. Rather, it will be shown later that dialogues within the text suggest that Torakichi himself understood that he had to self-edit his stories for his particular audience and also for Atsutane.

In chapter 3 it will be demonstrated that Atsutane's interview method favored certain types of stories and terminologies. This tendency became especially important in all conversations pertaining to Atsutane's new religious hero, the *sanjin*. However, before delving into the *sanjin*, first our attention should be directed to the scene and the setting for the introduction of the new medium and Atsutane's discourse about the new religious hero.

The Promoter's Venue

The Rise of Edo Academic Salons

For a discourse to be effective, it has to be propagated to an audience at certain sites from where it can continue to spread outward like waves in a pond. Most of Atsutane's written works were published and passed around among his friends, students, and patrons. Atsutane's school was notable for its use of printed matter to gain support among the literate masses, particularly among well-to-do peasants.[22] Ironically, even though Atsutane had strong arguments against a medium that used Chinese characters that supposedly distorted the meaning of the original Japanese words, he employed the medium liberally and enjoyed great profits from its use.

Although *Senkyō ibun* was described by Atsutane as a "secret" document, it was available at least to his students and his guests, and it was consulted for an abridged version of the Torakichi story that received a wider circulation. Moreover, the printed pages of *Senkyō ibun* reveal a different means of propagating Atsutane's *Senkyō ibun* message. Although a great deal of the contents of this "secret" work is a record of Tengu Boy

Torakichi being interviewed and answering questions, the question-and-answer sessions were not just one-on-one encounters. They were events held at people's houses, sometimes for special guests who came from far away or held important positions. The events often included fine food and drink, games, entertainments, and demonstrations of skill or magic. Certainly they included periods when Atsutane questioned Torakichi, but he usually did not do so alone; the other people in attendance felt free to, and they seemed anxious and privileged to join in.

Tengu Boy Torakichi was an attraction that drew many important listeners. He was put up and treated well by Atsutane in his own home because he delivered the message that Atsutane wanted him to. His role was to enhance Atsutane's status as the promoter of this great spectacle, and he verified Atsutane's discourse about the Other World while at the same time strengthening Atsutane's new ethnographic methodology.

The Tokugawa period is known for the rise of commoner culture in towns and cities and the proliferation of the private academy. With surplus wealth, surplus time, and the ready availability of books, would-be men of culture in the cities started to form study and reading groups, which sometimes had the opportunity to become larger, commercially viable private academies. The successful model of the private academy was Itō Jinsai's academy of Ancient Learning called the Kogidō.[23] It was likely envy of this academy devoted to Chinese learning that inspired Kada no Azumamaro's petition for an academy devoted to Japanese learning.

Motoori Norinaga's academy in Matsuzaka started out as a study group of friends who met at nights on the second floor of Norinaga's house. The academy was named the Suzunoya, the House of Bells, and it flourished even after Norinaga's death in 1801. Norinaga's two sons, Haruniwa (1763–1828) and Ohira (1756–1833),[24] worked to expand it after their father's death, and by the early nineteenth century it had branches in Kyoto, Osaka, Wakayama, and Edo. When Atsutane started his own study group in Edo in 1803, he was not yet affiliated with any established nativist school. From early on he actively distributed his work to other nativist scholars to elicit opinions and have them introduce his writing to the leaders of the important factions, perhaps showing that he felt the need or saw the wisdom in doing so to legitimize his work and attract a clientele.

In the early nineteenth century, Kamo no Mabuchi's school of nativism was still flourishing in Edo near where Atsutane lived. Mabuchi's most illustrious student, Murata Harumi (1746–1811),[25] was the teacher of Atsutane's contemporary Oyamada Tomokiyo. Harumi had emphasized the precise study of ancient poetry and even the composition of contemporary poetry as the proper activity of nativist scholars. Tomokiyo gained a reputation for his aptitude for *kōshōgaku*, or evidential studies, a kind of precise textualism. This was the character of the nativist study undertaken at the so-called Edo school of *kokugaku*. However, Atsutane was not drawn to poetics, at least not as much as he was to metaphysical speculation. Still, he did send out feelers in an attempt to be recognized by this group, but his attempt to join or to be recognized failed and so he looked elsewhere, to the Suzunoya. At that time, the Edo school was not the most important nativist academy in Japan.

In the first decade of the nineteenth century, the Matsuzaka-based Motoori Suzunoya had extended its influence into Edo. Despite this expansion, Edo *kokugaku* was still dominated by the students of the Kamo school based in Edo. Ban Nobutomo, a young scholar of the Edo Suzunoya, had yet to make a name for himself and was still far from what would be at the peak of his celebrity. While the Edo school had became known for its emphasis on poetics and aesthetics, along with the previously mentioned field of evidential studies, the reputation of the Suzunoya was more eclectic. Norinaga had defined four fields of study for *kokugaku:* theology, antiquarianism, history, and poetry. This school was certainly a better fit for Atsutane than the poetics and evidential studies of the Edo school; however, the fit was still far from perfect.

Atsutane met Ban Nobutomo, who was recognized as a student of the late Norinaga, and asked him to look at his work. Nobutomo seemed impressed enough to send the sample to Motoori Ohira of the Suzunoya in Wakayama, with whom Nobutomo was affiliated. At first Ohira was pleased with it, but he later received word that Atsutane had sided with the Edo school's Murata Harumi in a well-known debate with Izumi Makuni (?–1805).[26] This debate had involved some name-calling and deprecation of Norinaga's philological ability, and Ohira subsequently rejected Atsutane's request for affiliation. However, Norinaga's other son, Haruniwa, had no objection to Atsutane and so in 1806 Atsutane was officially accepted into Haruniwa's branch of the Suzunoya.

There was another important trend in the Tokugawa period that affected the scholarly activity occurring at these private academies. After the collapse of the Ming dynasty, a segment of well-to-do educated Chinese society left the political turmoil of their cities and retreated to the countryside to live as men of arts and letters, spending the bulk of their time writing and painting. Images of that effete, elite lifestyle came into Japan during the late seventeenth century, and a culture of the *bunjin,* the man of letters, came into vogue in the cities. The elite townspeople did not leave the cities for lives of reclusion, but they sought to emulate the literary and artistic pastimes of the Chinese men of arts and letters.

Of course, the supposed practice of art for art's sake is even more rewarding if it can be shown off so others can appreciate the genius, hard work, and suffering of the dilettante. Also, those who could not be artists sought out the presence of artists, and circles of the cultural elite came together and circulated artists and other curiosities through their academies and salons. The Edo school[27] academy and salon belonging to the previously mentioned Oyamada Tomokiyo flourished due to this trend favoring the arts. His salon was graced with the likes of famous Edo artists such as Santō Kyōden (1761–1816),[28] Shikitei Samba (1776–1822),[29] and Takizawa Bakin (1767–1848).[30]

It is easy to comprehend how the Edo school with its emphasis on poetry would be particularly suited for salon activity filled with elegant, tea-sipping poetry readings, but one might wonder how a salon dedicated to theology or history would hold up in this kind of competition for the cultural elite's attention. Modern stereotypes might incline us to think that Atsutane would steer clear of this salon activity, being a man of religion rather than a man of art. However, *Senkyō ibun* shows that Atsutane was quite active in this salon society. Atsutane organized and directed salon events to make new contacts and to impress powerful people as well as his student/patrons and his fellow scholars.

Atsutane's attraction was not a poetry reading or a musical performer. He offered up a Tengu Boy with tales of the Other World. The Tengu Boy not only told tall tales, but performed feats of magic. He danced exotic dances. He wrote in an unknown language. He predicted the future. He was a performer, whose performance and whose very existence "coincidentally" verified the theology and cosmology that was the focus of Atsutane's life's work.

Atsutane did not create this salon society, but *Senkyō ibun* verifies that this was already one of the main forums for communication in Edo.[31] Members of the cultural elite and the intelligentsia lived in close proximity and often dropped in on one another. The opening scene of *Senkyō ibun* takes place at Atsutane's home and the next scene at the home of a former student. Most of the scenes unfold in the parlors of teachers, students, or distinguished personages. Most of the important characters in the book live such short walking distances away from each other that servants are dispatched as frequently as modern cell phone calls. Before we examine exactly how Atsutane used Torakichi to take advantage of this forum for reputation building, we should first review how Atsutane managed to rise to this level of prominence in Edo society.

Atsutane's Personal Promotional Success

Atsutane was born into a samurai family in present-day Akita Prefecture. Due to circumstances, he left his family and went to Edo to seek his fortune when he was approximately twenty years old near the turn of the nineteenth century.[32] After a few years of subsistence living performing a variety of working-class occupations in Edo, he had the good fortune to marry and be adopted into the Hirata samurai family, hereditary retainers of the Bitchu-Matsuyama lord. His father-in-law ran a small academy based on the Yamaga Sokō[33] school. Atsutane was drawn to the Ancient Learning component of those studies and became fascinated by the nativist teachings of Motoori Norinaga.

As noted earlier, he was accepted as a member of Motoori Haruniwa's Suzunoya and set out to establish his own reputation and gather paying students in Edo. The early years seem to have been a continuing struggle racked with poverty and tragic events such as the death of his two young sons and his beloved first wife, Orise. For his scholarship, though, these seem to have been some of his most productive years, and there is evidence that he was gaining a reputation during that time as a Shinto scholar. In 1808 he received an appointment as professor of Ancient Learning for Shirakawa Shinto priests, yet he still kept his job as a working physician. His records show that even as a professor/physician his family fortunes still suffered.

Atsutane's fortunes seemed to change quickly in the year 1816, when he accepted a pupil named Yamazaki Atsutoshi[34] from present-day Saitama Prefecture. He was introduced to this new student by another student, a Shinto priest from present-day Chiba Prefecture, which Atsutane also visited in 1816 on what can been characterized as a fund-raising and recruiting tour of the Kantō. Atsutoshi was approximately ten years older than Atsutane and very impressed with his writings. He was not a Shinto priest but was reportedly "Shinto crazy." He was said to be fond of dreamily chanting Shinto prayers clothed in his own personal Shinto priest garments. However, what was most important for the future of Atsutane's school[35] was his status as a wealthy (cooking) oil merchant.

It was Atsutoshi's money that funded the publication of Atsutane's *The August Pillar of the Soul* and other important books. It was Atsutoshi's connections that allowed Atsutane to meet other rich and important people. One prime example of his important patronage occurred in 1820. Atsutoshi met with the lord of Tsugaru and impressed him with a copy of *The August Pillar of the Soul*, the publication of which he had funded. After that, Atsutane was invited to meet the lord, which led to the development of a personal relationship. Atsutoshi provided many such important introductions, and it has been speculated that Atsutane's recruiting tours through present day-Saitama and Chiba prefectures, and even his trip to Kyoto in 1823, were made possible only by the ready availability of Atsutoshi's money.[36]

The Kyoto trip is often considered the point in Atsutane's career where we can see the reward for all his hard work and ambition. On this trip to the old capital not only did Atsutane fulfill lifelong desires by paying his respects at the grave of his revered master Norinaga, as well as visiting other living prominent *kokugaku* scholars with whom he had only previously corresponded by mail, but he also received the honor of an audience with the emperor. His writings were presented to the retired emperor, Kōkaku (1771–1840) (r. 1779–1817), and he met with the reigning emperor, Ninkō (1800–1846) (r. 1817–1846), and various members of the aristocracy. Even more important for his work in 1823, the Yoshida family appointed him to serve as instructor to Yoshida Shinto priests. The Shirakawa and the Yoshida families controlled the licensing of the vast majority of Shinto priests in Japan, and Atsutane's popularity had both families vying for his good will.[37]

The good fortune of finding such a prosperous pupil did not by itself succeed in getting Atsutane to the Imperial Palace in Kyoto, but his recruiting trips, the circulation of publications, and the access to the inner chambers of the rich and the powerful were all essential to that end, which means Atsutoshi was essential to that end. The strong relationship between the master and the disciple was made even stronger when in 1818 Atsutane took as his third wife Atsutoshi's adopted daughter.[38] Atsutane biographer Tahara Tsuguo remarked that it was not difficult to notice the sudden improvement in Atsutane's fortunes after marrying for the third time. This marriage meant that Atsutane was freed from poverty and able to concentrate all his time and ability on spreading his doctrine, building up his school's enrollment, and enhancing his own reputation.

In 1816, the same year Atsutoshi became a student and the same year the name of the school was changed, the records for enrollment in his academy show a more than 100 percent increase. Eighty-seven new students enrolled to bring the total to 166. Also interesting to note is the change in the way Atsutane addressed himself in his letters, where we see him starting to refer to himself by the title "Hirata Daikaku."[39] The rapid growth of the school and the bestowal of honors and appointments for Atsutane himself clearly did not happen by accident. Atsutane was actively promoting his school and his teachings.

A passage in *Senkyō ibun* itself serves to verify that he already had a reputation for self-promotion at the time he met Torakichi. Otake Sensei, a respected scholar who ran his own academy, said about Atsutane, "I haven't met this Hirata yet, but if anyone can spread the Way of the Kami widely throughout the public, he's the one."[40] Atsutane's meeting with Torakichi must have presented itself as another opportunity to bring novelty and interest to his ever-expanding school and ever-increasing promotional activity. This new type of staged attraction allowed him to expand his methods of persuasion.

Prior to Torakichi's arrival, Atsutane had used lectures in official posts or as the head of his academy to get his teachings across. He also used the lecture circuit in the countryside and was known to circulate pamphlets to the literate peasants throughout that circuit. He also published works that were distributed throughout elite society by a network of well-placed friends and scholars.

Yamazaki Atsutoshi was not the only useful contact Atsutane made in Edo. His work also brought him the praise, assistance, and friendship of other important people. His best and most influential friends were Yashiro Hirokata and Hanawa Hokiichi (1746–1821),[41] two older *kokugaku* scholars with excellent reputations for scholarship and governmental bureaucratic influence and connections. They assisted Atsutane in various ways such as lending him money and vouching for his character. Two other famous late Edo scholars and artists he was known to keep company with were Murata Harumi and Kato Chikage, both students of Kamo no Mabuchi and scholars and poets of high repute. The list of other artists whose paths crossed his in Edo is distinguished,[42] which means that Atsutane socialized with the wealthy cultural elite who actively sought out the company and guidance of both scholars and artists.

Starting from the time Atsutane's school enrollment started to soar, there is also evidence of increased activity of contact with various daimyō in hopes of being hired by them in some capacity. One problem with meeting many daimyō was that Atsutane was already in service to and receiving a stipend from Lord Itakura, the master of the Bitchu-Matsuyama-han. In 1823, the same year Atsutane visited the emperor and received his Yoshida Shinto teaching appointment, he also managed to secure his release from Lord Itakura's service, completely freeing him to take the best offers available.

A few years earlier Atsutane had been hired by the Tokugawa family's lord of Owari to teach Ancient Learning and military studies. He also frequently visited the lord of Ki Province, important to him because that had been his master Norinaga's daimyō. At one point Atsutane sent Torakichi unaccompanied to Ki Province after receiving a request for a personal interview with the Tengu Boy. There is also evidence of strong connections with important samurai retainers from Satsuma Province. The political connection he seemed to covet most was with the Tokugawa lord of the Mito-han, with whom his friend Yashiro tried to broker a teaching appointment to the famous and influential Mito school. Unfortunately for Atsutane, this appointment could not be arranged, and in this one case, Atsutane's dealings with the Tengu Boy may actually have worked against him.[43]

In the midst of all this self-promotion activity in 1820, Atsutane gained custody of a Tengu Boy with firsthand testimony of life in the Other World, able to awe and surprise a public susceptible to that kind of persuasion. He promoted the Tengu Boy, took him on tour, and at times even loaned him out. Even though the Tengu Boy was a source of worry and a potential danger to the reputation of Atsutane's academy, he also clearly enjoyed some popularity in the Edo salons, and the written records of those occasions further served to keep Atsutane's school a hot topic among the people in the know. However, celebrity like that could not last forever, and in time Torakichi stopped attracting so much interest and attention.

Torakichi eventually lost his drawing power for Atsutane's academy, but not before he had served his purpose. Overall, the stir he caused in Edo salon society worked to increase the interest in Atsutane's Ibukinoya academy. A detailed look at some of the specifics of Atsutane's and Torakichi's salon activities as described in *Senkyō ibun* will show how Torakichi was used to create a stir, draw attention to Atsutane's school, enhance Atsutane's reputation, and propagate his Other World theology.

The Salons of *Senkyō ibun*

As we have seen, the *Senkyō ibun* text starts with an invitation to an interview with Tengu Boy Torakichi, about whom rumors have been reverberating throughout the salons of Edo. The first scene of the book sets the stage for the series of interviews that make up the majority of the text. One unintended benefit of the *Senkyō ibun* record is that it thickly describes Edo salon society, in which theories were introduced and argued and reputations were made and destroyed. This setting, the activities that took place there, and the participants in these salons are detailed within the text. These details give us a clearer picture of just how a new medium such as Torakichi was used and how the salon setting complemented this particular means of spreading Atsutane's new message. In other words, Atsutane received word of the Tengu Boy through this grapevine, and he decided to gain control of the boy and pass on his teachings through the boy by inviting friends, students, and all the important people who would come to his salon to view the novelty.

The first meeting of Atsutane and the Tengu Boy took place at an Edo salon, but even before the meeting, on the way to Yoshishige's house, when Atsutane asked if the boy's stories were credible, Yashiro answered, "According to Yoshishige, the other day when they were at Ninagawa's house."[44] Immediately, the book has introduced an important method for the propagation of a message in Edo in the 1820s. Certainly people met for friendly purposes, but no doubt it helped to have an attraction to get people to come over. Atsutane and Yashiro, in particular, were attending to see just such an attraction.

Atsutane met Torakichi a second time at Yoshishige's house, but for his third meeting with Torakichi he planned to organize a large affair at his own house. He cajoled Yoshishige into allowing him a third audience with the boy at his own house as soon as possible, since Torakichi had been saying that soon he had to leave for the mountains for the annual winter austerities. However, as explained earlier, after intently planning his first reception for Torakichi, Yoshishige cancelled on him at the last minute, causing severe embarrassment and disappointment for Atsutane, enough for Atsutane to take his wife and several others over to Yoshishige's house to complain directly. That night's entertainment did not work out, but Atsutane followed up, and soon Yoshishige gave in and granted Atsutane his own, and the first of many, salon affairs with Torakichi as the main attraction.

When Atsutane went over to register his complaint, as described earlier, he did manage at least to get more information about Torakichi from the boy's own mother. He later wrote that this information only whetted his appetite for more conversation with the boy and strengthened his resolve to somehow get Torakichi over to his house. He wrote:

> Although we thought Yoshishige's conduct was reprehensible, we had to win him over. So I sent presents and also asked Master Yashiro if he could go over as a friend and somehow persuade Yoshishige. On the afternoon of the tenth I sent a letter along with Yashiro saying that I was hoping that they could come over the following evening. I wrote that I was hoping to have Satō Nobuhiro[45] and also Kunitomo Yoshimasa[46] over to join us since I felt bad about having invited them from all the way over from Yotsuya only to have them go home disappointed earlier on the sixth. This was all to be conveyed by Yashiro in the hope that I could get an answer by tomorrow. Early on the morning of the eleventh there came word from Yashiro saying that Yoshishige had agreed to come over with the boy that evening.[47]

The quote shows just how anxious Atsutane was to have Torakichi come over and how important it was to have an attraction for his salon. The two invited guests were both students of Atsutane's nativist academy, but they were not just young disciples looking for some enlightened teaching. Both of them were accomplished intellectuals in their respective fields, and both of them left their marks in Japanese history. Atsutane hoped his academy would attract just such important people, not just for the monetary support but also for the reputation and social status, with the accompanying perquisites that came with being held in high esteem by men of acknowledged accomplishment and standing.

Atsutane seemed to place an importance on recording those in attendance at his salon events, and he often practiced this form of name-dropping in *Senkyō ibun*. This practice could possibly help to recruit those who were allowed to read the book as an enticement to entrance into his academy. Perhaps it also served to flatter those students who were already enrolled but whom Atsutane recognized for their attendance. Even before the particulars of the event, we are given the list of guests for the Tengu Boy exhibition.

> Now, on that day Igarashi Tsushima, priest of Suwa Shrine in Sasagawa village in the Katori district of Shimosa province, had come to Edo to study and was at my house. At half past the eighth hour, Master Yashiro and his grandson Master Jiro arrived. After that, Kunitomo Yoshimasa and Satō Nobuhiro came. By a stroke of luck, Aoki Namifusa also showed up. The Kotori family household all came. From the academy there was Takeuchi Takeo, Iwazaki Yoshishiko, and Moriya Inao among others.[48]

This listing of the attendees served as a list of witnesses who would be implicitly agreeing with Atsutane's record of miraculous stories, and it could also serve to reassure the reader that he was not dealing with one ideologue's delusion.

This meeting was especially important for Atsutane since it was the first time Torakichi had set foot in his house. Accordingly, he recorded the activities in expansive detail. First they brought out Atsutane's stone flute used in rituals for calling down the *kami*. Torakichi blew into it and the sounds were described as filling the heart with happiness. A general question-and-answer session started, and Atsutane claimed that everyone was both surprised and impressed. Torakichi was then questioned in detail about the guns of the Other World. Kunitomo, being the expert, led the questioning and was very impressed and convinced by the Tengu Boy.

Next Atsutane brought out the writing implements for Torakichi to demonstrate the writing used in the Other World. At this first meeting his writing was not deemed to be very impressive; it was only in later meetings that Torakichi "allowed" his hidden prowess and supernatural training to be revealed. Before the questions had been exhausted and after Torakichi had promised to teach Atsutane how to make a certain long flute used in the mountains, Yoshishige insisted they had to leave. Much to the disappointment of all in attendance, Atsutane's first showing of Torakichi left everyone wanting more. The next day, as a token of his appreciation, Atsutane sent over a servant with a promised book and a request for another visit with Torakichi at the next possible opportunity. The request was put off.

However, as explained previously, after Torakichi made his brief trip to the mountains only to be rebuffed upon trying to regain entrance to Yoshishige's house, he returned to Atsutane's house seeking shelter. The next morning, after performing his morning *kami* rituals, Atsutane immediately went over to Yashiro's place to inform him of the good fortune. Next, he sent word to Yoshishige's to explain why Torakichi would be staying at his house. We know that word of Torakichi's return spread quickly because Atsutane next provides another long list of the attendees[49] at that day's audience with Torakichi. Master Kotori was there. Ban Nobutomo, Nakamura Obinata, Aoki Goroji, and Masao from Sasagawa were all reported to have attended. Of course, Kunitomo Yoshimasa was also there to finish up the questioning about the guns of the *sanjin*. Yashiro and Master Hagiwara Senami were also there to ask more questions about the writing of the *sanjin*.

Another episode of typical Atsutane salon festivities is described by Atsutane's student Takeuchi Magoichi in his Atsutane-authorized minichronicle of Torakichi's special abilities *A Short Chronicle of the Divine Child's Possession Tales* (*Shindō hyōdan ryakki*). This work, which was written around the same time as *Senkyō ibun* and containing many similar passages, gives a prime example of the elaborate preparations and pains taken by Atsutane and his academy to celebrate and valorize both Torakichi and his supposed *sanjin* master. Takeuchi claimed that while secretly following Torakichi one day, he overheard him talking to an invisible interlocutor about his mountain master Sugiyama Sanjin's birthday the following day. Takeuchi took this secret information to Atsutane, who found it the perfect opportunity to throw a large party and official ritual ceremony. He hurriedly set about inviting his fellow academicians and other important personages.

Atsutane declared that they should spare no expense celebrating this special occasion, for which he would be the first and only person to be throwing a party. Takeuchi's book provides a long list of decorations and varieties of food for which they scoured the town. When everything was prepared and the guests had arrived, Torakichi set up the *himorogi*, ritual enclosure, before inviting his master Sugiyama Sanjin to enter, spiritually, that is. Then Torakichi made the obligatory ritual offerings, after which everyone feasted. When the feast was over, Torakichi himself provided the entertainment for the main guest, his master Sugiyama Sanjin, and the other celebrants by performing a number of dances using fans, bells, paper wands, *sakaki* branches, and bows. When the entertainment was over, Torakichi ceremonially sent his master back to the Other World. Takeuchi ends the description with another long list of names of the people who had come to witness this great first-time event.

As explained earlier, Torakichi stayed permanently at Atsutane's house from that time on, making many more appearances in front of Atsutane's guests. However, a salon presentation was not without a potential downside. Local dignitaries and authorities also sought Torakichi's company, and Atsutane occasionally had little choice but to send him out alone to what sometimes turned out to be performances in front of hostile audiences. One such situation turned out to be an ambush or a debunking session of sorts.

Torakichi later provided the details of the hostilities to Atsutane, who recorded that Torakichi had told the truth and done his usual act, only to be confronted by a certain hostile Shingon priest. Torakichi described this priest as both arrogant and ignorant and said he had simply reacted honestly by showing his disgust for the stupid priest. It is clear that this event did not bring Atsutane to doubt Torakichi's truthfulness or abilities; however, Atsutane clearly expressed his concern that this kind of episode would lead to unfavorable talk and rumors about his prodigy, which could lead to criticism of both of them. Before the event even occurred, Atsutane had sensed there could be trouble and wrote that he "faced Mt. Iwama and prayed [to Sugiyama Sanjin] at some length that Torakichi would be protected from a meeting leading to his embarrassment, since that kind of thing would prove to be extremely regrettable for me also."[50]

This kind of slander was something that clearly worried Atsutane, for he wrote more concerning this episode. Atsutane's trusted student Satō Nobuhiro informed him that Torakichi had said some vile words to the priest at the local dignitary's house. Nobuhiro had heard the news from someone who had been in attendance, and although Nobuhiro said that his informant had been impressed with the boy's abilities, still he felt that the overall impression had been negative and that the affair would lead to more slander and hatred. He further suggested that that kind of meeting be curtailed. Clearly, then, Atsutane was aware that what he was doing by putting Torakichi on exhibit was risky, not because he himself doubted the verity of Torakichi's testimony, but rather because salon society opinion could make or break reputations.

From Public Performance to Staged Dialogue

Torakichi's tour through the salon venues was important for the publicity and the shock value it lent to the supernatural superstar. Publicity for the superstar also meant more publicity for Atsutane's school. It is recorded more than once that people came to Atsutane asking to be allowed to see the boy. Still, we have also seen that the salon venue had its shortcomings, especially if the performance was not under close supervision or if Torakichi was asked to go beyond his normal repertoire. The topics of Torakichi's conversations and demonstrations in front of audiences were wide-ranging, but for his more focused probing on specific points of theoretical importance, Atsutane pursued a different mode of interrogation, the Socratic dialogue.

The five chapters of *Senkyō ibun* include a variety of narrative styles. The work begins with Atsutane narrating his first meeting with Torakichi and continues with the later meeting and interactions, along with descriptions of Torakichi's daily activities and his appearances at salon meetings. The progression is usually chronological, with Atsutane filling in background he has heard through other sources and adding his own thoughts and commentary about the boy. However, a major portion of the work consists of dialogue between Atsutane and Torakichi. Atsutane asks questions about the Other World and Torakichi answers, often in fairly extended fashion. Atsutane frequently asks follow-up questions for clarification or further details. Sometimes those dialogues inspire Atsutane to recount a similar story he has heard elsewhere that either backs up or adds variations to Torakichi's answer. Sometimes interlocutors other than Atsutane are introduced. The questions are not randomly arranged; questions on related topics are often grouped together, although at times similar questions are repeated in different chapters that sometimes result in different answers.

The dialogic form is crucial to Atsutane because it allows him to focus on the answers that are most important to him. Atsutane tells the first part of the work in a narrative form that introduces Torakichi and establishes his celebrity and credentials as a medium because this is the most straightforward way of explaining the importance of this discovery to his audience. Yet Atsutane chooses not to write the rest of the book as a running narrative description of what Torakichi had seen in the Other World.

The dialogue form allows Atsutane to decide what is important and allows the true evidence to come only from, and be heard directly from the lips of, the supernatural informant Torakichi.

Atsutane often criticizes text and the supposed verity of textual records of people's speech, but the fact is that he himself cannot get beyond it completely. He finds it easy to criticize Buddhist and Confucian texts because their numbers and the length of their histories led to contradictions and errors. Atsutane believes in an original truth, but he also believes that history has covered up that truth with layer upon layer of lies. His choice of an ethnographic interview method allows him to claim direct access to the truth with no historical layering of lies. He claims that having a living informant has an advantage over ancient writings in that his source can be questioned if the reader/listener doubts what he has been told. Certainly, Atsutane still produces written text, but he defends his writings by claiming they are subject to verification not available to any other ancient history.

The choice of this style of writing, then, stemmed in part from Atsutane's mistrust of history. It was also due in part to his privileging of oral modes of communication over written modes; more will be said about this in later chapters. Atsutane actively sought out all opportunities to conduct interviews with living informants, a method he would continue in his future research even when he was finished with Torakichi. He held a bias toward the belief that firsthand information from a living source who could be tested, analyzed, and judged was the most reliable type of information, much superior to histories that had traveled through many different centuries and many different interpreters. He surely hoped that many others would also believe he had found a trustworthy medium in Torakichi and that his actions of recording the words of his informant would not be seen as creating an additional medium between the reader and the truth of the Other World. If his recording was to be seen as a medium at all, he would rather it be considered transparent, not one that required his additional effort of translation, interpretation, or editing.

However, an unforeseen result of the employment of the dialogic style is that Atsutane makes himself and Torakichi into characters in a work of fiction. Atsutane often thinks out loud in this work, and he displays himself and Torakichi as human beings in a relationship that sometimes brings them joy and sometimes brings them into conflict. Atsutane styles himself as a reflexive observer of his interactions with Torakichi, yet he willingly relinquishes distance and objectivity in their conversations. Furthermore, as will be evident soon, Atsutane is prone to playing Socrates to Torakichi's Theatetus. He strives to help Torakichi discover the knowledge that he knows is within the boy himself. Atsutane is also privy to this knowledge, but he will not make the pronouncement for the boy. Torakichi's ultimate role and purpose is to act as the supernatural mouthpiece for Atsutane's message without letting the world know this is going on. Still, it is important to remember that biased Socratic dialogue is not only found in the works of literary philosophers of Plato's ilk, it can also be seen in many records of dialogues between modern ethnographers and their informants.[51]

The dialogic style employed in *Senkyō ibun* was important to Atsutane because he could control it, and it allowed him to direct Torakichi's claims of lived personal experience, not hearsay and knowledge based on books, toward the furtherance of his own scholarly and religious goals. Atsutane wanted his readers to believe that he was only posing questions and not providing the answers himself, but as will be shown in the next chapter, he was persistently and diligently searching for better questions in order to get better answers. He was a master of the "how often do you beat your wife?" type of question, but he deserves more credit than that, for he could be more subtle. The goal of the questioning was, of course, to provide first-hand evidence of the activities and makeup of the Other World, and just as important to introduce what was supposed to be seen as a new originally Japanese religious and cultural hero, the *sanjin*. This hero was to be a savior and a source of strength, wisdom, and pride in a time of impending internal and external crisis for Japan. The next chapter will explain just how this religious hero and superman, who was supposed to have been living and active in Japan since the beginning of time, was finally found and introduced to the world by Atsutane in *Senkyō ibun*.

CHAPTER 3

Manipulating the Medium
Separating the *Sanjin* from the *Tengu*

Atsutane's Other World

Senkyō ibun opens with a conversation between Atsutane and his elder confidant and friend, Yashiro Hirokata, in which the existence of a mysterious and supernatural Other World is a premise accepted by both parties. As explained earlier, for Atsutane, the Other World had the meaning of the normally invisible half of a universe made up of two worlds, one seen and one unseen. As he explained in his most famous cosmological text *The August Pillar of the Soul,* drafted in 1812, the unseen half of the universe was first mentioned in the ancient stories about Ōkuninushi ceding the land of Japan to the Imperial Grandson, Ninigi no mikoto. In these stories, in exchange for his peaceful generosity, Ōkuninushi was given charge of this Other World.[1] According to Atsutane's interpretation of the mythological concession, it was Ōkuninushi who received the better part of the deal. This was due to his belief that the Other World was the numinous world inhabited by *kami* and spirits, and as such also served as the wonderful realm of the afterlife for the souls of the Japanese departed.

However, this pleasant and reassuring Other World was also populated by a variety of creatures that were menacing to the world of humans. Furthermore, although it was difficult for humans to cross into the Other World and obtain any solid information about it, it was not difficult for the inhabitants of the Other World to cross over into the human world. Another point of interest in Atsutane's theory is that the Other World and this world tended to intersect in the wilderness; that is, in the mountains of Japan. Traditionally in Japan, even before Atsutane's speculative efforts, the mountains were seen as an entryway into the supernatural world.

According to Atsutane's cosmology, the Other World and this world overlapped, and it was in the mountains that the wall separating the two became porous enough to allow penetration by the human being.

Therefore, the topography of the Other World was exactly the same as the topography of Japan. When Torakichi described the landscape of the Other World in which he claimed to have lived for years, geographically speaking, he was only describing certain mountains in Japan about which any bold and resourceful human could also have known. Therefore, Torakichi's special contribution to Atsutane's theory of the Other World would lay in his discussion about its inhabitants.

Torakichi's Other World

Some of Torakichi's stories of the Other World concern its animal inhabitants. A few of his stories about the fantastic animal life are probably actually about animals we would consider commonplace. For example, Torakichi told an exciting story of a certain creature that flew down from a tree and latched on to his face. It was not a large creature, perhaps no larger than his face, but it could fly, it had claws, and it was fierce. Although Torakichi seemed convinced he had had a brush with something quite exotic, from his description, it is fairly clear that his ferocious battle took place with a flying squirrel, not a completely unknown or fantastic creature.

Torakichi told another story of being attacked by a dragon. One day he was wading through a stream when an animal in the water grabbed him and pulled him under. He escaped by fighting off the dragon, which from his description might be alternatively identified as a large snake. However, Torakichi insisted that a baby dragon had attacked him. In both of these examples the beasts of Torakichi's Other World are dangerous and ferocious, but his descriptions of them do not set them apart from animals in this world.

One story introduced another legendary but imaginary beast. Torakichi told of monkeys who resembled humans. The most interesting detail about them was that they could make a special type of liquor, which Torakichi reported to be especially delicious. Here Torakichi is depending upon legends of an orangutan-type beast, a *shōjō*, a hairy creature with a human face who was reportedly fond of sake. This story had been popularly told throughout China and Japan for centuries.

Senkyō ibun contains other stories in which Torakichi describes beasts not so easily identified in reality or in legend. One such example is Torakichi's account of a four-legged armored creature, a drawing of which is included in *Senkyō ibun*. According to Torakichi's description, this creature was as large as a horse and had iron needles sticking out of its body.[2] Its diet consisted simply of iron, and occasionally it would throw off sparks caused by the friction of its own body parts. Sometimes those very sparks would be the cause of its self-immolation.

According to Torakichi, most of the vegetation of the Other World was the same as that of this world, with one notable exception. Torakichi reported that there was a special type of tree, which he claimed could give off its own light.[3] He claimed that his *sanjin* master often used that kind of wood for his night lamp. Torakichi expressed surprise that people in this world did not use that special wood, and he offered to help out by finding some for Atsutane. However, except for the story of the glowing wood, the rest of Torakichi's descriptions of plants and grasses were of varieties recognizable by the Japanese of that time. Normal humans and *sanjin* used those resources similarly; that is, for food, medicine, or clothing.

The other living beings in the Other World described by Torakichi were *kami,* demons, *tengu,* and humans. Torakichi had little to say about the *kami* except for one isolated instance when he claimed that his *tengu/sanjin* master was also a *kami.* Usually he claimed ignorance of specifics about *kami;* for example, he stated that the *sanjin* in the Other World knew as much about the *kami* as the people of the world knew about the *sanjin,* in other words, very little. However, in spite of that statement, Torakichi did have many things to say about the *sanjin*'s role in service of the *kami.*

Torakichi affirmed the existence of varieties of demons. He spoke of demons in interviews, but usually not in great detail. He also drew some pictures of demons he claimed to have seen in the Other World, but they are comparatively unremarkable. Atsutane did not dwell on the subject because what he deemed to be interesting was that despite similarities of evil intent and purpose, Torakichi maintained clear distinctions between demons and *tengu.*

Atsutane asked, "When you say the world is full of demons [*akuma*] what do you mean? What's the difference between demons and *tengu,* and where do the demons live?"

Torakichi said, "I don't know where they live but they have many separate groups. If they were all together there would be a tremendous number of them. They are always flying around in the sky and causing calamities in the world. That is, if a person is evil, they increase the evil, and if the person is good, they obstruct his good deeds and cause evil thoughts to arise within him. They seek out the vanity and laziness in people and prey on those thoughts to bring about all kinds of calamities and disasters. They pervert people's thoughts toward evil things. They deceive humans by manifesting themselves in shapes and appearances that would appeal to each person. They can change into anything: buddhas, bodhisattvas, handsome men, beautiful women, and apparitions from hell or paradise. These demons attract any and all into their groups, and attempt to fashion the world to their own liking.

The demons I have seen with my own eyes look like the ones in the accompanying pictures.[4] The one moving the cart is called a *dairiki* [great power]. These are not the only two types but these are the types of demons that I clearly remember seeing. I don't know the name of the other demon drawn here. I drew him as I saw him, with chains hanging from his ears. Strings hang from the hands of the demons and they lower them to cause disaster to strike whatever they touch. In addition, they seem to have fur on their heads that looks more like iron needles. They pull on the strings hanging from their hands, but they can't catch good people with them. Also, they walk around peeking into people's houses. These demons are infested with horseflies. Also, there are some demons that have skulls for heads.

One of the reasons that *kami* exist is to rescue humans from all these kinds of demons running around. My master says that if people only knew how many of these kinds of demons were around, they would probably do the right thing more often.[5]

This was Torakichi's most detailed statement on demons, and some of the extant pictures show precisely what kind of beasts he was describing. Their reason for existence seemed to be to destroy good and spread evil. While Torakichi claimed there was a certain amount of protection from demons provided by strong moral character, he also insisted that demons could cause evil thoughts even among the good. Although their natural appearance was ugly, scary, and dangerous, they also had shape-shifting abilities. In other words, anything could be a demon in disguise.

The statement concerning the use of Buddhist heroes and Buddhist doctrines of paradise and hell sounds suspiciously like Atsutane. The question Atsutane asked that led to Torakichi's description seems to indicate that Atsutane was under the impression that a *tengu* was just a specific form of demon. After all, Atsutane's theory was that demons came from Buddhism, and a *tengu* was just one more kind of Buddhist evil. Torakichi's assertion of the demon's shape-shifting and buddha-imitating ability further reinforced Atsutane's associations of demons with Buddhism, but he made it clear that in his eyes *tengu* and demons were not always similarly evil in nature.

Tengu

Torakichi's specific pronouncement on *tengu* went as follows:

> Distinct from those kinds of things [demons], the thing called *tengu* arises
> naturally deep in the mountains. It happens that birds and beasts after liv-
> ing for an extremely long time, all of them, eagles, kites, crows, monkeys,
> wolves, bears, deer, or boar, turn into *tengu*. Birds grow arms and legs,
> and the beasts grow wings. In addition, the human soul after death and
> also the human while he is living can turn into *tengu*. However, the *tengu*
> who result from human transformation can be either evil or good. The
> evil *tengu* eventually join the ranks of monsters and demons. The average
> person cannot distinguish between the workings of the various types, and
> so they call all of them *tengu*. Therefore, someone like my master is called
> a *tengu* by the world, so I have come to call him a *tengu* for the time being.
> But the truth is that he is not a *tengu*. He is a *sanjin*.[6]

The bulk of the information given by Torakichi about the inhabitants of the
Other World concerns beings that fit into two categories: the *tengu* and the
mountain-dwelling humans, referred to as *sanjin*. Even so, Torakichi often
collapsed the categories; for example, he sometimes called *sanjin kami*,
called demons *tengu*, and used the terms *sanjin* and *tengu* interchange-
ably. In particular, when it came to the term *tengu*, Torakichi often used it
as a positive appellation meant to bestow a good and powerful status on
his master. This imprecision and ambiguity with some key terminology
proved to be troublesome for Atsutane.

This raises one of the most important issues in this study; that is, to
what extent the testimony of Atsutane's informant was influenced by Atsutane's expectations. For Atsutane, Torakichi was often painfully inconsistent in the terminology he used when referring to his master. Atsutane
recorded Torakichi as calling his master *kami*, *tengu*, great *tengu*, *sanjin*,
or great *sanjin*. When asked about the inconsistency, we have seen that
Torakichi could explain it away by saying that his master told him to refer
to him as a *tengu*, simply because that was the way the common person
usually referred to anyone who lived as his master did in the mountains.

According to one particular story, Torakichi's master told him he was
actually one of the famous thirteen *tengu* who live on Mt. Iwama.[7] However, as we have seen previously, Torakichi was also to insist that his master was not really a *tengu* at all. Torakichi claimed that the public was

generally misinformed and mistaken. People used the word *tengu* as a general term to include many different varieties of beings that inhabit the mountains. According to Torakichi, he only called his master a *tengu* as part of a deception orchestrated by his *sanjin* master for the furtherance of his master's secret (but altruistic) purposes.

At the time of his interviews with Torakichi, Atsutane was engaged in a wide-ranging program of studies of supernatural phenomena. In 1821 he wrote an introduction to a story he had heard of a man haunted by evil spirits called *Inō mononokeroku*. He did not write this as fiction; rather it was part of his new field of study, spiritual fieldwork. However, Atsutane's research on supernatural phenomena was not completely value-free. He held a special dislike for *tengu* when he conducted his research on them. This research eventually resulted in the publication of *Thoughts on Supernatural Beings of Past and Present* (*Kokon yomikō*), which exhibits his bias against them. Haga Noboru, a recognized expert on late Tokugawa nativist thought, referred to some of Atsutane's adopted son and successor Hirata Kanetane's writings to establish the context of Atsutane's opus on *tengu*.

As expressed in Kanetane's preface to this work [*Thoughts on Supernatural Beings of Past and Present*] "Many of my father's thoughts concerning supernatural creatures in this world are dependent upon the theories of Hayashi Razan," and Hayashi Razan's influence is strong here. Razan was strongly opposed to Buddhist demonology that spoke of supernatural creatures and hells and heavens. It is thought that this book [*Thoughts on Supernatural Beings of Past and Present*] was put together in 1822 almost the same time as *Senkyō ibun*. In the 4th month of 1828 Kanetane expressed the reason for the writing of this work, and the following explanation expresses Kanetane's thoughts that, concomitant with the corruption of the world, the number of *magakami* [*kami* of calamity] had increased. "When the trappings of Buddhism were brought over from China in the Middle Ages, it is thought that along with them came numerous supernatural creatures. Those people here [Japan] who were drawn into this Way eventually turned into those kinds of demons. They kept on increasing in number until finally there were great numbers of those evil things in this world." He claimed, in effect, that the increase in supernatural creatures corresponded to the increase in heresies such as Buddhism. Since Buddhist monks and *yamabushi* were *tengu*, Atsutane called them Buddhist Demons and said that these were people who had all fallen into an evil path. The ultimate point of the work [*Thoughts on Supernatural Beings of Past and Present*] was to clearly reveal that fact.[8]

So in short, Atsutane's works on *tengu* are biased by his hatred of them as Buddhists transformed. He had no doubt that *tengu* were real, but he also had no doubt that they were despicable.

When Atsutane used the word *tengu*, the denotation and the connotation were clear. He, unlike Torakichi, had no mixed feelings concerning the word and had no reason to be vague. As a result, again unlike Torakichi, Atsutane never tried to valorize the role of *tengu* and is also not under suspicion of changing his terminology and attitudes to cater to the religious likes and dislikes of different audiences.

A simple explanation of Atsutane's *tengu* theory can be found in the aforementioned *Thoughts on Supernatural Beings of Past and Present*. This work reveals Atsutane's assertion that *tengu* come in two categories. The first category is the *tengu* that is a bird or beast transformed over time.

> According to the stories passed down from the teachings of the *sanjin*, those things that the world calls supernatural creatures, or *tengu*, are eagles, kites, foxes, or a variety of other types of birds and beasts. After living for several hundreds or thousands of years, the birds grow hands from their wings, and they stand on the flesh that has grown onto their former bird feet. In the case of beasts, their front legs grow wings, and after a while they stand upright and change form to look like people. It is also said that among those that fly, there are some that fly without wings.[9]

Atsutane may be indirectly telling us that this is a story he heard from Torakichi. Torakichi would have been his most direct source for his quote, "teachings of the *sanjin*." If this is so, the explanation is surprisingly similar to something Atsutane attributed to Hayashi Razan some ten years earlier in his *The August Pillar of the Soul* (*Tama no mihashira*).[10] Therefore, if Torakichi did reveal these "teachings of the *sanjin*" to Atsutane, it was not new information. In any case, Atsutane's source for the second category of *tengu* is clear and seemed to work as justification of his prejudice against Buddhism.[11] That second category of *tengu* was a human who had been transformed due to some evil influence.

> As Razan Sensei explained, many [*tengu*] are Buddhist priests or *yamabushi* who have undergone demonic transformations. It is thought that the reason people began to call them *tengu* is that, with their big noses and their protruding lips, their heads look like *tengu* [the other kind of *tengu*, the animal transformation *tengu*]; furthermore, they live in the mountains and cause people misfortune, and so they came to be grouped with the other type of *tengu*.[12]

Atsutane's negative perception of tengu is made quite clear by these two statements. He found both types to be disgustingly bestial and that they "cause people misfortune."

Another aspect of *tengu* legend that tended to make their existence more believable was that they were often associated with actual historical figures said to be living and lurking in the wilds or in the dark corners of the Other World. In contrast to this, there was a similar if less popular practice of memorializing other historical figures wandering the mountains with the title of Sanjin. This coincidence naturally suggested that there were two kinds of beings, both formerly human, that existed in the supernatural environs of the mountains. The ones with the bad reputations were *tengu*, and the ones with the good reputations were *sanjin*.[13] At least this was the dichotomy on which Atsutane was relying to distinguish the supernatural figure he intended to praise.

Discovering the *Sanjin*

When asked about his mountain associates, Torakichi described a class of people who lived outdoors with relatively few possessions. These people seemed to live off the land and had neither stores of wealth nor incomes from steady occupations with which to buy food and clothing.[14] The main occupations he described for them were wandering from place to place, practicing asceticism, and offering prayers to *kami* or buddhas. His teachers and companions in the mountains were known by a variety of names, but the name given them by Torakichi when he spoke seriously and in praise of them in front of Atsutane was *sanjin*.

As the Chinese characters of the word indicate, *sanjin* are human beings that live in the mountains. They are people who have left society and have decided to live alone or in small communities of like-minded recluses. They come from any level of society and embark on this lifestyle at almost any age. The lifestyle of the *sanjin* was to be understood as pastoral and rustic, but at times *sanjin* were said to visit cities and towns, though their stay there was always meant to be brief. Someone making a long, slow trip that forced him to stay in the mountains for an extended period of time was not necessarily a *sanjin*.

The use of the two-Chinese-character compound for *sanjin* can be traced back to ancient Chinese texts,[15] and in Japan, Atsutane himself places them in the eighth-century poetry collection *Manyōshū*, and they are also to be found in the *Kokinshū* (903). Literati in China and Japan have used and on occasion continue to use *sanjin* as an honorific title.[16] However, prior to Atsutane's *sanjin*, it was not a specifically religious classification. In *Senkyō ibun*, Atsutane equates the term closely with *shinsen* and *sennin*, and his intent was to put the term on par with words usually used to describe Daoist Chinese immortals. Torakichi clearly stated that the Japanese *sanjin* and the Chinese *sennin*, the immortal, were to be considered similar but with important differences to be described later. This combination of characters would later become better known in Yanagita Kunio's *minzokugaku* studies as *yamabito*, but although the reading had changed, the meaning was still charged with nativist Japanese supernatural connotations.[17]

The *sanjin* characters themselves do not indicate a gender restriction, but in practice, *sanjin* were always male. Females who happened to wander into mountains were never called *sanjin*. In fact, according to Torakichi, women were prohibited by the *sanjin* from entering any mountain in Japan, all of which, Torakichi claimed, had *sanjin* living on them. Of course there was no official written code among *sanjin* that restricted women, as there seemed to be no written code establishing any rules for *sanjin;* for this, we must rely on Torakichi's word.

In addition, there was no official school of *sanjin* and there were no sects of *sanjin*. Torakichi claimed that *sanjin* worshiped *kami*, buddhas, or both. However, according to Atsutane, a true *sanjin* would be one who worshiped only the *kami*. Torakichi often distinguished *sanjin* by their mountain of residence. He also distinguished them by the particular deity they served and worshiped, which would also be related to their specific mountain. Given the fluidity of the term, one might think that to become a *sanjin*, one could just decide to leave home permanently to live in the mountains. However, in *Senkyō ibun*, the *sanjin* life was referred to as a fate, not subject to individual dreams or ambitions.

The physical model of the *sanjin* was Torakichi's master Sugiyama, often referred to as Sugiyama Sanjin. The first description of him came from the story of Torakichi's first encounter with him selling medicines by a temple gate. Torakichi described him as an "old man" of about fifty years, with a long beard and matted, messy hair. He carried a mat, a travel bundle, and a pot filled with pills. At a different interview, Torakichi said that his master looked to be about forty years old with hair that grew down to his waist. He wore a brass headband, and the jacket and the *hakama* of a *yamabushi*, which were both red. There are a few extant drawings of Sugiyama Sanjin, all based on Torakichi's stories, and in those his costumes vary greatly from the previous descriptions. Sugiyama Sanjin was also described as being taller than the ordinary person by about five inches. He was once described as often sitting cross-legged and forming a *mudra* called *nai* (internal transmission) while chanting mantra.[18] Torakichi said he usually carried a long sword in his belt. On occasion he would wear a *tokin* headdress, but not the usual *shugenja tokin;* his was described as larger and shaped differently. Many of these descriptions sound like Sugiyama Sanjin could be a type of *yamabushi,* but Torakichi clearly stated that in his way of thinking, or perhaps in Atsutane's, *sanjin* and *yamabushi* were completely different entities.

There are stories recorded in *Senkyō ibun* of *sanjin* who awoke one day and realized they had to leave home. These awakened *sanjin* then went off to live in the mountains and commune with nature. Eventually the beasts of the wild would come to accept their presence, and even in some cases feed and protect them. Quite often, it seems, *sanjin* started out as children who had been lured away or carried off to be servants of some established *sanjin.* In those cases, those master *sanjin* would become their teachers of the *sanjin* arts, and the students would become the bearers of the tradition.

Torakichi, of course, became a *sanjin* in the second way; that is, he was lured away by a *sanjin,* if not actually abducted by force. We know that Torakichi still insisted that his introduction to the life had been fated. In a few passages he lamented the difficulties of the *sanjin* lifestyle and declared normal human admiration for the *sanjin* path to be foolish. In other words, he reinforced the idea that in spite of how wondrous the abilities of the *sanjin* were, no one, and certainly not himself, would choose this type of life. However, the story of Torakichi's entry into the *sanjin* life complicated that assertion.

Descriptions of Torakichi's *sanjin* master served multiple purposes. First, accounts of his wondrous abilities added to the mystical aura of his student, Torakichi, making him stranger and more wondrous, which in turn made him more of an expert about the supernatural Other World. Concomitantly, this also made Atsutane an expert, not as a practitioner of the *sanjin* arts, but as the first scholar to reveal them. This gave Atsutane the important role of introducing and explaining these native Japanese arts to a benighted world, formerly duped and spellbound by Chinese, Buddhist, and Western discourses. These descriptions of the *sanjin* master also created the template for Atsutane's religious virtuoso. Torakichi's master was not just an ordinary *sanjin.* He stood as the representative of the whole community of *sanjin* who inhabited the mountains of Japan. That being the case, there was no question too small, too simple, or too mundane to ask about Torakichi's *sanjin.*

Atsutane was also interested in just how human the *sanjin* remained; for example, he asked about their sleep habits. Did they sleep, did they need to sleep, and if so, how much? Torakichi's answer was that of course

they sleep, often snoring very long and loud. They also got cold in the winter, and Torakichi gave detailed descriptions, complete with illustrations
of the special stuffed sleeping garments his master wore in the mountains.
They also needed to eat, and Torakichi devoted a great deal of time describing the recipes and eating and drinking habits of *sanjin*. Those types of
descriptions served to make the *sanjin* appear all very human, which con-
trasted greatly with what Atsutane would learn about their super powers
and their advanced technological abilities.

These questions about everyday life served to make Atsutane's study
of the *sanjin* resemble certain modern anthropological studies. Anthropologists do not only exoticize their object of study, they also focus on the
mundane activities that all human beings have in common. One extremely
basic but essential purpose of Atsutane's *Senkyō ibun* was to validate as
factual the existence of just such a living community of beings in the Japanese mountains.

Therefore, many of the questions were meant to discover just how
much the *sanjin* was like the common Japanese person. Some of these
questions even seemed to be exasperating for Torakichi. When asked
what he thought were stupid questions, Torakichi would give a curt stock
answer, that *sanjin* have and do just the same kinds of things that people
here do.[19] One of Atsutane's anthropological aims was to establish the *sanjin* as originally and basically human, or actually, originally, and basically
Japanese. His goal was to show to what great heights the Japanese could
and should aspire.

Torakichi said his *sanjin* master was called by several names, none
of which he said was his real name, which could not be revealed. Torakichi claimed to have surreptitiously discovered the true name, but, for
reasons he himself could not understand, could never remember it. He
often reminded his listeners that his master always enjoined him to keep
the name secret; however, he was allowed to reveal the Buddhist alias Sugiyama Sōjō.[20] This is another example of the tension that runs throughout
Senkyō ibun concerning the suspicious nature of the information given us
by Torakichi and Atsutane. Atsutane himself clearly recognized the tension and tried to use it to his advantage.

Secret Information or Disinformation?

The tension referred to above lies behind the cloak of mystery that Torakichi's listener must penetrate. A strange person who seemed to have some
sanjin credentials was claiming to be opening up and giving previously
secret information. There was obvious fascination and excitement among

those visiting the salon hoping for exotic information. However, the story-teller, Torakichi, started out by warning his audience that he could not be completely straightforward because the information was too complicated and too wonderful for even him, let alone his audience, to fully compre-hend. A second reason he could not be straightforward, he claimed, was that he was not allowed to pass on important information to those without the proper credentials. This was a storytelling strategy that asked listeners to conclude that even though they knew they were not getting the whole story and that what they heard was laced with fabrications and omissions, still there could be something substantial to it. The lure was that even though the storyteller was not always passing on the truth, he gave the impression that he might actually have it in his possession. That is the impression of Torakichi that Atsutane would have found most pleasing.

Of course there are negative ways of explaining this kind of evasive storytelling. Torakichi may only have been passing on stories he had learned in his time spent working in temples, or even from his own short excursions into the wild, without the benefit of secret instruction by *tengu* or any other supernatural being. Certainly the story of the medicine ped-dler climbing into a small pot and flying away could be recognized as a tale with Chinese precedent. Furthermore, Torakichi, originally born in poverty, was housed, well-clothed, fed, and given gifts and attention for telling stories like these, so he had motivation to lie. If not actually lying, Torakichi may not have been able to tell the whole story because he could not remember it correctly or had not been given full instruction. In other words, his claims of being sworn to secrecy may have been pre-emptive attempts to ward off criticism and ultimately cover for his lying or his inadequate storytelling capacity. There was also the possibility that some stories had been completely fabricated from his own fourteen-year-old resources, and the complexity of the fabrication and his intellectual limi-tations precluded him from crafting completely defensible lies.[21]

On top of that, Torakichi often admitted his contradictory stances, but he did not attribute any significance to the logical problems caused by the contradictions in his statements. For example, Torakichi claimed that once in the mountains just before he was to return to the world of mundane humanity, his master took him aside and specifically instructed him that as a *sanjin* he was compelled to act for the good of the world. In particular, his master Sugiyama told him never to be insincere when he spoke of his mountain experiences. However, Torakichi also claimed he was further instructed that the people of the world could not be com-pletely trusted, so there were still some things he was forbidden to tell at all, or at least to tell completely truthfully.

Even more direct examples of contradiction occurred again in the discussion of the importance of keeping one's true name concealed. Torakichi explained that he was instructed never to reveal the name of Katsuma, which was his master's name for him. In addition, he said he was instructed to refer to a trusted companion by an alias and not by his real name, which he then also immediately revealed. In other words, Torakichi often told what he said he was specifically instructed not to tell.[22] At the same time, he admitted he had been instructed to practice giving disinformation on certain subjects. The result for the listener, then, is that on the one hand the information may be valuable, but on the other hand, by Torakichi's own admission, it may be a lie. He may be the bearer of important information he cannot tell, or he may be saying he is forbidden to tell as a way of covering up the fact that he does not really know.

Torakichi's stance on his master's true designation, *tengu* or *sanjin*, is often inconsistent and confusing. Torakichi stated that he had been instructed by Sugiyama Sanjin to refer to him inaccurately as a *tengu* to continue the current state of mass deception. Torakichi then clearly betrayed the fiction his master instructed him to perpetrate by revealing to Atsutane's circle that Sugiyama was not really a *tengu*. Although he had betrayed his master's command on secrecy, he could defend this betrayal by referring to his master's instruction never to be insincere when speaking of his mountain experiences and by claiming he was following another of his master's instructions to carry out the beneficent services of a *sanjin*, which was the *sanjin*'s stated duty, at least among those he could trust.

Those he deemed he could trust were those who revered the Way of the Kami and despised Buddhism, at least after he came under Atsutane's sway. However, according to Torakichi, another one of Sugiyama Sanjin's instructions to him was never to disparage Buddhism publicly, another of Torakichi's master's prohibitions that was ignored after he came under Atsutane's tutelage. Still, the evidence is clear that Torakichi did not always actively agree and support Atsutane's radical hatred and condemnation of Buddhism, and on those occasions he could claim to have been honoring the teachings of Sugiyama Sanjin. In fact, it would not be hard to imagine cynically that this instruction not to disparage Buddhism publicly could have been "recalled" by Torakichi to protect himself when he found himself seemingly sympathetic to Buddhism. Although Torakichi portrayed his master Sugiyama as an ardent advocate of the Way of the Kami, it is clear by many descriptions of his practices, and by Torakichi's own direct admissions, that Sugiyama Sanjin also worshiped in Buddhist fashion to Buddhist deities.

As has already been made clear, Buddhist practitioners and the term *tengu* had often been associated, and usually not with positive connotations. Buddhists themselves did not often use the word *tengu* in a positive light. Sugiyama Sanjin's choice of the term for himself, according to Torakichi, was attributable to his noble intention to carry on his role as savior of the people anonymously, or if need be, as the object of scorn from the ignorant masses. Torakichi claimed it was a humble and well-intentioned deception designed to deflect worship away from Sugiyama Sanjin himself and onto the *kami*. Sugiyama Sanjin's use of *tengu* can also be seen as similar to the literary tradition of exalted persons taking on humble personal pronouns and titles. Therefore, his humility in using the term *tengu* was to be seen as enhancing his nobility. In any event, the continuing *tengu* association for his Sugiyama Sanjin must have been Torakichi's contribution, for it is unthinkable that Atsutane could believe that anyone would willingly embrace the title of *tengu*.

When Life Gives You Lemons: Atsutane Seizes an Opportunity

Atsutane wrote of his confusion upon first hearing Torakichi explain to some guests that it was correct to refer to all mountain practitioners as *tengu*. Later, when Atsutane was alone with Torakichi, he questioned him about the truth of that statement. As noted earlier, Torakichi recanted and said it was not accurate to say that all the beings on those mountains were *tengu*. On that occasion, Torakichi first used the excuse that he only made that deceptive statement because of specific instructions from his master. Moreover, in that particular exchange with Atsutane, he added another interesting statement to explain away his habit of making contradictory statements. Torakichi claimed that after meeting Atsutane and going back to the mountains to consult with his master Sugiyama Sanjin, he was given specific permission to reveal all secrets to Atsutane, whom the master deemed trustworthy. Cynically speaking, Torakichi had just attempted to explain why he should be allowed to say one thing to others and another thing when speaking with Atsutane.

In effect, this meant that whatever Torakichi said when not alone with Atsutane might not be true, yet the untruth could not be held against him. As convenient an excuse as this was for Torakichi, who we have seen was prone to contradicting himself, it was also convenient for Atsutane. This explanation could be used by Atsutane to claim sole authority in determining the true words of Torakichi and at the same time served to ease his doubt about Torakichi's prior statements that he found objectionable.

Still, by the same token, it also gave Torakichi the opportunity to manipulate Atsutane and others whenever he saw fit, and for his own personal ends. However, we will soon look into just who was manipulating whom.

Torakichi's "clever" attempt to gain forgiveness for any statements that did not fall directly in line with Atsutane's theories of the Other World certainly should have given Atsutane cause to doubt whether *sanjin* actually were fundamentally devoted to the worship of *kami* and opposed to Buddhism as Torakichi had sometimes, but not always, claimed. There should have been reason for him to doubt whether the distinction between *tengu* and *sanjin* had really been important for Torakichi before he met Atsutane. Certainly Atsutane was aware that when Torakichi was not alone with him, he did not make the distinction between *tengu* and *sanjin*. This definitely raised the possibility that the nature and the role of the *sanjin* as servants of the *kami* devoted to saving the Japanese race and the nation of Japan was a story designed for Atsutane's ears only. At several places in the text, Atsutane was specifically presented with the information that Torakichi told Buddhist-friendly stories when he was in different company. Atsutane's friends and associates came to him telling him he was being deceived, or else that there was talk of Atsutane's being part of the deception.

Senkyō ibun makes it clear that despite this palpable public distrust of Torakichi's honesty, Atsutane chose to discount the anti-Torakichi rumors, some of which he himself documented in writing. Certainly a factor in this decision must have been that Torakichi affirmed what Atsutane wanted and needed to have affirmed. Therefore, Atsutane chose to believe that Torakichi might lie to others but never to him because doing so strengthened his discourse about the unique nature of Japan. Atsutane should not be seen as a fool, nor should he be seen as a charlatan himself, knowingly using a liar for his own aggrandizement. Instead, his support of Torakichi was not the cementing of a conspiracy to deceive, but rather a stubborn refusal to have his long-sought-after supernatural informant fail him. Atsutane's sincere belief in the Other World helped him to rationalize and allowed him to downplay the blatant deception techniques used by Torakichi. What's more, textual evidence shows that not only did Atsutane allow Torakichi to change his stories to align with his teachings, he actually actively manipulated Torakichi to do just that.

Separating *Sanjin* from *Tengu:* Atsutane Draws the Line

When Torakichi did not seem to immediately understand the direction Atsutane wanted him to go with his stories, Atsutane would have to lead him by asking him certain types of questions. Examples of Atsutane's leading questions appear in records of conversations regarding the proper way of referring to the beings living in the mountains; that is, prompts to call them *sanjin*, not *tengu*. These questions demonstrate how the answers Atsutane seemed to want were coerced out of Torakichi's mouth. Incidentally, the interaction between them was similar to Torakichi's description of his childhood experiences of hearing strange voices, which he then would realize were coming from his own mouth. The leading questions will demonstrate that although Torakichi was the medium, the message was coming from Atsutane. An example of Atsutane's leading questions can be seen in the following:

> I [Atsutane] said that it was well-known that *tengu* would eventually have to suffer three heats,[23] so that three times a day fire would burst out of their bodies, and according to rule, they would be forced to drink molten iron, isn't this so?[24]

Here, Atsutane reminds Torakichi of something he should take into account; that is, it is not good to be a *tengu* because it always ends badly.
Another example is as follows:

> Don't the thirteen *tengu* get angry when you call them *tengu?* Isn't there some other name that they are referred to by over there?[25]

Here the implication is obvious: nobody, not even a *tengu*, would want to be called a *tengu*.
Sometimes the leading question was not enough, and Torakichi needed stronger reminders of the proper terminology.

> Torakichi had said that there were various differences among the *sanjin;* still it was correct to refer to them all as *tengu*, which is common practice. When he said that, I [Atsutane] kept it in mind with the intent of asking him about it some other time. Since we were in the midst of a crowd, I made a note of it, which I put in my sleeve, and then later we went home. The next day when we were alone I asked him if he shouldn't just refer to them as *sanjin*, and he replied that he didn't do that. I reminded him that recently when he went to the mountains he himself had me write the word *sanjin* in the poems I wrote for him.[26]

Atsutane was clearly unhappy with Torakichi when he did not maintain a clear distinction between *tengu* and *sanjin*. Furthermore, from this passage it is also clear that the distinction was not important for Torakichi.

Leading questions and statements like those above were supposed to induce Torakichi to talk in more detail about *sanjin* and to eventually have him disavow his statement that they were the same as *tengu*. Some of these questions seeking affirmation of a *sanjin* occurred following a conversation about the thirteen *tengu* on Mount Iwama. On this occasion Torakichi had maintained that his master Sugiyama was one of those *tengu*. In this conversation we see that Torakichi started to realize that he should not call his master a *tengu* in front of Atsutane. It was at this juncture, as a reaction to that realization, that Torakichi then claimed that his master had instructed Torakichi to refer to him publicly as one of them to assist him in keeping his secret identity.

When dissatisfied with the answer, Atsutane then asked Torakichi what was quoted previously; that is, if he thought the *tengu*, especially his master, must be angry at being called a *tengu*, and so was there not some other name to refer to those who are not really *tengu*. Torakichi at first replied that his master and his associates did not care what those in the human realm might call them, and that humans called every strange creature in the Other World a *tengu*. However, he later gave in to Atsutane's insistence on some distinction by adding that there actually was a distinction made in that realm and that in fact four of the thirteen *tengu* were actually called *sanjin*. The rest were true *tengu*, beings who were transformations of eagles, kites, or such things. To add a touch of verisimilitude, Torakichi also threw in a comment that the *sanjin* all had to laugh when they saw the shrine talismans picturing them as having large noses and wings.

An important point to remember when analyzing this dialogue is that according to Atsutane's own record, being called a *tengu* did not bother Sugiyama Sanjin himself, nor did Torakichi ever express regret that Sugiyama Sanjin was known as such. In one dialogue in *Senkyō ibun*, Torakichi referred to his master as Great Tengu. Only later, upon prompting by Atsutane, did Torakichi change to the word *sanjin*. As we have already seen, the *tengu* references bothered only one person in this dialogue. The only person who asked for another way of referring to humans in the mountains was Atsutane. Torakichi simply accommodated him with what was a generic term not directly associated with any particular religious connotation.

The evidence is clear that the term *sanjin* did not occur consistently in Torakichi's speech, and when it did, it was in response to Atsutane's desire to hear it. Judging by the relative frequency of the appearance of the two terms, Torakichi preferred *tengu*. It was Torakichi who avowed to Atsutane at their first meeting that his master Sugiyama and the many other human inhabitants of the mountains revered the *kami*. However, it was Atsutane who made the decision to concretize the terminology, using the word *sanjin* to designate Torakichi's master Sugiyama and his *kami*-worshiping practices.

Atsutane's own record demonstrates that his questions prompted and at times badgered Torakichi into assertively and definitively claiming that his master was actually a *sanjin* and not a *tengu*. The dialogue between Torakichi and Atsutane went back and forth, and slowly but surely gave birth to a *sanjin* devoted to the Ancient Way supported by Atsutane. Torakichi's master, most likely a man living life as what we would identify as a *shūgenja* and what the nineteenth-century Japanese might tend to pejoratively call a *tengu*, was transformed into an Ancient Way *sanjin* by the Socratic method.[27]

Torakichi as Mouthpiece for Atsutane's Theology

In Atsutane's *The August Pillar of the Soul* in 1812, he introduced his idea of the soul and the afterlife. In brief, he asserted that all Japanese people had an intangible soul. The flesh eventually rotted away, but the soul was eternal. After the death of the body, the soul could either become a *kami* or a demon; that is, the souls trained in the true Way of the Kami became *kami* and the others turned into one of a large variety of demonic beings, *tengu* being one of them. Both the *kami* and the demons lived forever in the Other World, overseen by Ōkuninushi.

This bifurcation of good and evil souls resembles the traditional Chinese belief in cloud souls and white souls. A detailed look at Atsutane's soul theory does indeed show just how indebted it was to China's earliest traditions. Of course, Atsutane would not admit the debt but would instead place the origin of those traditions in Japan's ancient past. Atsutane's deep dependence on Chinese culture will be discussed in detail in the following chapter. In *The August Pillar of the Soul*, however, Atsutane ignores the Chinese connection and chooses to defend his claims for the soul and the afterlife with historical evidence pieced together from his interpretations of the classics of Japanese history.

In Atsutane's theory, the death of the body actually could lead to a good end:

> People exist in visible bodies for as long as they are in that visible world. When they die and return to the dark mystery, the soul at last becomes *kami*. Then, the actual amount of spiritual matter of which they are com-

posed separates out into noble and vile, good and evil, and hard and soft. The most surpassing among that spiritual matter becomes like *kami* from the Age of the Kami, of such grand quality in no way inferior to the *kami* of the Age of the Kami. All should know that in this they are no different from the *kami* at the beginning of time. . . . Ōkuninushi who exists there in his unseen form lovingly attends them. Lords, parents, wives, and children all live in comfort and prosperity, just as they had in the revealed world.[28]

However, he also had this to say about the way things could go badly after death:

The ancient stories explain why the *tengu* living in the Other World are so numerous. The stories say that they are people who died with extreme amounts of evil or bitterness in their hearts. They were so evil or so bitter that immediately after they passed away, they instantly joined that group. While some tend to overlook those kinds of stories as just the idle chatter of Buddhist priests, I have long suspected that there was some merit to them.[29]

It is interesting to note Atsutane's willingness to believe the "idle chatter of Buddhist priests" when it supported his own contentions. It was quite satisfying for him when elsewhere he highlights the fact that Buddhist priests also maintained that certain famous Buddhist priests were actually *tengu*. However, even more interesting to note for the argument here is the similarity between Atsutane's statements on the soul and what the illiterate and uneducated Torakichi was recorded to have said in *Senkyō ibun*, written ten years after *The August Pillar of the Soul:*

I [Atsutane] asked, "What have you heard from your master concerning the destination of the soul?"

Torakichi replied, "First of all, the human soul can be good or evil, and moves toward becoming firmly and completely one or the other, and then never perishes. In fact, there is no time when souls firmly composed of evil intentions can ever perish. They join the ranks of evil demons and eternally receive the punishments of the shining *kami*. The souls firmly composed of good intentions receive the blessings of the shining *kami* and become *kami* who protect the world until the end of time."[30]

Here we clearly see that Atsutane's theological speculations about the destination of the soul have been backed up by Torakichi and are actually the same teachings of Sugiyama Sanjin in the Other World, or at least that is what Atsutane would have us believe.

Other similar episodes are recorded in *Senkyō ibun*. In these exchanges, it seems highly likely that the words coming out of Torakichi's mouth merely serve to verify Atsutane's teachings. A good example of this, but not the only one, can be seen in the following episode when Torakichi comes to verify Atsutane's assertion that the most important principle of popular *kami* worship is the bond between the common Japanese person and the tutelary *kami* who is devoted to his or her protection.

In this particular episode, Torakichi was involved in a conversation with Atsutane, Yashiro Hirokata, and a Master Kurahashi,[31] who seemed to be a frequent visitor to Atsutane's salon. At its start the conversation was about mysterious strangers who kidnapped innocent people for their own selfish purposes. Torakichi explained that *kami, tengu,* and *sanjin* thought of humans as mere dolls and often did with them whatever they pleased. Yashiro then offered a story of *kami* coming to the rescue of kidnapped people, and Torakichi agreed that this had happened. Kurahashi brought up another story of a kidnapping by strangers with mysterious powers. He explained that the episode was resolved and the victim was rescued when the family prayed to their tutelary *kami*. Atsutane then brought up the stories of *Record of the Haunting of Master Inō,* for which he would write an introduction in 1821.

I [Atsutane] heard the story of a ghost named Sanemoto Goroēmon who appeared directly in front of Inō Heitarō in Bingo Province. When it happened, Heitarō called on his tutelary *kami*. The *kami* then suddenly appeared before him, formally dressed, but with only the upper half visible, and then remained by his side.

Then I said this to Torakichi, "I think that when Heitarō thought of the tutelary *kami* and then was visited by him, the protection of the tutelary *kami* saved him from being killed by the ghost. In the story of the man who had his voice borrowed by the stranger, the stranger was fearful of him praying to the *kami* of Sumiyoshi. In the story of the abduction of Noyama Matahyōei's child Tajirō, the leader of those strange men feared that Matahyōei would pray to the *kami,* and so they returned the child. When I look at all those facts it seems that even in the case of *sanjin* or *tengu* abduction, the words of the tutelary *kami* cannot be resisted. Furthermore, when it comes to ghosts, they cannot harm anyone who is protected by his tutelary *kami*. What are your thoughts about this?"

Torakichi said, "You are absolutely right. *Sanjin, tengu,* or whatever, if there is a tutelary *kami* that tells them to return someone, they must follow those orders. However, if someone is abducted and the parents or concerned parties' prayers aren't completely wholehearted, and therefore don't have proper influence in the Other World, then, in some cases, the abductee is returned as an idiot. Because of that, when I was abducted into the Other World, my master repeatedly warned me against saying anything to my parents. I too came to fear being returned as an idiot."

This was just as I [Atsutane] had thought and recorded in detail about the tutelary *kami* earlier in *Koshiden* and *Tamadasuki*. All people should be aware that every minute of every day they are dependent on the blessings of these *kami*. I wonder why it is that in spite of this fact, people do not think enough of the tutelary *kami* and have faith in other *kami* or buddhas.[32]

Torakichi need not have been rehearsed the night before to say exactly the right thing in response to the leading questions of his interlocutors. The personal touch he added to the story, his master's warning to him, is both clever and self-serving. Atsutane's reference to his own writings for detailed explanation of the teachings, along with his lament that these teachings are so little heeded, are also clever and self-serving. It is passages such as these that inform us that *Senkyō ibun* is not just the chronicle of Torakichi's testimony, but also a forum for the teaching of Atsutane's new theology. These kinds of exchanges serve as Other Worldly validation of the correctness of Atsutane's own previous individual speculations.

Another example of Torakichi's verification of Atsutane's opinions comes from the wealth of criticism of Buddhism found in *Senkyō ibun*. Torakichi's own words, recorded faithfully and perhaps gleefully by Atsutane, give his plain and open opinion about Buddhist professionals:

I [Torakichi] hate the way most of the people who join the Buddhist priesthood defraud the public, steal, adorn themselves, act so proud of their individual temples, and then look down on everyone else. I have always hated them. . . . My master was alive long before Shakyamuni, and he has told me over and over again that the Way of the Buddha is all about deceiving stupid people. It is a way composed only of fantasies about Shakyamuni.[33]

This master mentioned here is, of course, Sugiyama Sanjin, not Atsutane, as the viciousness of the commentary might suggest. In this passage, Atsutane gained not only Torakichi's verification but also the verification of an inhabitant of the Other World, who was purportedly alive long before Shakyamuni Buddha. Statements with similar criticisms of Buddhism from Atsutane's earlier writings will be discussed in detail in chapter 5, which describes how *Senkyō ibun* works as a critique of Buddhism.

Even the scholar Kamata Tōji, who does not suspect Atsutane of intentionally indoctrinating Torakichi, points out a statement credited to Torakichi from *Senkyō ibun* that he could not believe the boy was capable of producing by himself. In that passage, Torakichi waxed philosophical about the evils and dangers of being proud of one's own erudition. Kamata brings up Atsutane's own tendency toward pretentiousness when extolling his own "humble learning" and concludes:

> It is difficult to imagine that the fifteen year-old Torakichi was solely responsible for these words. It is likely that Atsutane's own attitude toward learning is reflected here to a very considerable extent. What Torakichi said was a reproduction of what Atsutane appears to have repeated on a daily basis.[34]

Kamata's last sentence should be kept in mind when determining just how much Torakichi's nativism depended on his new master's techniques of indoctrination.

Torakichi or Atsutane, Whose Voice Do We Hear?— Scholars' Opinions

Perhaps the most detailed study of Atsutane's life and work was conducted by the Japanese scholar Watanabe Kinzō and published in 1942. In a decidedly friendly analysis of Atsutane's scholarship, Watanabe concludes that Torakichi was just a flash in the pan who ultimately could not fulfill his promise. In other words, Torakichi was a fake, but Atsutane was one of many who were deceived by the boy and was not involved in any deception himself. Watanabe describes Torakichi as just another wunderkind who appeared out of nowhere like a shooting star, quickly gained a wide following, and was eventually done in by his inability to consistently deliver and live up to his reputation and promise.

Despite the above-quoted questioning of Torakichi's originality, Kamata Tōji is also kind to Atsutane's integrity. Kamata excuses Atsutane by diagnosing him with a peculiar psychological inclination to be attracted to a boy with such promise. Kamata emphasizes the tragedies in Atsutane's life that led to his deeply held wish to once again see his lost loved ones. In other words, Kamata concludes that Atsutane was taken in hook, line, and sinker by someone offering a channel to the Other World.

Kamata is convinced that Atsutane identified with Torakichi, who had faced many hardships just as Atsutane had in his youth. Moreover, Kamata suspects that Atsutane even identified with Torakichi's *sanjin* master. As evidence for these claims he cites Atsutane's portraits of the three of them and notes that all three men had similar facial features, particularly the noses and ears. Kamata also suggests that Atsutane might have thought of Torakichi as one of the two sons he had lost, being that they would have been in the same age range.

Kamata is attempting to examine and flesh out Atsutane's work, placing him in the role of patriarch of modern Japanese spiritualism. Therefore it is understandable that he would not find Atsutane guilty of too much premeditated manipulation of the medium. However, as explained earlier, Kamata clearly recognizes Atsutane's influence over Torakichi, but at the same time echoes Watanabe by arguing that Torakichi bewitched Atsutane. In effect, Kamata is saying that Torakichi bore the responsibility for parroting Atsutane's teaching too well.

Koyasu Nobukuni and Haga Noboru also do not find Atsutane guilty of any covert manipulation of the medium, even though they both point out uncanny convergences of Atsutane's and Torakichi's claims about the Other World. Koyasu concludes that Atsutane was taking Torakichi's stories at face value, then reconstituting them into evidence for a complete and consistent Shinto cosmology. He sees Atsutane and Torakichi as working in concert as part of a process of intellectual history that would create a modern worldview for nineteenth-century Japan. At his most critical, Koyasu claims that Torakichi was often Atsutane's echo, but an echo that provided verification of a mystical and divine sort.

Haga gives Torakichi, not Atsutane, the credit for distinguishing *tengu* from *sanjin* and *sennin* from *sanjin*. However, this conclusion ignores the many instances when Torakichi waffled about such distinctions. Furthermore, Haga places no importance on analyzing the context of the questioning that led to Torakichi's "independent" discovery of the *sanjin*. In Haga's defense, he was examining Atsutane and Torakichi's relationship only to characterize their cooperative efforts to create a new concept of Japanese folk religion. He saw them as agreeing on several ideas; namely, the soul, the afterlife, and the importance of local *kami*, those which would later be exploited and developed by Yanagita Kunio.

In the early postwar period, Donald Keene expressed some doubt about Atsutane's commitment to truthfulness in his work. Keene cites Atsutane's willingness to use Torakichi's stories of his moon flight alongside reliable scientific information as an example of Atsutane's determination to use any kind of evidence to support his theories. However, by the 1970s Keene's opinion of Atsutane's attitude toward Torakichi had grown less critical.[35] At that point he said he did not think Atsutane was gullible, but noted that nowhere did Atsutane admit to any disbelief or doubt as to the veracity of Torakichi's fantastic tales. Keene also noted that many learned men of the era found Torakichi to be credible, and he ends up concluding that Torakichi must have been a very convincing child prodigy. In other words, his conclusions are quite similar to those of Watanabe and Kamata.

A little-known American scholar of the 1960s, Walter Odronic, who completed a detailed study on Atsutane and is still the only person to have published a complete translation of an Atsutane text in English, could not even entertain the possibility that Atsutane believed Torakichi. Instead, he characterizes Atsutane's dalliance with divinely inspired children as a shameful attempt to deceive his public. Although Odronic recognizes Atsutane's ability to believe in what we would now call the supernatural, he does not explain why he assesses the Torakichi affair to be simply a hoax. Odronic just leaves us to conclude that his assessment is based on his intuition or the limits of his own credulity rather than any particular evidence or compelling analysis.

Mark McNally's understanding of the relationship between Atsutane and Torakichi has Atsutane simply following a trend of antiquarian studies pursued by other *kokugaku* scholars of the period. McNally concludes that Atsutane was interviewing Torakichi merely to amass a store of "friendly" empirical data on the Other World, which Atsutane assumed to be the same spirit realm he had been hypothesizing about in his earlier texts. McNally also incorrectly asserts that Atsutane never inserted theology into their conversations and never asked Torakichi to interpret his assertions about the Other World.[36] In other words, McNally does not require that we consider the question of whether the ethnographer was influencing the answers of the informant or whether the informant was deceiving the ethnographer.

By far the most interesting commentary on the power relationship between Atsutane and Torakichi, and on the true source of Torakichi's phenomenal knowledge, was offered by Atsutane apologist Origuchi Shinobu.[37] Origuchi suggests that Torakichi's knowledge came in great part from his former master, who was most likely some kind of yin yang specialist. However, Origuchi also asserts that there certainly were occasions when Torakichi said things that could only have come from Atsutane's teachings. Origuchi's explanation for those occurrences was that Atsutane held a kind of hypnotic power over Torakichi that enabled Atsutane to plant suggestions in Torakichi's mind, which then prompted him to make his answers correspond to Atsutane's desired result. Origuchi further insists that Atsutane had the power of a spiritualist that resulted in an unintended brainwashing of Torakichi. Due to the brainwashing, Torakichi naturally answered in a manner that pleased his new master. In other words, Origuchi concludes that Atsutane did not intentionally coach Torakichi to say what he surely had to have been taught by Atsutane.[38]

All the scholars named above missed, overlooked, or just were not interested in clear and abundant evidence of Atsutane's manipulation of the *Senkyō ibun* narrative and narrator. This has resulted in a critical devaluation of the craftsmanship that went into the making of this text. In fairness to those scholars, in every case their main interests lay not in narrative analysis, but rather in characterizing Atsutane's political impact on the future. Yet for this study, it is more important to understand how Atsutane constructed this fictional text itself rather than how this fiction may have led Japan to where it is today. If Atsutane's literary devices, which mask the true origin of what he has recorded, are not understood, they will continue to work their deceptions on present-day readers and scholars, and *Senkyō ibun* will remain in its present state, misunderstood as a quaint example of nineteenth-century folklore and superstition.

Atsutane Doth Protest Too Much

A few final examples of authorial manipulation of the reader should reinforce the contention that Atsutane desperately wanted his readers to believe that *Senkyō ibun* was a true record of testimony from the Other World, when in fact it is a fictive record bearing witness to Atsutane's public relations and recruitment initiatives. These examples come from a section at the end of the first of the five chapters of *Senkyō ibun*. This particular section was written in reaction to vicious slander leveled against Atsutane and well-publicized criticisms of his relationship with Torakichi. For Atsutane, this was particularly distressing criticism since it came from inside his Shinto or Ancient Way community and not from the so-called sinophiles or Buddhists, from whom it would be expected.

Atsutane recorded that he first heard these slanderous rumors from sympathetic men of integrity who were appalled that an honorable man such as himself could be treated so cruelly. One of the reports is recorded as follows:

> [The informant said], "The other day after I had arrived for a lecture at Otake Sensei's school, Shinto priest so-and-so came along and said the most slanderous things about you. What the man was talking about concerned the boy's statements about the Other World. The Shinto priest

called you the 'Mountain Master,'[39] and said that the boy was only allowed to say what you taught him to say. Also, he said that what you were saying about obtaining the stone flute through some divine inspiration was all a lie.[40] The priest is spreading the word that you got the flute from an antique dealer whom the priest also knows and who owned that flute himself for a long time. He also said that the antique dealer was very upset about what you were saying about how you obtained it."[41]

In another report, a certain Shinto Priest Haruhiko, friendly to Atsutane, had dropped in on an acquaintance, only to hear this Mr. X (there are blanks in the document where the name has been removed)

viciously slandering me [Atsutane] in the same manner as had happened at Otake's place. Mr. X said that I should also be considered guilty of luring in and carrying off the boy a short while back. Haruhiko left Mr. X's place as fast as he could and rushed over to tell me the story, and to check on how I was getting along.[42]

Atsutane went on to say:

There are many other people who have been slandering me about this Torakichi affair. They spread hateful rumors like, "Hirata has made up incredible lies in order to spread his own theories. He says that the late Master of the Suzunoya Academy [Motoori Norinaga] became a *tengu* in the Other World and sent this boy to tell everyone that the conditions of the Other World are exactly as he [Hirata] has always been saying." There are also people who say things like, "he wrote a book containing Age of the Kami Japanese writing, but he wants everyone else to think they are the real thing. To do that he taught them to the boy and made him say that they are writings from the Other World."[43]

It is strange that Atsutane's first response to this slander is to lament his tortured and misunderstood existence starting from his childhood. He seems to be looking for sympathy.

I was born unlucky. From the day I was born and left on a straw mat, I have not known the loving hand of a parent. It does no good to speak of it now, but I was passed from hand to hand, from the care of the nursemaid to adoptive parents, and was plagued by those cruel circumstances until I reached my twenties. Then, from the first time I set foot in Edo to this very moment in my life, I have had to endure every kind of trouble and sorrow there is. Since we are supposed to learn from our sufferings in the temporary existence in this world, I have accepted it all as merely my burden in life. In spite of all my troubles, everything I read and write is for the purpose of strengthening my resolve to follow the Ancient Way. I earnestly endeavor to clarify the True Way of the world, I certainly do not take the affairs of the Other World lightly, and my heart also goes out to birds, beasts, insects, fish, and even trees and grasses. Yet, how much more so does my concern extend to all other people, for whom I always do my utmost. I am constantly and secretly doing good deeds for others without any intention of seeking credit for them. No matter what anyone says about me, I have made a point of never doing the slightest thing of which I should be ashamed, and never for an instant have I wished ill upon anyone else. So why in the world do so many people viciously slander me by making up lies like the ones I just heard? Why in the world would people I have never seen or heard of, and who have no reason to hate me, make up such lies about me?[44]

Perhaps he first opts for a defensive strategy, looking for sympathy, because he truly feels injured. In short, his argument above seems to say that his lifetime of suffering and ignominy is evidence of his inner nobility, and he implies that the righteousness of his cause and his good intentions alone should mean that he deserves to be believed and trusted despite any evidence of wrongdoing. This defense of his integrity is, of course, no defense at all, because the criticisms are actually accurate descriptions of his deceptive and manipulative practices. His choice of defense here is clearly to play the victim and ask for pity from his supporters, most likely because he cannot prove his accusers wrong.

The chapter ends with a second kind of response, one that some might find more believable because it is an appeal to authority rather than pity. Still, this second defense also has its own shortcomings. Atsutane writes that an old friend, a Shinto priest who was an official at the Inner Shrine of Ise and had studied under Norinaga, visits him. The priest questions Torakichi and studies some of his writing. After careful deliberation, the priest concludes that Torakichi's master must certainly be a true *sanjin*. In addition, the priest relates a tale of his own frightening encounter with creatures from the Other World, and he is also able to confirm that these Other Worldly creatures left him alone when he invoked the authority of the *kami*. What this evidence actually proves is that Atsutane and Torakichi had managed to convince some very important people in the Shinto world and that those people were willing to back up Atsutane's story.

In spite of Atsutane's dual defense strategy of claiming discrimination and injury and calling on an important witness to defend his assertions, in fact his very own written record, *Senkyō ibun*, supports most of the charges of those who slandered him. Above all, the written record proves that Atsutane either put words in Torakichi's mouth or browbeat him into supporting his theories. In *Senkyō ibun* it is also plainly written that Atsutane's students physically carried off Torakichi and confined him in Atsutane's residence. Also in that record, Atsutane writes that in the first month of their relationship Torakichi was given a volume of so-called Age of the Kami Japanese characters to verify with his own master Sugiyama.

That Atsutane would receive criticism and suspicion for his relationship with a supernatural Tengu Boy should have been expected. In fact there is another written record verifying that Atsutane expected it but hoped to avoid it. Still, he could not restrain himself from publicizing this suspicious relationship in the short work by his student Takeuchi Magoichi called *A Short Chronicle of the Divine Child's Possession Tales* (*Shindō hyōdan ryakki*), whose distribution he authorized. In that work there is the following note verifying Atsutane's fear of scandal:

> Note: The stories of this divine child are all relevant to the Ancient Way. Being wary of public gossip, the teacher is still not talking to outsiders about this divine boy's ideas.[45] The fact is that the divine child's assertions coincide with what the teacher [Atsutane] had already recorded in detail in his work, *Koshiden*. Because of this he has been deeply anxious people will suspect that the divine child's stories have been made up simply to legitimate his own theories.[46]

That Atsutane spent so much time defending himself against criticism in *Senkyō ibun* suggests that this criticism was so harsh and well-publicized among his inner circle that he could not avoid doing so. Overdefending in the manner shown above was a subtle admission that he was aware of weaknesses in his defense. In fact, some of the charges were undeniably true. It is clear that Torakichi was abducted and that he had been taught Atsutane's theories and doctrines; he lived in Atsutane's academy of Ancient Way religion. Finally, he was a poor boy with no real home and no place to go, and he must have realized what lay in his own self-interest.

In conclusion, Atsutane's "secret" recorded dialogues with Torakichi were orchestrated toward a purpose: to hone Torakichi's supernatural testimony into a consistent story that supported Atsutane's Ancient Way ideology so that Torakichi could be personally presented at interviews and tell "his" story of the goings on of the Other World. Atsutane's most important ideological goal was to establish a class of religious virtuosi working for the *kami.* The interviews with Torakichi fleshed out this design to give birth to the concept of a new native Japanese religious culture hero. This hero's *raison d'etre,* and the reason he was sought out and discovered by Atsutane, was twofold. The first was to fulfill the role of legitimator of a new discourse on Atsutane's Other World. The second was to provide an alternative native Japanese religious virtuoso who could undermine claims of foreign cultural superiority.

In essence, Atsutane felt that Japanese religion needed its own legitimate entry into the contest for the world's most powerful religious virtuoso. Through Torakichi's descriptions of his master, we see the model for Atsutane's champion and learn his capabilities and his religious mission. This new and improved *sanjin,* with his newly elaborated skills and abilities, must be understood in the context of the heroes and the cultures against which he would have to be measured. His functions should be put in context to evaluate his role in Atsutane's new Ancient Way cosmology and theology. The following three chapters will detail this *sanjin*'s abilities, created as they were to bolster supposed deficiencies in Japanese native culture vis-à-vis Chinese, Buddhist, and Western cultures.

CHAPTER 4

The Critique of China and Defense of Native Culture

Atsutane's Stance on Cultural Borrowing

Atsutane's overall objective in his research was to rediscover what was originally Japanese and to rid Japanese culture of all foreign influences so that native culture could be revalued and understood as superior to other cultures. However, in pursuing this objective he had a habit of appropriating his so-called original and native Japanese ideas from foreign cultures. For example, his version of *jindai moji*, or the native Japanese writing system, which he claimed was developed in Japan's mythological Age of the Kami long before contact with the continental cultures, was criticized by important people[1] within his own *kokugaku* movement for being an imitation of *hangul*, writing from the Korean peninsula.

What is most paradoxical is that Atsutane habitually appropriated ideas from the very cultures with which he was competing and of which he was critical. The first glaring example from *Senkyō ibun* is the very word *sanjin*, which is one Chinese character radical short of being the same character combination that makes up the Chinese word for Daoist immortal. The imitation is obvious and intentional, and there is no attempt to disguise it, although we will see later how Torakichi clarified the difference between the two beings. This chapter will detail many more appropriations of Chinese culture.

There are also many examples in *Senkyō ibun* of Atsutane's appropriations from Buddhism, which is particularly startling in light of his often-expressed negative opinions about that religion. Specific examples of his debt to Buddhism will be given in the following chapter. In addition, as noted earlier, it is clear from reading Atsutane's *Outer Chapters of Our Doctrine* that he had been able to obtain writings on Christianity translated into Chinese. It has been further asserted that in Atsutane's new theological system, Ame no minaka nushi simply replaced the Christian God the Father, with two other creator *kami* filling the slots for the Son and the Holy Spirit to fill out the trinity of creation for the Shinto Zōka no sanshin.[2] Furthermore, Atsutane's new heaven- and hell-like afterworlds, with Ōkuninushi sitting in judgment, have also been evaluated as results of crypto-Christian influence. Atsutane, of course, would claim that the influence went the opposite way, but his own words admit that he read translations from Dutch books and recognized a similarity and connection between Christianity and his own Ancient Way.

> Far to the west of India there are countless countries, and even in all those countries, there is a tradition which says the gods of heaven created every-thing, starting with heaven and earth, and ending with human beings. This can be clearly seen when you look at documents from Holland. Any-way, the fact is that all the countries of the world speak in unison of a tradition of gods who live in heaven and create all things. While we doubt the verity of their stories, we know that they contain a small connection to our divine country's traditions.[3]

Much more about Atsutane's secular appropriations from the West will be explained in detail in chapter 6.

Atsutane was learned in various fields of scholarship. In his many works he proudly displayed his knowledge of theories and teachings originating in other cultures. He, of course, given his nativist agenda, was highly critical of those Japanese who were supporters of foreign theories and propagators of foreign teachings. He was quick to point out foreign "corruption," even in revered texts praised by other nativists. For example, in the *Nihongi* we find one of the earliest collections of stories relating to the creation and history of Japan. Yet this history differs from the *Kojiki* in that it also records variant versions, in contrast to the *Kojiki*'s single story line. The first creation story from the *Nihongi* describes an undifferenti-ated egglike substance dividing into distinct parts. Atsutane claims that this story was not originally Japanese and is clear evidence of Chinese cor-ruption that affects this whole work. In *Essence of the Ancient Way* (*Kodō taii*) he writes:

> At this point in time, because of the Chinese language embellishments of the *Nihongi*, we have lost the facts of the ancient past; moreover, this has given birth to the mistakes of later generations. If I were to mention one or two, first, there is the beginning of the volume of the Age of the Kami,[4] where it says "In ancient times before heaven and earth had divided and yin and yang were not yet separated in a nebulous mass like a chicken egg," up to "and later a *kami* was born from it." This is from the Han docu-

ments called *Huai nan zi* and *San wu li ji*.[5] The editor's intent was to add embellishments by appropriating from various places, even passages from foreign documents.[6]

In spite of his assertion of foreign influence, the very same structure he identifies in the *Huai nan zi* is clearly at work in the model of creation he eventually authenticates for his own cosmogony. Again in *Essence of the Ancient Way* he writes:

> So from a single object, something like a horn shot up, moving all around. The tradition calls it a reed shoot, because it sprouted up quickly just like a reed shoot would. Nevertheless, the body of the object that arose . . . was pure and bright. And, that thing became our very sun.[7]

Later in the same work he writes:

> In the beginning of the world from the single object floating in the middle of the great sky, a reed-shoot-like sprout arose to the heavens. Also, from the bottom of that single object another object, the root of heaven, descended and took form. From that, Kuni no toko tachi no kami[8] and Toyo kumu nu no kami[9] were created. The object that descended has been called Ne no kuni or Ne no katasu kuni,[10] but this later split off and has become the very moon we behold with our own eyes.[11]

Even though Atsutane does not make the connection that "yang goes up and yin goes down" or that "sun is yang and moon is yin," it would seem impossible that these connections eluded him and that he failed to notice how the structure of his story and the *Nihongi* story he condemns are related. More evidence of his acceptance of this Chinese model appears in his published defenses of fellow *kokugaku* scholar Hattori Nakatsune's[12] heliocentric theory.

Appropriating models from other cultures is a practice often repeated throughout the history of the expansion and interaction of Asian religions. Particularly in China, Buddhism, Daoism, and Confucianism had been trading and fusing paradigms for more than a thousand years before the resultant conglomerate of three different religious traditions, each composed of multiple schools, reached the forms studied by Atsutane in nineteenth-century Japan. In Japan, the Shinto tradition that Atsutane is associated with started as *kami* cults that grew in power and complexity in the medieval period by distinguishing their identities from the core Buddhist traditions. In a later development, as Neo-Confucian discourse grew in popularity, some Shinto scholars incorporated ideas, structure, and models from that tradition to revitalize and stimulate Shinto activity. Atsutane certainly had plenty of historical precedent and was in good company in his cultural borrowing activities, and in that sense was following Japanese tradition.

Although religious innovators before Atsutane borrowed ideas, few came straight out and admitted to a lack of original thinking. Instead, they came up with creative ways of claiming originality. One way to insist upon originality for a borrowed idea was to claim divine revelation, while another was to claim to have found a "new" ancient text. Atsutane's way of claiming originality was a little different. His claim was that his information, while not new, was original in the strict sense of the word. He asserted that scholars up to that time had held a deeply flawed understanding of the true "origin" of ancient religious ideas.[13]

Specifically, his claim was that Japan was the first land created in the world. That being the case, it follows that the only true stories about the creation must have originated in Japan. Following Atsutane's logic, unfortunate contact with non-Japanese sources corrupted the original stories, resulting in the Chinese elements of the *Nihongi*. The original stories had diffused throughout the earth, and in time they had almost all been corrupted. For example, the Japanese creator pair Izanagi and Izanami came to be known in the West as Adam and Eve. For Atsutane, one fortunate result of this diffusion was that some truly original components of early stories that had been forgotten in Japan could be rediscovered in other countries' corrupt stories. The forgotten stories or story components were currently mislabeled as foreign, but according to his theory, were actually originally Japanese. Therefore, Atsutane could claim that he did not borrow or appropriate foreign stories; he simply reclaimed ownership of Japanese stories. He writes:

> Japan is the root of the world. Due to this fact, in all matters Japan is superior to all countries, and therefore all foreign nations must be inferior to Japan in all ways. This we should always keep in mind. Also, for this same reason, all foreign countries' ancient legends are similar to our country's legends, even though they cannot be expected to have been transmitted in precise detail. This is analogous to stories of events in the capital being passed along to the countryside of the provinces; they will certainly not be exactly like the originals in the capital.[14]

Japan is of course the capital in this metaphor and the provinces are the rest of the world, with all the associated rustic deficiencies.

Atsutane had a further argument he used to justify his appropriation of ideas of foreign origin. Compared to most other nativists, Atsutane had an expansive and visionary view of *kokugaku,* the literal meaning of which is national learning, but which actually means Japanese learning. He once performed an analysis and ranking of all existing classifications of learnings and, not surprisingly, found Japanese learning to be the best. However, his decision was not based on the idea that Japanese knowledge had exclusive secrets unknown to the rest of the world. On the contrary, his vision of Japanese learning was that it was all-inclusive, in fact proprietary of all the best knowledge in the world.

> Now the reason I say Japanese learning is the broadest is, as I said above, that it is composed of various kinds of studies, including but not limited to Confucian learning and Buddhist learning. The ideas and the experiences of those Ways all are packed into Japanese learning. Just as in the saying, "the water of the eight directions and nine fields flow into the river of heaven without overflowing," every kind of learning is combined together in it, like the downstream flow of all rivers toward the great ocean. Because they are mixed together in this way, they have affected the minds of many people, and many of those people cannot separate right and wrong amidst all this information. Thus, many are confused. For this reason, if we do not separate Japanese learning into its components, the beneficial parts of the True Way will not be revealed. In order to arrive at a point where we can try to reveal the matters that harm the True Way, we must first learn about those previous [harmful] matters in order to identify them.[15]

According to Atsutane, then, it was both fortunate and unfortunate for Japan that every learning under the sun seemed to have been mixed together and collected there. But that being the state of affairs, he thought they should all be considered Japanese learning. Furthermore, having all kinds of knowledge was good, but if one was without the ability to make judgments about quality or truth; that is, that all things Japanese were superior and original, then just having a vast amount of knowledge was not to be praised. It followed then that knowledgeable Westerners, Chinese, Buddhists, or even Japanese sinophiles could not be considered ultimately admirable, no matter how much information they had.

This line of argument gave Atsutane license to use any foreign idea as his own. Yet for some reason he chose to eliminate one certain powerful and popular method for merging foreign traditions. This concept, which he argued against, was correlative thinking; that is, linking ideas, institutions, and symbols to natural phenomena in order to lend naturalness and credence to human artificial constructs. This type of cosmological thinking was ancient in origin and was also used quite often in the Japanese medieval period. It is especially conspicuous in Ryōbu Shinto and Ise Shinto texts.[16] For those who used this system, the matching of one set of fives or one set of sevens with other recognized sets of fives or sevens seemed to add to their cosmological importance and their truth value and believability. For example, in one typical medieval Buddhist-influenced Shinto text, the *Tenchi Reikiki,*[17] the sixteen generations of *kami*[18] of the Ise Shinto[19] tradition validate the sixteen arhats of the Buddhist tradition and vice versa. Or the seven buddhas of "history" equal the seven generations of heavenly *kami,* and the five buddhas of the mandala equal the five generations of earthly *kami,* and so on.

Atsutane was not in favor of this kind of cosmological model, at least not with the fives and sevens readily available to him; that is, fives and sevens that were often seen as typifying and perhaps strengthening Chinese or Buddhist traditions. His denial of fives and sevens was absolute, and his condemnation of those who would use them was complete.

> All the "seven generations of *kami* of heaven" and the "five generations of *kami* of earth"[20] have never been seen in the ancient documents. It is a vulgar explanation of later generations that carelessly makes claims that are forced into seeming to correspond to heaven and earth, without considering the meaning of events or even [the facts of] the ancient past. However, today's scholars, without analysis, sagely speak of "heaven seven, earth five." They say that after Emperor Jimmu there were human kings and therefore this corresponds to the three sources.[21] . . . Or else, they say the seven generations and the five generations are modeled on the seven stars of heaven and the five phases. They even make up explanations by matching up the eight hexagrams. The fact that they do this is all due to the self-serving theories of the recent generations of followers of Chinese reasoning. People who are fond of Buddhist theories say that the seven generations are fashioned after the seven buddhas of the past. This type [of talk] fouls and stains the ears. It makes me sick and is truly dreadful.[22]

Again, the particular efficacy of the numerological model lies in its ability to make associations and confirm relationships of theoretical amounts with actual amounts. For example, the idea of five elements or phases sounds plausible because we all have five limbs on our bodies or five fingers on each hand. Thus, the model is more effective for one who wants to establish equivalences, that is, to extend established legitimacy to another concept. In other words, this model is effective if one wants something to be considered *like* something else, or *as good as* something else. Clearly this was not Atsutane's hope for his Ancient Way.

Sanjin: The Chinese Connection

As mentioned in the beginning of this chapter, the term *sanjin* is closely related to if not directly based on the Chinese term *xian*, Daoist immortal, or *sen* in Japanese. In fact if one were to take the character for *xian*, separate it and read it from right to left, one would see the compound *sanjin*. It is clear from the description of the *sanjin* that the similarities go beyond the written representation and are not merely coincidental. However, Torakichi made it clear that the Chinese Daoist immortal should be referred to in Japanese as *sennin*, while the word *sanjin* was reserved for the native Japanese practitioner. Torakichi added that the two kinds of beings were familiar with each other and had traveled back and forth to each other's lands of origin, but they were categorically different.

Of course, we should remember that Torakichi's first meeting with his master was taken directly from the legends of Fei Changfang and Sire Gourd mentioned earlier, so Torakichi owed his own entry in the realm of the immortals to Japanese retellings of a famous story from Chinese religion. Partly owing to the importance of that connection, the *sennin* in *Senkyō ibun* received no especially harsh criticism. However, Torakichi also made a point of establishing an important religious difference between the immortals of the two countries. The *sanjin* was not concerned with benefiting himself, as was the selfish Chinese immortal; his religious role required service to others.[23] Torakichi had detailed explanations of the religious functions of the *sanjin*, but that will be presented in the following chapter.

The connection with the Chinese immortal was not made lightly. Atsutane was clearly impressed and fascinated by the practices of the immortals, and his *sanjin* stood to gain by the association. The connection with the tradition of Chinese immortals served to make all mountain practitioners seem numinously charged and probably in possession of supernatural abilities. Furthermore, giving them this *sanjin* title suggested that all people dwelling in the mountains were possibly part of an organized religious movement, even if no such movement actually existed.

Linking the *sanjin* to the Chinese immortals associated the actions of the Japanese practitioners with Daoist longevity theory and practice, called *shinsen shisō* in Japanese. These ideas had been developing in China a thousand years before the beginning of Japanese history, surely another reason why Atsutane desired the association. Stories of the Chinese immortals were older than the Buddhist Sutras. Longevity practices were some of the earliest recorded practices undertaken to become a spiritual being with access to a special world. This ancient story line from China was the model for Atsutane's "new" story line told through his supernatural medium Torakichi.

Atsutane's interest in Chinese history and religion is easy to substantiate; there are hundreds of pages of his writings to document that fact. On the one hand, he criticizes the Chinese by derogating their national character, saying that a nation like China that has a history full of killing its own leaders produces a race of people who are deceitful traitors by nature. On the other hand, Japan, he claims, with its unbroken line of emperors, is exactly the opposite in that regard. However, despite the criticism and the rejection of Chinese character, Atsutane envies China's antiquity. This envy is shown by his claim that China's cultural antiquity rightfully belongs to Japan.

Senkyō ibun was written in 1822 during a period of great activity in Atsutane's scholarship. Two years later, in 1824, he produced a work on China, *A Biographical Essay on the Yellow Emperor (Kōtei denkikō)*. In this work he tells the story of China's Yellow Emperor, but in truth, the Yellow Emperor story is used to focus on a detailed discussion of Daoist longevity practices.[24] In 1824 he drafted another work, *A Chart of the True Form of the Five Peaks (Gogaku shinkeizu)*, clearly showing his continuing interest in ancient Chinese Daoist philosophy and techniques. Also in that year, he drafted a revision of his daily worship ritual that included a new verse worshiping and honoring the *sanjin* of Japan and China.

In his corpus of writings there are also a number of undated works that all directly concern Daoist longevity practices.[25] He also wrote works about Lao Zi, the *I Jing*, tortoise shell divination, and the list goes on. The long list attests to his interest in ancient China, with particular focus on ancient Daoist practice. Perhaps the best example of his interest in Chinese religion and its relationship to his Ancient Way practice, especially as it concerns *Senkyō ibun*, is seen in his 1825 work *The Biography of Immortal Master Ge (Kassenōden)*, which is his biography of the Daoist[26] philosopher-practitioner Ge Hong (283–343), with special emphasis on all the immortality practices discussed in Ge Hong's work *The Master Embracing Simplicity (Baopuzi)*.

In *The Biography of Immortal Master Ge*, Atsutane writes:

An explanation concerning the realm of the immortals appears elsewhere in a work called *Senkyō ibun*, which is a secret record chronicling my investigations of it. The time will come for it to be released to the public, for they should read about this. Anyway, [Ge Hong's] teachings concerning the realm of the immortals, about which I was just writing, were perfected and practiced by the original practitioners of the Way of the Kami. The traditions of celestial immortals and terrestrial immortals can be seen in classical sources on the *kami*. However, these groups must not be confused with the heavenly *kami* and earthly *kami*. (The celestial immortal resembles the heavenly *kami* and the terrestrial immortal resembles the earthly *kami*, but there is such a difference in the spiritual energies that it does not matter how hard one studies or how diligently one perseveres on the immortal path, the two must be seen as separate and never mistaken for one another.) [27]

As much as Atsutane obviously admires ancient Chinese religion, he refuses to recognize the source of those traditions to be the Asian continent or to give Chinese religion any claim to superiority. He claims that all these religious elements and practices, which he so admires and studies in such detail, originated in Japan. His theory, of course, is that at some point long ago, these traditions were transmitted from Japan to China. Then, at another point in time much later, they were brought back to Japan in a corrupt form. An important element of that corruption is the great lie told by sinophiles that these ideas had no precedent in Japan, but had originated in China. As strained as this line of argument may be, Atsutane uses it repeatedly to fend off any charges of borrowing from China.

Nurturing the Life of the *Sanjin*

Just as Ge Hong knew the various ways of "nurturing the life" [28] of the Chinese immortal, Torakichi claimed to know the way of the proper care and feeding that would maintain the existence of the miraculously long-lived being the *sanjin*, the Chinese immortal's Japanese counterpart. Their eating habits were of great interest to Atsutane. In *Senkyō ibun*, he expresses his desire for the longest life possible, which explains his interest in all *sanjin* physical techniques that would increase the health of the body. His interest in this subject also led him to the writings of Ge Hong, who had recorded his own famous compendium of techniques for immortality, or at least for transcendence of the common human lifespan. For the sake of verification of his new medium, Torakichi, as well as his own desire to live a long life, Atsutane was on the lookout for any overlap of Torakichi's stories and Daoist immortal practices. His concern for a longer life and

Torakichi's flattering reassurances that he would be granted one can be seen in the following conversation vainly recorded by Atsutane.

I [Atsutane] am so busy with my writing and with the visitors who keep constantly dropping by that everyday Torakichi would hear me complain, "The days and even years are just too short!"

Torakichi said that feeling was a good thing, because it was a sign of long life. His master had told him the following about that. "Two years of my [Sugiyama Sanjin's] life feels as short as the length of one day in the common man's life. That is because my lifespan is so long. Bugs and birds have short lives. Bugs such as the fly, even though born in the morning to die that night, do not think their lives are short. This is because they are short-lived. People who achieve much in the world are long-lived even though they feel their lives are short. This is a sure sign of accomplishment. For example, take someone who dies at fifty. That person does not know it, but he should have been dead at forty, but he lengthened his original lifespan to die at fifty. Achieving things in this world is better than any other method for lengthening one's life."

There are many who think that this is true. There is the story of the woodcutter who ventured into the Other World and while he thought he had spent a single day watching a game of *go*, actually several years had passed. And conversely, once a person went to the country of Huai An and thought that one instant was actually several years, because he was in the world of short-lived bugs.[29] When you try thinking of it in this way, it actually would be natural [for those in the Other World] to feel that the time of the long-lived human is actually short.

In addition, I [Atsutane] have been thin since I was a child and have always envied heavy people. I have tried eating lots of food to strengthen my body. But I have always been exasperated because there was never even the slightest result. Torakichi heard me say this.

Torakichi said, "My master is always saying that people with very little flesh have light bodies so that even their thoughts are close to the ethereal *kami*, which is a mark of long life. So he eats specially prepared food without any meat and sometimes when he feels heavy he drinks reducing medicines and sometimes also drinks vinegar. Therefore, there is no reason to worry yourself over being thin."

Also, since I [Atsutane] find it very annoying when my nose hairs grow way out of my nostrils, I keep tweezers close by me so I can readily pluck those hairs. Upon seeing this Torakichi said, "Long nose hair is a sign of long life and my master believes they should never ever be plucked. My master's nose hair is extremely long. Five or six have grown out of both nostrils and are so long that they are indistinguishable from his moustache. The master takes great care of that nose hair."[30]

The following exchange reveals that Atsutane was thinking he could hope to find in Torakichi's stories something even better than Chinese models and practices of longevity.

Nakamura Noritaka once told the following story.
There once was a man from X village, X district in Enshū.[31] He was an incorrigible hoodlum in his youth. He was punished with banishment for the crime of swearing at an official. He immediately left that very day to enter the wilderness cut off from all human societal interaction. For five years he did not venture out of the mountains. Then one day he returned to his hometown saying he wanted some clothes. When the villagers asked, "How have you been living in the mountains for all these years?" He said, "I am living in harmony with the beasts now. I make food and have a way to cook it without pots. I do not feel inconvenienced in any way." After that he would return to the village about once every three years and gradually came to take on the appearance of a Chinese immortal.
Torakichi said, "To become like a Chinese immortal you don't need to have any special physical characteristics referred to as 'immortal bones.'[32] Anyone who spends thirty years deep in the mountains will eventually be accepted by the beasts that at first dislike and flee from him. Eventually they will start to bring him all sorts of food to nourish him and then they will work for him using the special powers they possess. So it is just a matter of time until that person starts becoming like the Chinese immortal."[33]

The story and Torakichi's response to it reveal that he did not think much of the run-of-the-mill Chinese immortal, and it also suggests there was something more to the Japanese immortal *sanjin*'s regimen that made them special. Atsutane and the other salon visitors questioned Torakichi to find out what part nutrition might play in that special regimen. The following is a broad sampling of the conversations on that subject.

I [Atsutane] asked, "In the Other World, are there any special life-nurturing practices?"
Torakichi said, "Just the usual things. All in all, I have nothing particularly special to tell about life-nurturing practices."[34]

Here Torakichi seems to demur, but Atsutane will not be put off so easily.

I [Atsutane] asked, "The Chinese immortals have many cinnabar elixir[35] formulae for living long without aging. Do *sanjin* mix and drink those kinds of cinnabar elixirs?"

Torakichi said, "I have never seen the mixing of that kind of cinnabar elixir. However, there is a concoction my master always drinks. You make it by heating a quantity of citron seeds in top-quality sake. You simmer them well over a medium flame until they dissolve into a mush. Separate out the dregs and add dried ginger powder and white sugar and then once again mix them over a flame. Pour out lumps about the size of a thumbnail on a wet board. After they have cooled and hardened, scrape them off and store them in a jar. The master partakes of this concoction constantly. This is a medicine that regulates the chest and belly. It also takes care of any congestion."[36]

I [Atsutane] said, "According to Tōun's[37] stories, the *tengu*[38] diet consists of pine needles, bamboo leaves, and other tree leaves. Also, occasionally they catch fish and eat the flesh. Or else, they catch baby monkeys, cook, and eat them. The thing called *tengu* fire in the remote mountains are fires from when they cook, and because these fires are actual fires, bits of charred bamboo leaves can be found at those fire sites, all of which is visible to the human eye. However, the phenomenon of foxfire[39] is not real fire and so nothing has been burned. Anyway, do they really sometimes eat that kind of food?"

Torakichi said, "They do sometimes eat pine needles, bamboo leaves, and other tree leaves, but they don't always eat that. Occasionally they will eat foods that have been pickled in an equal amount of salt. Once anything has been pickled in an equal amount of salt it's all right for them to eat it. Also, they eat fish and birds, but they never eat things like monkeys. This is not just for the reason that eating beasts is abhorrent to the *kami*. The mountains are the property of the beasts, so to live in the mountains and eat beasts is simply not allowed. Of course that is the way it was at the mountain I was at. Tōun was from over there at Mt. Kompira, which is a place I don't know about."

I asked, "According to Tōun's stories, since gold, silver, rice, and coins were the exact worldly treasures that humans worked so hard for, the use of gold and silver was disavowed over there, and even the smallest grain of rice was rejected as a means of sustenance. What is your opinion on that?"

Torakichi said, "Gold, silver and coin usage goes on just as I told you earlier, and it goes without saying that they eat rice. However, I don't know how things are over at Mt. Kompira."

[. . .]

Torakichi said, "whatever kind of bird they have, they prepare it in the same manner as people here prepare chicken. They remove the skin completely, strip off all the flesh, grill it with salt and eat it. Sometimes, when they catch a lot of extra pheasants, they'll pickle them in salt and dry them, only to grill and eat them later. Birds are the most important part of the *sanjin*'s diet. Bird meat is exceptionally light and that enables them to fly. There was one time when even I went thirty days eating nothing but birds. My body felt so light I felt as if I could fly. They also say that people who eat only birds are especially long-lived."

I said, "Among the common folk rabbits aren't considered to be beasts. Even the nobility eat rabbits by classifying them as a type of bird. How about *sanjin*, do they eat rabbits?"

Torakichi said, "They never eat any other beasts, but even in the mountains rabbits are called a type of bird and are eaten. The crown of the rabbit's head is especially nutritious for humans. Since this meat is considered to be medicinal, they especially prize eating it."[40]

Perhaps remembering that Torakichi's master is not the normal, run-of-the-mill *sanjin* or *tengu* in the Other World, Atsutane tailors the following question to focus on his special status and powers.

I asked, "Are there set eating habits for Great Tengu?"[41]

Torakichi said, "Since they have special powers they eat whenever they want, and whatever they want appears before them to eat. Besides that, in the case of the thirteen *tengu*, every day the villages each prepare offerings, so even we followers can eat our fill of that. However, the actual offerings do not diminish, they remain as they are. Yet, the *tengu* do partake of them. And you might think this strange, but after I go back there please try leaving something on the altar that you want to let me eat, and the next time I come I will give thanks to you."

I asked, "Do they cook anything by themselves to eat?"

Torakichi said, "They have cooked for themselves. But the offerings from the believers in the villages around Mt. Iwama are enough so they don't have to."

I asked, "When they cook what do they do for pots and kettles?"

Torakichi said, "They have all those kinds of things over there. When there's something they need but don't have, they go to somebody's house and borrow it. They return it when they are finished with it. But even when they borrow something the family thinks it's still there and so they aren't aware of the borrowing."

I asked, "Do they eat fish, fowl, or the five pungent plants?"[42]

Torakichi said, "They eat fish and fowl either boiled or fried or else they eat them raw. The *kami* only despise the eating of four-legged beasts, so those they never eat. That would be extremely defiling. Doing anything that the *kami* despise should be avoided. They say that doing such things will lead you down the paths of evil. Leeks are the only pungent foods they eat."[43]

Atsutane's guests were also interested in the foods of the *sanjin*, and he also records their questions and Torakichi's answers to them.

A certain person, while eating with Torakichi, asked him, "What kind of vegetable dishes do they usually eat in the Other World?"

Torakichi answered with a smile saying, "I always have trouble with those kinds of questions. Since they have supernatural powers, whatever they want to eat immediately appears before them. Therefore it is no different than the foods in this world."

But this person was persistent and said, "But that being the case isn't there something they eat that we in this world don't usually eat?"

Torakichi said, "If you take young pine cones which haven't yet opened up and peel off the covering and pickle them in salt after boiling them, they are very tasty. Also, they often eat a vegetable dish of Japanese cedar buds pickled and washed after the salt has completely soaked in. These two foods act like an ointment for your mouth. Also, young pine needles pickled in an equal amount of salt are eaten. Everything, when pickled with an equal portion of salt, can be turned into a food. This means that one can survive by eating only that sort of food. You can even eat bamboo leaves. Furthermore, even moss on a pine tree can be eaten in *mochi* if carefully washed. Steam the *mochi* rice and mix the moss in while pounding it and it's not bad at all. In addition, if you wash and dry clay over and over to remove all the sand, roll it into dumplings and bake it, it is perfectly edible. All of these are foods that give sustenance. My master said that if people only knew they could always eat these kinds of things they would never be troubled by famine."

Then someone asked while they were drinking green tea together, "Do they have tea in the Other World?"

Torakichi said, "They don't use the same kind of tea leaves they use here. They take cherry tree buds, steam them until they are soft, and then leave them to dry. You can then boil and drink it like tea. Also, the teacakes they eat have grilled chicken or fried red beans inside them."

Again someone asked while eating *mochi*, "Do they eat *mochi* in the Other World?"

Torakichi said, "Certainly they pound and eat their own *mochi*. But since we're on the subject of *mochi*, when they say "kaki" *mochi* here in this world, this refers just to the way it is cut. But in the Other World, when they say "kaki" *mochi*, it means dried *mochi* with fresh, tart, de-seeded persimmons mixed in with the *mochi*. These are especially delicious when eaten flame-roasted. However, you cannot roast the *mochi* on the same day you pound it. Not only for *mochi*, but also generally speaking, it's better to avoid as much as possible reheating anything that has already been boiled or grilled. Of course, bean paste and soy sauce have been made by cooking, but since these are things you heat with water to eat, reheating them is not really a problem at all."[44]

As interested as Atsutane is in *sanjin* eating habits, he does not seem disappointed that Torakichi's information about the proper care and feeding of *sanjin* contains nothing especially supernatural or even alchemical. Perhaps it only reassured him of his personal religious conviction that dietary and external alchemical practices were secondary and inferior techniques for those lacking in faith in the *kami*.

Atsutane's Pre–*Senkyō ibun* Medical Theories

In Atsutane's time, Japanese medical practices owed a great debt of gratitude to their Chinese antecedents. Atsutane should have been well aware of this, seeing that he began his study of medicine at age eleven under the tutelage of his uncle and held employment as a physician at the same time he worked as a teacher, lecturer, and master of his own academy. In 1810 Atsutane drafted the medical text titled *The Essence of the Way of Healing* (*Idō taii*), also called *The Peaceful Stone Hut* (*Shizu no iwaya*). This draft of his comprehensive and detailed theory of the art and science of healing was completed ten years before Atsutane was to meet Torakichi.

In this work Atsutane actually denies the Chinese beginnings of Japanese medicine and claims that the ultimate source of all healing practices and remedies is the *kami* of Japan; namely, a pair named Onamuchi and Sukunabikona. In Aston's translation of the *Nihongi* it is said of these two *kami*:

Now Oho-na-mochi no Mikoto and Sukuna-bikona no Mikoto, with united strength and one heart, constructed this subcelestial world [the Japanese islands]. Then, for the sake of the visible race of man as well as for beasts, they determined the method of healing diseases. They also, in order to do away with the calamities of birds, beasts, and creeping things, established means for their prevention and control. The people enjoy the protection of these universally until the present day.[45]

Atsutane understood both diseases and calamities to come from the invisible Other World, so it was logical that he should search for supernatural or metaphysical solutions to problems caused by metaphysical beings. Atsutane's teacher Norinaga, a physician himself, distrusted the common treatments offered by Chinese medicine and instead recommended invoking *kami* to cure illness.

Atsutane explained that although this wondrous and divine healing knowledge was originally imparted to the ancient Japanese, much of it had been lost since the Age of the Kami. However, the true healing knowledge imparted by the two *kami* of healing was not irretrievably lost; it had been preserved in the Other World. Some of this preserved knowledge was spread to the various other lands as the supernatural beings made travels and occasionally allowed the divine knowledge to diffuse to foreign shores. Fortunately, there were some wise foreigners who managed to preserve the healing traditions, most notably in China. One of the reasons Japanese and Chinese medicine were so similar, he claimed, was that the Chinese received all their correct knowledge of healing from Japanese supernatural sources.

One of those Chinese Atsutane praised for preserving the ancient *kami* tradition of healing was Ge Hong, who was well-known in Japan in Atsutane's time for his *shinsen* teachings and practices. In essence, Atsutane's theory of the Way of Healing was very similar to, and most likely dependent upon, ideas from Chinese magical medicine that developed during the early stages of the growth of the Daoist religion in China.[46] Many Daoists believed that one of the leading causes of physical illness was a soul influenced by evil demons into longing to corrupt the very body it inhabited, leading to sickness, death, or transformation into a demon itself.[47] Many among them felt that the most certain method for fighting off evil demons was to discover their names and give them commands, either orally or in written form on a talisman, to leave or surrender. In other words, they believed that demons followed a code of conduct as in a kind of Daoist legalistic worldview.[48] Atsutane wholeheartedly accepted this theory and this technique for controlling demons. Years later, at one juncture in his conversations with Torakichi, he confirmed the continuation of this belief in spiritual hierarchy with his supernatural informant in the following quote, presented earlier in a different context.

> It seems that even in the case of *sanjin* or *tengu* abduction, the words of the tutelary *kami* cannot be resisted. Furthermore, when it comes to ghosts, they cannot harm anyone who is protected by his tutelary *kami*. What are your thoughts about this?"
>
> Torakichi said, "You are absolutely right. *Sanjin, tengu,* or whatever, if there is a tutelary *kami* that tells them to return someone, they must follow those orders." [49]

As for other possible non-Daoist sources of inspiration for his medical theory, in general, in *The Peaceful Stone Hut*, Atsutane had little favorable to say about Buddhism. His negative attitude held true for the most part when he assessed the effectiveness of Buddhist medical practices. He claimed that as long as Buddhists placed the buddhas over the *kami* their practices could never be as powerful as *kami* healing rituals. One notable exception to his disdain for the healthful benefits of Buddhist practice was the introspective meditative practice recommended by the Zen priest Hakuin (1685–1768), but the exception is more comprehensible when it is noted that Atsutane actually praised this as an effective method of cultivating one's *qi*, which brings the practice back into the *shinsen* fold. [50]

Unexpectedly, Atsutane often praised Western medicine, which he came to know primarily through translations of Dutch anatomy books and through students in his academy who had also absorbed much of the current Dutch studies. He was impressed by stories of its accuracy, but at the same time he condemned as barbaric the dissection of the human bodies required for such accuracy, although he did not have that same reservation concerning the autopsy of animals. However, as we can see in *The Peaceful Stone Hut*, whenever he would praise any foreign skill it would always be accompanied with a disparaging remark that explained what might have looked like a recognition of foreign superiority. He claimed that one reason the Westerners would know more about illness than the Japanese is that they were physically inferior and prone to illness, so naturally they would have had more experience with it.

Torakichi's Brand of Medicine: Recipes for Remedies

Being an accomplished physician and pharmacologist, if not an alchemist, was an important feature in the identity of the Japanese *sanjin*. Atsutane's nativist culture hero's first appearance in *Senkyō ibun* was in a medical role when Torakichi first spotted his *sanjin* master-to-be selling pills on the street. Fourteen-year-old Torakichi himself was to become a healer. On the very day that Atsutane had Torakichi dragged into his house, Atsutane found he had come down with a fever that forced him to his bed. He later recorded that Torakichi came to his bedside and administered a fever-cooling spell that quickly made the fever go away.

On several occasions the visitors to Atsutane's salon asked Torakichi about the medicine practiced in the Other World. Torakichi was almost always ready with recipes and regimens used to cure all sorts of complaints and diseases. On one such occasion the Atsutane student and noted scholar in his own right Kunitomo Yoshimasa put the following series of questions to Torakichi:

> Kunitomo Yoshimasa put a question to Torakichi saying, "A certain person asked me. . . . This person was extremely frightened by thunder. Just before he knew it was coming, his head would start to hurt so much that he would end up lying on the floor. Often when the thunder was intense he would black out. Isn't there any way to stop this fear of thunder?"
>
> Torakichi said, "The way to do that is to dig a cave-like hole on top of the highest mountain you can and stay in it overnight. When you're in there take a handful of earth from inside the cave hole and also a live root from any old tree, wrap them together in paper and save it for later. When it thunders hold that package on your navel and stay perfectly still until you're completely calm. But this isn't just effective for thunder, if you put it on your navel it also keeps you from getting dizzy when you're in a high place, or you're riding on a horse, in a cart, or on a boat. Also, I hear that if you stay in that hole for a time longer, this is also effective in curing nervous conditions."
>
> Kunitomo said, "Every year around Matsudai in Shinshū there are outbreaks of dysentery which are so bad that they even cause a great many people to die. Someone asked me if there wasn't some way to fix this tragic situation. What should he do, do you know of some cure for this?"
>
> Torakichi said, "My master probably knows some method of preventing the spread of those outbreaks, but I don't. Yet if you wipe the slime off the back of a loach with a spatula so that you get a good-sized portion of it; and then mix that with sugar and drink it with cold water every morning; or, if you eat some charred loach every day, then you won't get diarrhea. Or, even if you already have it, do this and you'll get better."
>
> Kunitomo said, "I was also asked by someone if there was some way for a childless woman to get pregnant."

Torakichi said, "That woman should take a clean stone picked up either at a shrine or on a riverbank, and every morning facing the rising sun while holding the stone up to her forehead, pray to the sun saying the words, 'please grant me a child.' Eventually when she does get pregnant she should have accumulated a large number of stones. She should store all of these stones near the place that she found them, for it is said that those stones will serve as protective charms for the child's life and should insure that it survives childhood safely."

Kunitomo said, "A person asked me if there weren't any spells for when you're deep in the mountains or in some village and you want to prevent or remove the curse caused by evil *oni* [51] or demons or wild beasts there. Isn't there something for this?"

Torakichi said, "There are those kinds of spells but I haven't learned them yet. I have, however, learned how to make some protective talismans and these are spells that are not to be passed around carelessly. If they are for Hirata Sensei then I can pass them on, otherwise I have only carved some in wood for personal use. When I'm in a strange and dangerous situation with a likelihood of being attacked by wolves or some other vicious beasts, or else if I'm in a fix in mountains suddenly enveloped in clouds or mist, then I'll break out these talismans. When it's a case of something visible like wild beasts, I can show them these talismans, and after I do I definitely won't come to any harm." [52]

On another occasion another curious visitor led the questioning:

Kōno Daisuke asked, "There is a twenty-five- or six-year-old man who suffered from syphilis, but has recovered for the most part; however, he still has a persistent cough. Various doctors have treated him with this and that, but he hasn't been cured. What medicines are effective for coughs?"

Torakichi said, "For coughs cut up some fresh pine needles and fry them until they're black. Boil that down together with an equal amount of mustard greens before ingesting it. This works for all coughs."

Kōno said, "A certain woman has a sickness called *shōkachi*. [53] The pain is unbearable and even though several doctors have done their best, they haven't been able to cure her. Is there any medicine for this kind of sickness?"

Torakichi said, "Heat six *momme* [54] of salt until only four *momme* are left. Then add one *gō* of water and boil it down to one half or five *shaku* of that. Then add two *gō* of water and boil that down to one *gō*. Drink it all at once. After a while you will start to feel some pain, but when you do, add six *gō* of water to ten *momme* of alum [55] and drink this after having boiled it down to four *gō*. This is especially effective medicine for gonorrhea and *shōkachi*. Or else, you could boil down bush clover grass that grows on plum and pine trees, and use that. This too is miraculously effective for gonorrhea and *shōkachi*. At times when plum trees don't have bush clover, you can use the moss instead."

Note: Heat a *mon* coin in lamp oil and swallow it. This is helpful for rigid stomachs.[56]

Then there was this interesting and sad case for which he had a novel and no doubt painful solution.

A certain person said, "There's a man who is about thirty years old. From when he was a child and into his twenties he was subject to chronic seizures, but otherwise he was very quick-witted. However, after receiving prayers and medical treatments he seemed cured except he developed a kind of amnesia and no longer could interact in society. He is not thought of as a complete idiot because there are still times when he acts and speaks intelligently. On top of all this he doesn't have even the slightest sexual urge. Is there some way to cure him?"

Torakichi said, "Since he developed those symptoms as a transformation of his seizures, treatments for seizures should still work. To do that first set up two lenses in a telescope and put water with dissolved rouge in [a cylinder] between them. Then use this to look at his body in the sunlight. Usually you will be able to see places from his shoulders to his hips or on his arms that show discoloration when reflected through the red glow of the glass. That is where the poisons have collected. Trace black ink lines around the places with the poisons. Fashion copper vessels about two inches deep in the exact shapes as those places. Heat up good quality *shōchū*[57] as hot as he can stand and pour it in the vessels. When it cools down remove the *shōchū* by soaking it up with a cloth and then replace it with more hot *shōchū*. Repeat this over and over until these spots look like they are covered with a red lacquer.[58] At that stage the bad fluid will start to come out. As you are doing this over and over the poisons will gradually all come out, and when they are all gone he will get better."[59]

On another occasion Kunitomo led off with more questions:

Kunitomo Yoshimasa put a question to Torakichi, saying, "A certain person asked me to ask. . . . Isn't there some kind of medicine that can cure the sicknesses which the medical treatises label incurable, such as paralysis, tuberculosis, stomach ailments [cancer?], and leprosy? What about those?

Torakichi said, "For paralysis eat blackened toadstools that grow on plum trees. For tuberculosis char female and male geckos individually and without letting the sick person know, slip it into whatever you feed them. . . . For stomach ailments the fresh liver of a crane is effective. For leprosy take a piece of cotton soaked in *shōchū*, light it, and while it is burning pat it down repeatedly [on the afflicted areas]."

Somebody asked, "I know someone who suffers from gout. Isn't there some treatment for that? Also, do you know any medicine for burns or hemorrhoids, and do you know any methods to stop bleeding?"

Torakichi said, "For gout, char flattened moss from a plum tree, knead it with rice starch and smear it on. This has a potent effect. For burns, mash young Japanese cedar leaves and cold rice together and smear this on. If you do this over and over, the heat will be drawn out of the afflicted area, the pain will go away, and it will heal without leaving a scar. For hemorrhoids, first dry out clumps of algae that have washed up on the seashore, and char them before applying. To stop bleeding a Kumano fire starter[60] is very effective. And I just remembered something. When I came back from the mountains I was given a small round pale black stone. Wherever I pressed it even the worst bleeding would magically stop. But I forgot where I put it and now that I think of it I really regret that."

Someone asked, "For years I have suffered from colic and spasms. Do you know of any medicine for those things?"

Torakichi said, "For colic, char some silver vine powder and bitter oranges, combine equal portions, and drink the mixture frequently. For spasms, pickle a *kangarasu*[61] in a chamber pot for thirty days. Wash it and blacken it without gutting it. Eat that mixed with an equal part of the powder of the fried shell of the red conch. These cures are effective for gas, heartburn, and all other stomach ailments.

(Note: Electricity cures spasms. Kakidōshi grass[62] cures spasms.)[63]

Once one visitor asked if there was anything good to use for contagious eye diseases, "crazy eyes," pus-filled eyes, and bloodshot eyes.

Torakichi said, "For those things [eye ailments] one should find a small flat stone and write 'tiger eye' on both the front and the back. Heat this in a fire and then drop it in water. When its cools, use it as an eye patch. After warming the eye like this several times the eye should get better."[64]

Another visitor asked him if he didn't have some effective plaster formulae which he could pass on.

> Torakichi said, "In the mountains plasters are made of cedar leaves, sweet grasses, and green tree leaves boiled in sesame oil. When it turns black remove the dregs. Heat that remainder together with red and white wax. To test when it is done, drip a little water on it. Let it cool until it is hard and then it can be used for swellings and things like that. In addition, we sometimes flatten out some lead and boil it in vinegar for a couple of hours and this can be applied and used to shrink all sorts of swelling and also promote quick healing." [65]

He was also asked how to cure other types of swellings:

> A certain person asked, "Do you know any spell for lumps in your throat, and what do you do for a swollen tongue?"
>
> Torakichi said, "The characters of the ancient poem [left blank], and for the swollen tongue charred maggots spread on the soles of your feet should heal that." [66]

Torakichi also had cures for very minor ailments. When asked about dog bite treatment:

> Torakichi said, "I heard that if you combine equal parts of the best powdered tea with baked alum and drink it with water, you'll get well quickly." [67]

He also had some advice for snake bites:

> Torakichi said, "When you are bitten by a pit viper you should put *kushi-gaki*[68] on the bite. These vipers have long needle-like teeth that break off in the flesh when they bite. Those broken teeth are harmful, but the *kushi-gaki* will draw them out. Also, if you put *kushigaki* on a viper it will die. *Kushigaki* is just like poison for a snake." [69]

An alternative cure for poisoning in general was offered at another juncture:

> "As for poison antidotes, take rice stalks at planting time, clean off the dirt and put them in a pot. Cover, heat, and start steaming them until water starts condensing on the lid, then take the stalks out and mix them

together with an equal amount of charred black *mochi* rice (if there's no *mochi* rice then *mochi* itself is fine) and ingest this mixture. It works wonders both as a poison antidote and also for food poisoning."[70]

Kunitomo Yoshimasa asked, "Someone asked me to ask you if you had something to help people who were walking long distances."

Torakichi said, "My master should be able to tell me, but I haven't heard anything from him about it, yet just the other day someone else told me about a special treatment that helps you walk long distances for days without getting worn out. You mix equal parts of *daiō*, *saishin*, and *uzu*[71] and then knead that into deer fat. Apply this to the soles of your feet and the soreness will soon be gone."[72]

A good example of the extraordinary range of diseases that could be cured by the *sanjin* came up when Torakichi was told a story of a certain woman who went to sleep during the middle of the day only to find that a snake had crawled into her vagina and would not come out,[73] which led to the woman's subsequent death. Torakichi claimed that *sanjin* medical knowledge could have saved the woman.

Torakichi said, "When a snake enters the vagina or the rectum and does not come out, one should take five *shaku* of sake mixed with one *gō* of tooth dye, heat it and drink it and the snake will come out. However, it is quite rare that a snake would impregnate anyone like that. And, in addition, drinking that mixture is also good for curing snake bites."[74]

So far, we have seen Torakichi fielding questions about diseases and ailments that plagued the human realm, then, at some point the questioning turned to sickness in the Other World.

I [Atsutane] asked, "Do they get sick in that world?"

Torakichi said, "My master has never been sick, but his followers have gotten sick. Still, even then at most those were stomach aches, swellings, scrapes, or cuts. They take pills for stomach aches. When they have swellings they use their long nails to scratch them open and scrape out the pus. Then, of course, they rub leaves, grass, or else dirt or whatever is handy on that area. They have similar treatment remedies for scrapes and cuts or else they cure them by licking them or chanting spells."[75]

I asked, "What is in those pills, and are there other good medicinal formulae?"

Torakichi said, "Red earth[76] and *kitsune chabukuro*[77] are mixed together thoroughly, kneaded, rolled in rice, and covered with red clay or bamboo leaf. This is medicine good for all stomach aches even those caused by tapeworms. Or, you can take *tajima*[78] seeds and mustard leaves and any of the hundred grasses, boil them all down, then remove the dregs, knead them thoroughly and they will work to cure chest congestion, stomach spasms, or worms.

Burns caused by either hot water or fire heal well when you cover them with plasters of heated clams or field poppies. They also use boiled carrots for burns. They take carrots grown without fertilizer and without washing off the dirt or removing the fine roots, tie them up with a rope and dry them in the shade. After boiling these they allow the water to cool and then cool the burns in that water. When they do that the water gets hotter because it is drawing out the heat, and the pain suddenly goes away and the burn heals without scarring. Similarly the budding leaves of Japanese cedar crushed together with rice and liberally applied will also get hot like that. If you keep reapplying it, it also stops the pain.

To cure poor circulation you should apply a paste of red and black pepper dissolved in water. As for other formulae or remedies, I will teach you about them as I remember them."

It seems that the cures for the problems of the lesser *sanjin* under the tutelage of the Great Sanjin Sugiyama are not of a completely different nature than those meant for the people of this world. The major difference seems to be that the inhabitants of the Other World have only common complaints and no debilitating or life-threatening problems.

At one point Torakichi's knowledge of Other Worldly drug preparation techniques was summarized by Atsutane under the heading of a single day's record.

The Conversations of the Nineteenth Day of the Fourth Month (1821)

He said that the practice of medicinal remedies consists of thirty types but the information given herein should prove sufficient.

For the preparation of *korafu*,[79] first grow carrots where the soil is poor and dry. This should produce warped dwarf carrots. The roots will be stunted and likewise the seeds. The next day after removing the seeds, dust them with powdered red pepper mixed with powdered dried sardines. Plant those seeds in a box with about seven inches of sand which has been washed carefully to remove the dirt mixed with the scum left over when making tofu and leave the box out in the sunlight. In time as soon as buds start to sprout bring them into the shade. When they get too big, sprinkle them with red pepper and reduce their moisture. When you do that you produce carrots with skinny leaves, stems, and roots. But don't just pick them when the cores start to show. Carrots that are raised this way have far superior medicinal powers than large carrots.

To prepare the roots of the three-leafed parsley in order to make them into medicinal remedies, plant them just like the previous carrot example and let them grow in the sunlight. Mix this powder with sulfur and heat it in water, then apply it to contagious spreading skin rashes. (Red bean powder.)

The way of preparing snake gourd[80] is the same as the others. It is used for eyes, burns, gonorrhea, and *shōkachi.*

The way of preparing crazy eggplant[81] is the same as the previous methods. You use the root either pickled in a persimmon soup or powdered. It is effective for swellings or cuts caused by blades. Furthermore, wounds caused by blades which have had this applied to them will not worsen.[82]

The way of preparing *daiō*[83] is the same as the others. It is used for all illness.

Horse bezoar[84] and whole *reishi* mushrooms (horse bezoar alone is fine) powdered and kneaded with castor oil before prolonged storage underground are used as ointments on cuts and boils. It is powerful, miraculous medicine.

Take carp or crucian carp raised in fresh pure water and after making them spit out all the mud inside them, put them in a glass container with the lid sealed tightly. Wrap that in paper, coat it with lacquer, and, after allowing it to harden, bury it. Dig it out after about ten years and wrap the carp in silk wadding and dry them in the shade. Pulverize it after it has dried. This medicine is used to improve blood circulation. Or, the powder can be applied as an eye ointment.

A shell shaped like this [picture of a small corrugated cylinder] attached to the back of an abalone, when rubbed on the body, does wonders for eye illnesses.

Dried lizards mixed with jimsonweed powdered and kneaded into rice is a medicine for stopping decay and degeneration. Also a little bit of lizard is used as medicine to induce vomiting. This is for times when you have swallowed poison or when something you have swallowed has gotten stuck.

Put some turpentine in a box or, even without a box, bury it. When this is pulverized and applied it is an effective remedy for swelling.

He says they do not check the pulse.

When you apply powdered jimsonweed dissolved in rice bran lard as a treatment for dark spots or rashes, they clear up immediately.[85]

There was one recipe for a preventive medical potion to fight off evil vapors:

I [Atsutane] asked, "Since you live in the mountains, do you know of some protective remedies taken to fight off evil vapors in the mountain air, the steamy fog after a storm, mist, or dew?"

Torakichi said, "If you char the plum fruit until it is no longer sour (or dry it) and put it in sake and drink it, the mountain storm vapors will not affect you even should they swirl around your entire body." [86]

Many of the ingredients used in Torakichi's remedies have multiple precedents in Chinese texts. Cinnabar, of course, is a key ingredient in some alchemical elixirs of immortality touted by Ge Hong and the earlier alchemists to whom he gave credit for his recipes. Other of Ge Hong's eight minerals are included in Torakichi's recipes, but the malachite, orpiment, and mica crystalline minerals were absent from Torakichi's inventory. Ge Hong's fondness for spontaneous growths such as mushrooms and other types of fungi are also well-represented in Torakichi's lists of ingredients, as are many herbs, gourds, vines, and other similar types of potent and poisonous vegetation that multitudes of Chinese and Japanese physicians, healers, and alchemists have favored for more than two thousand years.[87]

Atsutane's Japanese Language Theory

Atsutane wanted to make a clear distinction between the two similar religious heroes, *sanjin* and *sennin*. The distinction was based on country of national origin and religious purpose, but it was demonstrated and made easily discernible by choosing a slightly different arrangement of Chinese characters. This little sleight of hand can be seen as a foreshadowing of Atsutane's hope of establishing a clear linguistic differentiation between things originally Chinese and things originally Japanese. In 1821, a year before Atsutane wrote *Senkyō ibun*, he wrote *The Sacred Letters of Japanese Traditional Script* (*Kanna hifumiden*), which contained what Atsutane maintained were examples of the original writing used by the *kami* in Japan before Chinese characters were imported and adopted. This was most likely the work accompanying *The August Pillar of the Soul* he sent with Torakichi to be reviewed for accuracy by Sugiyama Sanjin. As mentioned earlier, the review was short but favorable with the comment that it was incomplete. Or at least, that is what Torakichi reported to Atsutane.

Establishing a clear linguistic separation and difference from China was not a project or goal that originated with Atsutane. This was a project undertaken by several of his predecessors. Norinaga, in particular, theorized about the difference and made that difference an important point in the constitution of a purely Japanese identity. Norinaga's linguistic claims concerning the ancient Japanese language were central to his method and to the conclusions of his research.

Norinaga's claim was that the ancient Japanese language was a transparent medium that truly expressed direct experience. That is to say, there was no confusion of meaning, nor was there any deception in it. The *kami* communicated to humans in that language. The humans directly experienced the truth of the words and responded truthfully.

Atsutane, who styled himself as Norinaga's legitimate successor although there was little more than dream evidence supporting that claim, accepted and parroted many of Norinaga's arguments and stances. He too valued speaking over writing, judging the written word to be just another layer separating the word from its true meaning. Although he practiced a different brand of philology[88] than Norinaga, he too believed *kokugaku* required the study of ancient texts, just as his self-styled teacher had. He too believed that the Japanese language should be cleansed of harmful Chinese influences and that prior to those influences it had reflected the true Japanese spirit, just as Norinaga had claimed.

In one scene recorded in *Senkyō ibun*, Atsutane sent over to Torakichi's first benefactor Yoshishige's house a book by Norinaga called *Restraints for a Lunatic* (*Kenkyōjin*). This book was written by Norinaga in 1785 and was a critique of a work by a Buddhist named Fujii Masamichi (1732–1797). This man had written *An Attack on an Eruption of Words* (*Shōkōhatsu*) in 1781, in which he argued that the ancient Japanese language had never existed in a pristine state but from its beginnings had been continually influenced by exposure to the language systems of the Asian continent. Norinaga blamed this book's mistaken premise on "Chinese mind."[89]

As much as Atsutane owed to Norinaga, which was a great deal, he departed from him on certain key issues. It has already been noted that the destination of souls was a much nicer place in Atsutane's cosmology than it was in Norinaga's. Another point of departure was Atsutane's assertion that the ancient Japanese had their own independent writing script during the Age of the Kami, which was replaced when Shōtoku Taishi (574–622) started the wholesale importation of continental ideas in the late sixth and early seventh centuries.

Jindai moji

Atsutane believed in something called *jindai moji*, native Japanese writing script from the Age of the Kami.[90] Serious speculation that such a thing

existed started in the middle of the Kamakura period. Urabe Kanekata in
the *Shaku Nihongi*, circa 1301, declared that Izanagi and Izanami must
have used Japanese writing when they performed scapula divination and
that Kōbō Daishi's *Iroha uta* was probably a re-editing of original Japanese
characters. Inbe no Masamichi asserted in the *Nihon shoki jindai kuketsu*
(1367) that until the time of Shōtoku Taishi, pictographic Japanese characters and Chinese characters were used in combination. In addition,
Yoshida Kanetomo (1435–1511) claimed in the *Nihon shoki jindaishō* that
the *iroha* and *katakana* were the creations of later generations. However,
the fifty sounds actually originated in the Age of the Kami, when there
was a several-thousand-character *jindai moji* writing system created by
Izanagi and Izanami, the mythical creator couple. Yoshida Shinto teachings claim that Shōtoku Taishi replaced that writing system with Chinese
characters and that from then on the *jindai moji* fell into disuse, but were
still transmitted within the Yoshida family. Accordingly, the idea of *jindai
moji* spread along with Yoshida Shinto.

In the Tokugawa period there were rumors of the existence of two
secret *jindai moji* texts, *Hijin no sho* and *Satsujin no sho,* and also of bamboo slips handed down in Izumo and Atsuta, both sites of ancient shrines,
that transmitted the *jindai moji*. In addition, *jindai moji* theories other than
Yoshida's began to arise. Atobe Yoshiakira (1658–1729) of Kikke Shinto
first presented the traditional twelve horary signs as a concrete array of
jindai moji characters. They were declared to be a part of the tradition
coming from Yamazaki Ansai (1619–1682) and so were adopted into the
traditional teachings of Kikke Shinto.[91]

Surpassing Yoshiakira's *jindai moji*, which only had twelve characters,
was the *jindai moji* theory introduced in *Sendai kuji hongi taisei kyō*. This
text explained that there was an ancient forty-seven-sound edict from the
sun goddess Amaterasu to the earth god Onamuchi. This was represented
as a sound chart, which supposedly had been transmitted to the ancient
shrines.[92]

Unfortunately, according to the text, those particular *jindai moji* characters were not passed on. Instead, the text showed only the Chinese
characters, supposedly chosen and exchanged by Shōtoku Taishi, that
corresponded to each sound of the original *jindai moji* chart. Later on,
associations between *jindai moji* and Chinese characters became one of
the foundations of doctrines supported by different theorists for the unification of the three religions.[93] Explanatory texts appeared showing various
relationships between the Japanese sounds and the corresponding Chinese
characters. However, these texts could not escape the fatal criticism that

while arguing for the existence of *jindai moji* and their sounds, they could not present the *jindai moji* themselves. In reality, these speculative teachings were based on variant sounds and meanings of the Chinese characters themselves.

In 1778 the aforementioned Buddhist Fujii Masamichi claimed to have come into possession of a secret scroll from which he published forms of the forty-seven characters, which he called *hifumi*. He also claimed authenticity for additional charts of two types of cursive characters, which were supposedly based on transmissions from ancient shrines. After this, various other arrays and systems appeared as the overall interest level in *jindai moji* theories grew. While on the one hand, well-known Shintoists, Confucianists, evidential historians (*koshōgakusha*), and *kokugaku* scholars such as Yoshimi Yoshikazu, Dazai Shundai, Ise Sadatake, and Motoori Norinaga all denied there was such a thing as *jindai moji*, on the other hand there were some famous scholars, such as Arai Hakuseki (1657–1725), who at least maintained a neutral stance.

Atsutane authored *The Sacred Letters of Japanese Traditional Script* in 1821. In it he collected fifty different types of examples of divine characters. He examined and expounded on various theories, among them his colleague Yashiro Hirokata's theory, which said that the twelve horary signs were Ryūkyū Island characters published in a work called the *Ryūkyū shintōki*. Atsutane's conclusion was that there were two forms of block and cursive writing, *hifumi*, which were to be recognized as genuine *jindai moji*. His opinion did give strength to the affirmative arguments concerning *jindai moji* in the late Tokugawa period. Nevertheless, arguments denying it were in the mainstream. Ban Nobutomo reaffirmed the theory that the *kana* syllabary was derived from Chinese characters. He pointed out that Atsutane's *hifumi* was extremely similar to *hangul* and completely rejected all *jindai moji* theory. Yet even this did little to dampen the Atsutane faction's support for the theory.

The charts Atsutane published and deemed to be *jindai moji* are part of the traditional holdings of the Grand Shrine of Izumo. Atsutane's publication shows the block character forms and *katakana* alongside their cursive character forms. They are arranged in a sequence called the *hifumi uta*. Atsutane felt confident in *jindai moji* research because his chart showed a relationship of correspondence between two different types of character forms from two different textual sources. The block characters supposedly came from the previously mentioned secret source called the *Hijin no sho* and the cursive characters supposedly came from one called the *Satsujin no sho*. In short, Atsutane denied the charges of appropriating *hangul* and in turn criticized his detractors essentially for supporting a *kana* syllabary sound chart established under the influence of Buddhism and Chinese culture.

Torakichi's *jindai moji*

In *Senkyō ibun,* Torakichi is offered up as living proof of Atsutane's *jindai moji* theory. Before Atsutane met Torakichi, he maintained that the *jindai moji* were either secretly preserved in shrine vaults or left in the charge of mysterious people somewhere in the mountains.[94] His student Satō Nobuhiro had shown him one such example from the mountains, and he claimed to have had other remote sources. Given this, it seems not unreasonable for Atsutane to hope that Torakichi had been exposed to the true characters of Japan while he was with the *sanjin* in the mountains. Torakichi did nothing to dispel that hope.

In several places in the text, Torakichi's calligraphic skills were put to the test. The demonstration of the writing of the Other World was one of the standard entertainments in Atsutane's salon. At a certain point in the evening, paper, brush, and ink would be brought out and characters would be brushed by Torakichi and passed around for the gathered scholars to comment upon and analyze. Torakichi seemed to understand the importance of performing well in these demonstrations, and once he even blamed the quality of the writing tools he was supplied with for a poor performance before a difficult audience.

Of course, Torakichi was basically illiterate. He could read and write only a few Chinese characters and on important occasions he always asked Atsutane to write for him. However, Atsutane claimed that Torakichi could write in a script unknown to any of the salon guests, one which Torakichi himself could not read. Torakichi claimed that he had only gone so far in his *sanjin* writing courses; that is, he had not yet had to study the meanings of what he wrote. Furthermore, he said he had only had the opportunity to practice a limited set of characters and variants of those characters. Atsutane recorded his suspicions about Torakichi's not knowing the meaning of what he wrote. However, strangely enough, he wrote that he did not doubt that these were real characters from the Other World; rather, he doubted Torakichi's claim of not knowing the meaning. Atsutane suspected that Torakichi might be holding back some secret information.

At one such salon demonstration of his calligraphy, there was talk about the origins of Torakichi's writing style. The general opinion was that it resembled an ancient style which one guest attributed to Kūkai. One guest stated that this would make sense since Kūkai had entered the world of the immortals long ago and still could be passing on the tradition there. Atsutane's opinion, which he claimed was also backed up by Torakichi and Torakichi's master, was that Kūkai, as good as he was reputed to be, could not have mastered this ancient style, so this writing script must have originated in the Other World.

At one interview Torakichi explained the calligraphy training in the Other World in great detail, adding to the believability of the claim that there was an entire secret writing system practiced in the mountains of Japan by a society of *sanjin*.

> Torakichi said, "For hand training, in the beginning I would hold fine sand in my hand and practice drawing circles in it. From there I moved on to triangles. After that I got used to drawing squares. . . . Next, I got used to writing the *Seimei kuji* [95] clearly and perfectly. After a while I was able to write them skillfully with the brush even in my sleep. After that I learned characters. The teaching method had me learn one character at a time along with all its alternate forms." [96]

Torakichi added that the writing technology was no different in the Other World. They used the same kinds of brush, ink, and paper.

At one interview session, Yashiro produced an ancient document he had acquired and asked Torakichi to analyze it. It was a test of his calligraphic knowledge and ability. Torakichi noticed two different styles and said that one belonged to a man and the other to an old woman, and he also commented generally on the age of the document. Yashiro proclaimed his analysis to be correct, and Torakichi's stock rose.

The description and the questions about Torakichi's writing knowledge ventured off into the religious and supernatural at times. Torakichi claimed to have expert knowledge of the drawing of protective amulets and talismanic tallies. Atsutane also spent much time on Torakichi's writing of the magical *kuji* and variants of it. Torakichi explained techniques for performing these letter spells and their efficacy. Not once were these techniques attributed to other traditions such as Daoism, Buddhism, or Shugendō. Atsutane's Ancient Way medium introduced them; therefore, Atsutane claimed them for the Ancient Way.

Arguments about *Kishin (Kijin)*

The subject of the supernatural, or ghost and spirits, stood as a point of controversy between Atsutane and certain intellectuals of his time whom he and Norinaga had classified as sinophiles. This is particularly relevant for *Senkyō ibun* considering that Sugiyama Sanjin and Torakichi were sometimes considered to be *tengu* themselves, which would make them supernatural beings. In Atsutane's time the existence of this type of being and other strange beings like devils, demons, ghosts, and goblins were often matters of serious debate. In fact, if supernatural creatures were ultimately found to be fictitious, superstitious fantasies, or even superfluous realities, then Atsutane's whole worldview would have crumbled.

One reason his opponents in this debate were classified with the sinophiles was the word used to describe the topic; that is, *kishin*, a character compound that literally designates demons[97] and *kami*. This subject is found in Confucius' *Analects*, but Confucius' treatment of the concept was ambiguous and evasive.[98] In other words, the uncertainty and ambiguity of his treatment of the spirit world stimulated debate throughout the centuries and across religious traditions throughout East Asia.

Tokugawa period Neo-Confucian Shinto had fused *kami* with *ri*, or principle. As a result, *kami* had become more than a god. It had become an abstract concept occupying the central position in the Neo-Confucian metaphysical framework. On the downside, *kami*, although not specifically denied the property of physical existence, did suffer a loss of materiality.

The trend for the Ancient Learning scholars was to deny both the Neo-Confucian Shinto abstraction and also the contention that the *kami* should be respected more than the early Chinese sages. In the Ancient Learning teachings, the *kami* were recognized as beings whose purpose was to help create ethical people and governments. In other words, they were seen as tools subordinate to the more classical ethical ends of the ancient way of the sages.

Atsutane's entry into the nativist academic fray can be marked by the publication of his first two works denouncing the mistakes of his so-called sinophiles. The third effort, *A New Discussion on Gods and Demons (Shinkishinron)*, which would fifteen years later be published in a revised version called the *Kishinshinron*, was presented to the Suzunoya nativist academy as an example of his readiness to be accepted as a legitimate follower of Norinaga's brand of anti-Chinese nativism. *A New Discussion on Gods and Demons* contained Atsutane's mature arguments against the previous sinophilic discourse on the status and nature of *kami* and spirits and established his own stands on those questions. Obviously, Atsutane disagreed with both the Neo-Confucian and Ancient Learning interpretations. According to Atsutane, the *kami* were individual beings, not principles. Furthermore, in his theology there was nothing that should be more exalted than the *kami*. The role of the human was to serve them and thank them.

Atsutane's method in *A New Discussion on Gods and Demons* was to read and analyze the ancient Chinese texts in order to interpret them. In other words, at this point he was necessarily and deliberately using the philological strategies of his predecessors and enemies, especially Ancient Learning scholars, whose school is usually credited for spreading the method to Japan from China. However, even at this early juncture in his career, Atsutane's conclusions differed from previous ones based on those texts and even from those of his revered teacher Norinaga.

Atsutane developed a new understanding of the reason for the existence of evil in the world, and he denied that *kami* would cause bad things to happen to good people. According to Atsutane, demonic forces, not *kami*, caused evil, as Norinaga concluded. He claimed that *kami* cherished the good and always reacted to destroy and sweep away defilement, impurity, and corruption. Therefore, they were only responsible for destructive acts in punishment of evil. It has been suggested that this innovation in Atsutane's theology came from his reading of the forbidden Christian texts. Whatever the origin, Torakichi told many stories that confirm Atsutane's assertion that the *sanjin* punished evil at the behest of the *kami*.

Critique of Neo-Confucian Shinto

Another text prior to *Senkyō ibun*, *The Essence of Popular Shinto* (*Zoku shintō taii*), was drafted in 1811. This early work contains several fine examples of Atsutane's attitude toward scholarly schools in Japan, which he believed were slavishly sinophilic. This work shows Atsutane's bitterness about the situation in Japan, where even Shinto, the so-called native religion centered on *kami* worship, had become influenced, even dominated, by Neo-Confucianism. He further argues that many of those who opposed Neo-Confucian influence, the Ancient Learning school for example, were really only seeking to replace that Chinese influence by another sort of Chinese influence.

One complaint he has against the so-called sinophiles is that they suffer from a type of Japanese inferiority complex. He charges that sinophiles claim to have adopted Chinese teachings because they believed that Japan is a country without any of its own. In particular, he levels this kind of criticism against the practitioners of Yamazaki Ansai's Suika Shinto, a popular Neo-Confucian blend of Tokugawa Shinto.

> Confucians today demean Japan by speaking ill of it. They say that Japan is in a regrettable state. They declare with shame that India has Buddha's teachings, and China has what the Confucians call the Teachings of the Sages, but poor Japan is a land without teachings.[99]

He continues by commenting on one of Suika Shinto's theological writings.

> When you look at that book, Shinto is all mixed together with the impudent theories from Chinese classics. The text is fashioned to resemble Shinto ritual prayers and Shinto purification prayers. Then they name this fallacious Way Rigaku Shinto [Studies of *Ri* or Principle]. *Rigaku* is what they first called the theories of the Cheng brothers [100] and Zhu Xi during China's Song dynasty. The truth is that these teachings stole their main ideas from Zen Buddhism. [101]

By this last sentence we see that not only is Atsutane dismissive of the teachings because they are Chinese, he also finds them fatally flawed by their Buddhist origins. An association with Buddhism was never flattering when it came from Atsutane. Notice also that the Chinese scholars were accused of stealing the bad ideas. In other places Atsutane had already pointed out his belief in the inherent thieving nature of the Chinese.

Another passage from *The Essence of Popular Shinto* provides a clearer idea of what Atsutane means by Chinese thinking, what it is and how it differs from Japanese thinking. The passage also shows how Chinese thinking had corrupted ideas of Japanese superiority, which he felt should have been obvious to the superior intellect of the Japanese.

> First of all the principle of the superiority of the *kami* is an inestimably wondrous thing. The fact that the common person's mind does not understand this principle, as it should, is because the Chinese have muddied the reality of what we experience every day with the idea of Universal Principle. The foolish idea that biases them, that all things that ever were on heaven and earth are nothing other than principle, has resulted in all the people of Japan being confused and corrupted by the Chinese classics. They think that only Chinese ideas are wise, forgetting that wondrous principle [of the *kami*], and consider themselves wisest of all things. They do not believe in the ancient traditions [of Japan] and they perversely explain the miracles of the Age of the Kami by making them part of the Universal Principle. [102]

This is an accurate description of the way Neo-Confucian Suika Shinto was put together, and it was no great feat that Atsutane was able to discern this. It had never been a great secret, just an obvious way of combining two important discourses in the Tokugawa period.

Atsutane's typical criticism of Neo-Confucian Shinto and "Chinese thinking" was a condemnation of abstract thinking. He characterized "Chinese thinking" as pushing abstraction to an absurd level so that people were unable to understand what was right before their eyes. In other words, thinking too much was bad; common sense, at least native Japanese common sense, was good.

Atsutane was also not impressed with the school of Ancient Learning that boasted of great scholars like Ogyū Sorai and the Itō family scholars. This school claimed that the work of Song Neo-Confucianism, characterized by Zhu Xi, only served to add another layer between the original teachings and the true meaning of the Way of the Sages, written centuries before Zhu Xi and the Cheng brothers' ideas were added. Ancient Learning scholars believed they had improved upon studies of ancient Chinese knowledge and brought scholarship closer to the truth of the ancient Chinese sages.

In Atsutane's opinion, Neo-Confucians were not merely sinophiles who had adopted Chinese thought. Worse than that, they had also stooped to the level of stealing Indian thought.

Atsutane writes:

> When Zhu Xi was asked about his teachings on gods and spirits, particularly if gods and spirits existed, he said, "One cannot say for sure that they have a material existence, but one also cannot say that they do not have a material existence." [103]

Atsutane felt that this kind of response was strikingly similar to and probably appropriated from the wisdom sutras of Buddhism, particularly the parts of those sutras devoted to existence and nonexistence.

He continues in the next passage to say that the Ancient Learning school in Japan was no improvement in original thinking on the subject.

> Those called the Ancient Learning scholars argue against Song Confucianism. For example, Mononobe Sorai and Itō Tōgai certainly also pondered their existence. . . . Concerning that, first Sorai in his book discussed gods and spirits saying "sometimes I am with those who say they exist and sometimes I am with those who say they do not." When Tōgai spoke of them he said, "I have not fully explored whether gods and spirits exist or not, but it would be well worth figuring out." So how about that? They are not one bit different from Zhu Xi. Are they not simply following his same way of thinking? And if they are following Zhu Xi, then do they not support the same meaning as the Buddhist Sutras? [104]

One last example from *The Essence of Popular Shinto* should give a clear understanding of Atsutane's contempt for Confucian scholars of any ilk and for followers of any Shinto that was based on Neo-Confucian principles such as Suika Shinto. After an introductory paragraph wherein he ridicules the Chinese-inspired theory that things naturally come in sets of five, such as the five phases, organs, flavors, colors, and the like, he laments the extent that such Chinese thinking has infiltrated Japan.

> Certainly it would be better if our countrymen did not imitate them. Isn't it tragic that they believe whatever the hairy Chinaman says? I think the students of popular Shinto and the Confucians are the kind of people who, for example, if a Chinaman told them that dung was bean paste, would gobble it up right away.[105]

In *Senkyō ibun* the response and opposition to schools of Chinese learning is represented by Torakichi's mountain education and Sugiyama Sanjin's teachings. At one point Atsutane asks Torakichi if he has ever heard about Chinese learning. He writes:

> I [Atsutane] asked, "I have heard Sugiyama Sanjin knows quite a bit about Buddhism, but I wonder if he didn't also lecture in depth on the teachings of Lao Zi or Confucius, or on the teachings of other Western Lands?"
> Torakichi said, "I heard about Lao Zi and Confucius from somebody somewhere, but I didn't hear about them in the mountains."[106]

Also,

> I asked, "Does Sugiyama Sanjin have a library of Confucian classics or Buddhist sutras?"
> Torakichi said, "I know only a little about those things, but my master doesn't even have one scroll of them."[107]

In *Senkyō ibun*, Atsutane set down his clear belief and stand on the existence of *kami* and spirits, in obvious opposition to both Neo-Confucian scholarship and Ancient Learning scholarship in Japan. After *Senkyō ibun*, he continued to write about *kami* and spirits, but he had different sources and methods than he had had in the early stages of his career. His earlier philological attempts to attack sinophilic anti-*kami* discourse were replaced by fieldwork into the supernatural. On one level, *Senkyō ibun* defines a new attempt to criticize sinophilic discourse, but this time it comes through ethnographic record and visits to Edo salons with the so-called Tengu Boy Torakichi as his anti-Chinese spokes-spirit.

For someone who made the argument that the written word was an inferior means of communication, especially in a written language like Chinese so completely foreign in origin, Atsutane certainly relied heavily on it for his own studies and scholarly production. His readings on Chinese history were comprehensive and his scholarly output was phenomenal. The more we learn about his interest in and devotion to ancient Chinese literature, the more hypocritical his complaints about sinophiles and their influence sound. Perhaps recognition of this very contradiction in the most important aspect of his life, his religious scholarship, spurred him to work toward becoming less dependent on the written word.

Whatever the impetus, philological method clearly had limitations Atsutane was not willing to accept. He could not count on it to produce the answers for which he was searching. Torakichi delivering his staged tirades supported by Atsutane's philological argumentation brought an increased chance of effectively delivering Atsutane's desired message. Chinese and Japanese scholars Atsutane hated for their love of Chinese culture had introduced and paved the way for the nativists, Atsutane included, to use philology. However, this method privileged the group that had either the oldest or the most revered documents, which naturally led to the dominance of ancient Chinese classics over the relatively new Japanese texts. Atsutane was being as innovative as possible in his attempts to turn the tables on his hated sinophiles who held such a strong methodological and historiographic advantage over him and all other proponents of Japanese superiority. In the next chapter we shall see how he employed his new medium to criticize Buddhism while at the same time appropriating whatever he liked from it to give shape to his own version of the native Japanese religion practiced by the native Japanese religious hero, the *sanjin*.

CHAPTER 5

The Critique of Buddhism and Defense of Native Religion

Anti-Buddhist Discourse

Senkyō ibun is filled with anti-Buddhist rhetoric, as are many of Atsutane's writings. The usual way Atsutane countered Buddhist discourse was by direct criticism and slander of Buddhist beliefs and practices as well as the believers and practitioners. The new method of attacking Buddhism in *Senkyō ibun* was the creation of an alternative religious virtuoso that equaled or surpassed the champions of Buddhism. Through the new medium of Tengu Boy Torakichi, the native Japanese *sanjin* was discovered and presented as a Japanese human who had become a superhuman hero much like, but better than, the bodhisattva of Buddhism, the immortal of Daoism, and the saint of Christianity all rolled into one.

In *Senkyō ibun*, Atsutane both attacked Buddhism and built up his Ancient Way. One specific type of attack, seen in great length in an earlier and more specifically anti-Buddhist text called *Laughing Discourse after Emerging from Meditation* (*Shutsujō shōgo*), was based on Atsutane's contention that human beings have a type of genetic, hereditary religion that cannot be changed.

> What the people who take the tonsure do is degrade the *kami* of this august land by making them seem to be in service of the Buddha Dharma. What should we think of this? First of all, it is unthinkable that one would degrade the ancient *kami* who created this very heaven and earth, and who deserve great respect by mere virtue of the fact that they are our own ancestors. Even if Shaka was someone to be respected, he should be viewed suspiciously as a foreigner, whereas our ancestors are our true roots. Still there are those people who fawn over foreigners. They flatter foreigners by saying that they will reject their very own lords and parents for them. They reject the premise that their own august country's *kami* are superior to all others. It is bad enough when we hear our own lords and parents slandered, but it is unthinkable that one of us would actually join

in. It is a strange world in which people reject the idea of honoring their own parents.[1]

This genetics of religion attack was further developed in *Laughing Discourse after Emerging from Meditation,* as Atsutane used his interpretations of Asian and Western sources to characterize the nature of the people of India, the country that gave birth to Buddhism. He assassinated the character of the people first by denigrating their climate. The land was too fertile; the temperature was too hot. Therefore, the people did not have to, and were physically unable to, work hard. According to Atsutane, they had a tendency to rise up against their lords and fathers. Furthermore, they were dirty, mistaking cow dung for air freshener. In other words, they were lazy, backstabbing, and smelly; therefore, their religion was one fit for lazy, smelly backstabbers.

This genetics of religion argument also surfaced in a few places in *Senkyō ibun.* In an argument with a Buddhist priest during a salon session, which Atsutane could not attend, Torakichi told his Buddhist adversary:

> Even though you say that my stance of revering the *kami* is untenable, Buddhism was not something that originated in this country, but *kami* are things that come from this country. Because the others here and I are descendants of the *kami* we must stay obedient to that path. My master teaches the true way that should be revered before all others. Therefore if you priests had any noble qualities at all you would give up Buddhism and return to faith in the *kami.* Even though you say you despise the *kami* you are still not a descendant of the Buddha, and as a person born in the land of the *kami,* saying that you despise the *kami* means you despise this land and yet you must live in this land. People who call themselves priests are all like you.[2]

Although Atsutane was not in attendance, his genetics of religion argument was. Torakichi claimed in the quote that his master, meaning Sugiyama Sanjin, taught the true way, the Way of the *Kami.* However, in this instance, it seems more likely that this Ancient Way medium was spouting Atsutane's message.

We see this same argument come out of Torakichi's mouth again at another juncture in *Senkyō ibun.*

> This faith in the Buddha Dharma among the people is the same as not thinking that this body is precious, the same as wishing for it to be something else, such as turning into some vile buddha. This land is not the

Buddha's land; it is the *kami*'s land. We should realize that all of you and I also, as the descendants of the *kami*, would all eventually become *kami*. Many of the *kami* we worship at the shrines were originally human. All the people of this world are noble and splendid. They would know this if they worshiped the Daimyōjin or any *kami*, and not some buddha. People wanting to become a buddha are just like people wanting to become *sanjin* or *tengu*; they don't understand. Buddhist priests say they give people Buddhist names so they will change and become buddhas, but not being the descendants of the Indian Buddha, they do not become buddhas. They are the descendents of *kami*; in other words, the peach tree grows from the peach seed, just like the plum tree grows from the plum seed.[3]

Once again Torakichi attributed this wisdom and the argument to his *sanjin* master, but it sounds much like Atsutane's argument from years earlier.

Another way both Torakichi and Atsutane argued against Buddhism was by directly criticizing Buddhist practices. In one statement Torakichi condemned Buddhist priests by attacking their supposed denunciation of male-female sexual relations. He started his argument against them by saying that there are no living beings, fish, bugs, birds, or beasts that do not have sexual relations. Furthermore, the august intent of the *kami* is for the multiplication of the human race. This condemnation was in need of clarification because, according to Torakichi, *sanjin* also abstain from sexual relations with women. In fact, women were not even allowed in *sanjin* areas of the mountains because they were regarded as impure and defiled.[4]

In their defense, Torakichi claimed that *sanjin* practiced purity and abstinence because doing so brought supernatural power and long life. The result would be the same for the Buddhist who did the same, but most Buddhists, he charged, did not honor those vows and did have sexual relations with women. Besides the *sanjin*'s ability to actually carry out this vow of abstinence, he added that the difference between the Buddhist denial of sexual relations and the *sanjin* denial was that *sanjin* only recommended this practice for themselves and did not claim this would be suitable for the rest of the world as the Buddhists did. Torakichi also added that *sanjin* prayed daily for the fertility of the land and the fertility of humanity, while the Buddhist did not.

Another criticism of Buddhism leveled by Torakichi was his assertion that most Buddhist priests were hypocrites. As mentioned above, he claimed that although priests preached celibacy, they themselves were guilty of wantonly satisfying their lustful urges. He said they preached against meat eating yet satisfied their own hunger by eating four-legged beasts, which, according to him, was considered by the *kami* to be an abomination. In a strange twist, Torakichi once took a Buddhist priest to task for not properly shaving his head and not wearing the three robes, the prescribed Buddhist garb, in the manner expected of a true priest. However in that case, there appeared to be a personal reason behind the criticism. Torakichi readily and loudly admitted that he hated this particular Buddhist because the priest had invited him over with the hidden intent of publicly testing and embarrassing him. In other words, Torakichi's anti-Buddhist tirades were not based strictly on nativist principle.

Chinks in Torakichi's Anti-Buddhist Armor

As stated above, one type of anti-Buddhist strategy Atsutane used in *Senkyō ibun* was to ridicule Buddhist practices. However, the ridicule did not always originate with Atsutane the author, or even Torakichi his main narrator. Sometimes other participants in salon activities would add grist to the anti-Buddhist mill. Curiously, Torakichi did not always make the most of his many chances for dishing out harsh anti-Buddhist rhetoric.

On one occasion a visitor named Tsuchiya Kiyomichi offered the following negative criticism. Atsutane records:

> Tsuchiya Kiyomichi said, "How about the fact that when one hunts monkeys or rats and is about to kill them, the animals put their hands together in a pleading fashion. Some say that since Buddhism is more than two thousand years old, even beasts assume Buddhist postures in imitation of that Way. I say it is time to put that theory to rest. My guess is that it is not that the beasts have learned the postures of Buddhism. We know that originally the Buddhist hand posture was something started in India, so I say the opposite. This posture was learned from the beasts. Actually, I have heard that my opinion is also written somewhere in ancient Chinese texts."
>
> Torakichi said, "These praying and bowing postures are not just limited to monkeys and rats. In the mountains, bears stand up and face the morning sun. Many times I have seen them bowing and praying."[5]

This is an interesting exchange because the ridicule intended by claiming that Buddhist practice comes from imitating bestial sources was watered down by Torakichi's additional example of the bear. First of all, facing the sun and bowing was part of Atsutane's morning worship ritual. Was Torakichi commenting similarly on the worship of the Ancient Way?

Was he praising beasts for worshiping the *kami?* Was he defending Buddhism or just the ritual postures of bowing and praying? Whatever the case, his response seemed to neutralize that particular attempt to bestialize Buddhism. This was one case that suggested that Torakichi was not instinctively anti-Buddhist.

However, at another time when the talk had turned to snakes and dragons, Torakichi told a story of how once he and his master climbed down into the hole of a nine-headed dragon avatar. He claimed it looked something like a blue-green snake with multiple heads. The large heads had ears, the small heads had teeth, and the dragon would send blue clouds out of its mouth that made the hole smell of blood. Sugiyama told him there was nothing to be afraid of, but Torakichi was frightened and left. Something from the cave was stuck to his foot and he noticed it looked like a Buddhist sutra. He then looked around and noticed that there were lots of pieces of Buddhist sutras all around. He also realized that the blue vapor was actually poisonous, but due to his master's special protective power, he said, he was not adversely affected in the least.

In this impromptu story of the nine-headed dragon avatar, Torakichi linked Buddhism to a dangerous bestiality.[6] Buddhism was not only bestial; it was hideous and poisonous. Still, the superior power of the *sanjin* rendered the Buddhist poison ineffective. This brings up another recurrent motif in Torakichi and Atsutane's anti-Buddhist rhetoric. They did not claim that Buddhism was ineffective and powerless. On the contrary, they granted Buddhism great power to do harm, and of course blamed it for the corruption of Japan. Naturally, they claimed that the Ancient Way was stronger than Buddhism, but that Buddhism was still a force with which to be reckoned.

This somewhat respectful stance was reinforced in another exchange when a student of Atsutane appeared proudly displaying a metal statue of Shōten, or Kangiten, the elephant-headed god of Esoteric Buddhism. The student said he had won the statue in a debate with a *yamabushi* and was wearing it as a decoration. Elsewhere in the *Senkyō ibun*, Torakichi admitted that his master Sugiyama also performed Shōten worship, but he claimed it was only for apotropaic purposes. He claimed his master respected the power of Shōten but did not revere him.

Atsutane argued that the Shōten image must be thrown away. One of his arguments against Shōten was the familiar one against all defiled foreign religions, and followers of the Ancient Way should not possess images of those impure foreign gods. Atsutane added that Shōten worship was done for selfish purposes, to build up personal power but not to help the greater world. Atsutane declared that altruistic motivation was the measure of a worthy practice. He said that even if Shōten helped the student to gain control brutishly over others, they would always remain resentful of their new master and never serve him willingly, and this method thus would only lead to criticism and slander. Atsutane concluded that although it had some power to it, it was a half measure at best.

Atsutane suggested to his student that he throw the statue into a river or an ocean. He warned that if those who practiced Shōten worship had weak minds, they were in danger of becoming attached to it, even though it had no ultimate value. In other words, not only was it a futile practice, it had an addictive power, making it harmful for the user. Torakichi claimed that even though Shōten did not actually exist, the statue should not be thrown in the river or the ocean. He felt if it were thrown where some net could raise it, there was always the chance it could end up duping more foolish people. He suggested that the best thing to do was to melt it down, destroying it completely.

Although Torakichi reinforced Atsutane's claimed that Buddhism was inferior to his Ancient Way, he clearly feared and respected the power of the foreign religion. Although Atsutane admitted that Buddhism had power, he still limited his appreciation of that power to include only the ability to deceive and corrupt the practitioners and the ability to prevent the *kami* from receiving their deserved reverence. For all their similar rhetoric, a careful reading of *Senkyō ibun* demonstrates that Atsutane and Torakichi had basically differing attitudes toward Buddhism. Torakichi, unlike Atsutane, had spent time training to become a professional Buddhist and seemed to have retained a feeling of reverence or at least fear for the religion. Furthermore, Torakichi's actions after finally leaving Atsutane's house strongly suggest that his anti-Buddhist reactions were simply inspired by his current situation.

Possible Buddhist Influences on *Sanjin* Abilities

Atsutane used Torakichi to further his critique of Buddhism. But it is a fact that Torakichi had previously spoken in praise of Buddhism, at least when he was at Yamazaki Yoshishige's house. Given Torakichi and his master Sugiyama's knowledge and practice of Buddhism, it should be seen as inevitable that the *sanjin*'s supernatural abilities and powers would mimic those of Buddhist heroes; that is, buddhas, bodhisattvas, eminent monks, and patriarchs. Of course, due to Atsutane's affinity for the tradition of Chinese immortals, it is also natural that some of the supernatural powers attributed to the *sanjin* can also be seen in Daoism and traditions other than Buddhism. The effect of all those combined influences on Atsutane's

Senkyō ibun was that Buddhism was not used only as a model for imitation for the Ancient Way and its heroes, but also as a standard to be surpassed.

Torakichi reported that his *sanjin* master Sugiyama was unbelievably old and was fated to live much longer than he already had. According to Torakichi, Sugiyama's lifespan had been set at sixty thousand years, and this was so long that whenever Sugiyama would count his age he would call six hundred years "one." He referred to himself as "seven," which meant he was approximately forty-two hundred years old by human count. This of course would make him older than the historical Buddha, and would also give him a lifespan comparable to the amount of time allotted for the future Buddha Maitreya to preach the dharma.[7] Torakichi himself said his lifespan had also been determined in the Other World, but it had been set at a very modest, almost human, one hundred years.[8] This would make Torakichi's lack of supernatural ability understandable, but it would still make him privy to the secret information of that world.

Torakichi claimed that when the *sanjin*'s fixed number of days was finally over, his physical form would disappear and he would become a *kami*. However, there were some *sanjin* who were said to be ageless and who would be active in the world for as long as the world lasted. For Atsutane's Ancient Way to have a hero that lives a long time or is nearly immortal does not substantiate a claim of cultural borrowing. However, the idea of a being that exists as long as the world system exists is a strong hint that Torakichi had been exposed to ideas that can be traced to the Indian Buddhist idea of finite world systems. But there is no absolute way to fix the source of the influence for either Torakichi or Atsutane.[9]

The *sanjin* certainly possessed supernatural powers. Episodes of flying were recurrent in Torakichi's stories. Torakichi himself could not fly, but he claimed to have been flown all over the world and to the stars by his master. As related earlier, one mode of air transport was the gourd that contained more than it should have been able to and that flew at amazing speeds. This, as we have seen, was a variation on a tale of Daoist immortals.[10] However, in most of Torakichi's stories about flying with his master, Sugiyama Sanjin did so without the gourd, which also made him resemble a flying Buddhist arhat.

For centuries before Atsutane's time, the power of flight had been important in stories of the supernatural powers of Daoists and Buddhists. That the *sanjin* could fly must have pleased Atsutane, and he must have been even more pleased when he learned that his native land's culture hero also had the power to fly at supersonic speeds[11] as well as speeds more suitable for sightseeing and comfortable aerial viewing. In addition, the *sanjin*'s ability to fly was not limited to the earth's atmosphere. He could fly to distant stars and through the holes in the moon.[12] Of course the creation of a flying hero does not constitute cultural borrowing, yet Buddhist and Daoist heroes flew, and a *sanjin* hero who was capable of supersonic and space flight certainly equaled, if not surpassed, his continental competition.

Another power of the *sanjin* was the ability to make alter egos. Sugiyama Sanjin could create doubles and triples of himself and therefore was able to be in many places at once. This ability to have multiple bodies was again not limited to one religious tradition;[13] still it was very important to the understanding of the Mahayana bodhisattva and buddha.[14] This seems to be a very useful power, and Atsutane's *sanjin* never took second to any other religious hero. Therefore, it is not surprising that he too could pull this trick off.

The subject of this alter ego ability arose when Torakichi was asked if his mountain master did not miss his presence. Someone wondered if there was not work to be done on the mountain for which a *sanjin* would require a novice and servant such as Torakichi.

> Torakichi said, "When my master felt that certain things could not be accomplished because there were not enough people around to do them, he was not in the least bit inconvenienced because he could always call upon his many alter egos."[15]

When he was asked for an explanation of how his master produced these alter egos, he replied:

> Torakichi said, "Whenever he needed alter egos he would pluck hairs from under his lower lip, chant a magic spell and any number of people who looked just like the master would appear. However, I do not know the words of the incantation."[16]

The *sanjin* also had the power of invisibility, another power occasionally attributed to the Buddha. This power was sometimes referred to by Torakichi as his master's "shadow" form. According to Torakichi, the advanced *sanjin*, at least one more advanced than Torakichi, could not be seen unless he allowed himself to be seen.[17] When Torakichi was with his *sanjin* master, he too was invisible to human eyes, but of course he lost this advantage when he was away from his master.

This subject came up in the following:

Atsutane asked, "At Atago shrine there are lots of worshipers, the Head of the Shrine along with many Shinto priests, and some others. When those people gather there on the grounds in such numbers where does that large a number of *tengu* hide?"

Torakichi said, "Even when the worshipers come in droves and even when the head of the shrine shows up, people from the seen realm cannot see the *tengu*. The eyes of the common people of the world can see great distances, but even when we are close by they won't notice us if the master prevents them. Whenever I go anywhere with the master, I can see other people, but those people don't see me even when I'm right beside them. Now that I've come back among the humans they can see me when they look at me. Yet if I went into the Other World, even if I were beside some normal human, he wouldn't be able to see me. Moreover, with their super-natural powers, whatever they build can't be seen. . . . They just think of a house and suddenly it's there."[18]

Atsutane had been curious about the living conditions at Atago shrine. Torakichi explained how easy it would have been to build residences, but actually the thirteen *tengu* chose to dwell in the shrine itself, at least when it rained. This prompted a question from Atsutane concerning how the thirteen *tengu* with each of their three or four servants lived in the two rooms that made up the Atago shrine. Torakichi said this was not a problem for them. A large number could enter and there would always be plenty of extra room, which of course was due to their supernatural pow-ers. In other words, in addition to being invisible, great numbers of *sanjin* could exist in a space that would not be considered large enough for the average human being. This explanation of how so many *sanjin* or *tengu* could live in a small shrine was later used by Atsutane to verify that eight million *kami* could be enshrined in the *kamidana* of every household. This would also explain how the *sanjin* could fit into a small flying gourd.

Sanjin could also fire flames out of their bodies. This will be of interest later in the discussion of the *sanjin*'s role in national defense. The ability to shoot fire is a foreseeable power for supernatural beings, but for Bud-dhists it should bring to mind Shaka returning from Tsusita heaven and the bodhisattva of the Lotus Sutra, who both shot a combination of fire and water from their bodies.[19] The rest of the *sanjin*'s violent repertoire was based on conventional and unconventional technological weapons that will be discussed in chapter 6.

Torakichi was not exhaustive in his imitation or rather his matching of power for power in the makeup of the nativist culture hero. There are a few traditional Buddhist powers that the *sanjin* lacked. For example, the *sanjin* was not able to read minds. Torakichi liked to tell stories in which he occasionally was able to lie to or otherwise fool his *sanjin* master. However, in his visits to foreign lands, Torakichi's master was able to understand all foreign languages. His mind could pick up the meaning of the voices and in that way understand them. He could also understand the voices of birds, beasts, and even insects. Besides his telepathic shortcomings, there are also no stories that reveal exceptional visual or auditory abilities. Of course, the final two of the traditional six Buddhist spiritual penetrations[20] are theologically incompatible with Atsutane's religious thought and are, not surprisingly, left out of the *sanjin*'s repertoire.

Seeds of *Sanjin* Ambivalence toward Buddhist Practice

One interesting variation from Atsutane's theme that all Buddhist practice is bad, unless it can be claimed as originally Japanese, crops up in some of Torakichi's discussions of the *sanjin*. As stated earlier, Torakichi had not always publicly declared his hatred of Buddhism. On certain occasions he told of the many Buddhist practices he encountered in the mountains and in his own personal experiences being associated with two different Buddhist temples. Unfortunately for Atsutane's nativist project, Torakichi could not always be consistent in his stance toward Buddhism and also could not deny the Buddhist practices undertaken by his *sanjin* master.

Although Atsutane would surely have wanted a perfect Ancient Way hero, he did not edit out all the discrepancies between what Torakichi claimed to be his master Sugiyama Sanjin's practice and a perfectly native Japanese practice celebrating only native *kami*. Therefore, in *Senkyō ibun*, Torakichi at certain points admitted that his master followed Buddhist practices. When such a revelation was made it was quickly followed by an explanation, which was an attempt to mollify the concern of those, primarily Atsutane, who would think that admission of adherence to Buddhist practice would be tantamount to a betrayal of the Ancient Way. At the very least, this kind of admission could have impeached Sugiyama's credentials as the model for Atsutane's culture hero *sanjin*, but ultimately it did not seem to matter.

As an example of a serious Buddhist intrusion into Sugiyama Sanjin's practice and the excuse used to explain it away, there is the following exchange between Atsutane and Torakichi.

Atsutane asked, "Is it true that your master in the Other World practices Fudō, Dakini, Shōten, Marishiten, Izuna, or any other of the various worship rituals that spring from Buddhism?"

Torakichi replied, "My master worships some from among those, but the truth is that they are just names attached to beings which do not really exist, and so he is not really fond of the worship of Kannon, Fudō, or Marishiten. But he has a stronger dislike for the worship of Dakiniten, Izuna and Shōten, because they are served and worshiped by *tengu*, foxes, demons, and things like that, and therefore, he has always advised against that kind of worship."

Atsutane asked, "I don't understand why he advises against practicing them, yet practices them himself."

Torakichi immediately replied, "Since Dakiniten and Izuna worship is for foxes and *tengu*, my master does not practice them. But he does occasionally practice Shōten worship. The reason he does is because Shōten creates obstacles for the world, and it is another name for the *kami* of obstacles, so he performs this worship so that this leader of demons will not make any obstacles for him. But this is a far cry from the way the Shugendō practitioners do it, because they do it to get worldly benefits for themselves. The truth is that my master's principal purpose is to earnestly worship for worthy ends. He prays for peace in the world and prosperity for all people. In general, he performs his practices in order to be a true *kami*, and they are based on the Way of the Kami. However, he also performs practices which come from Buddhism, or which have become connected to those practices in today's world. He uses the two mandalas and, beside his *kami* altar, he also prepares the *shumidan*[21] and performs Buddhist prayers so that other forces in the world will not hinder his other practices. The people of the world today believe in all those kinds of things and not this land's own *kami*. My master insists that their worship of such things and their negligence of the *kami* results in the *kami* being stripped of their spiritual authority."[22]

In this strange, contradiction-laden exchange, it seems that Torakichi's strategy was to admit that his master performed Esoteric Buddhist practices, but also to weakly defend his master's legitimacy by claiming that he actually did not like doing them. What is even stranger is that in another conversation introduced earlier, he claimed Shōten to be nonexistent. Yet in this passage, he claimed that Shōten was a powerful *kami* leader of demons whom his master reluctantly placated. Finally, he ended his weak defense with a kind of lament that repeated Atsutane's earlier claim that worship of buddhas diminished the *kami*. Nevertheless, he refused to recognize his *sanjin* master's role in that process and that he himself had been caught in a contradiction.

In another interview Torakichi was confronted with how he described his master Sugiyama during his stay at Yoshishige's house. One visitor to Atsutane's salon claimed that when Torakichi was at Yoshishige's house he had described his master as having the shaved pate of a Buddhist priest. The visitor also claimed that Torakichi had said his master often sat in the lotus position making *mudra*. He further claimed that Torakichi had said his master would face west and chant to the buddha of that direction. The visitor continued with a laundry list of other charges that incriminated both Torakichi and his master as Buddhist sympathizers, if not Buddhist practitioners.

Atsutane reported that Torakichi's face was flushed when he heard these accusations, but he soon defended what would have been the disastrous revelation that Torakichi's *sanjin* master practiced Buddhism. Torakichi denied the charge that he had said all those things. He claimed that the people who had visited Yoshishige's house had been telling all sorts of lies.

Torakichi claimed to have been misquoted regarding his description of Sugiyama's appearance. According to Torakichi, he had described his master as follows: His hair was long and hung down in back, and he did not wear red robes but rather an outfit that resembled ancient hunting clothes. He did not sit in anything like a meditation posture, but sometimes when he was deep in thought, he would sit down with his hands before his stomach, close his eyes, and break into a chant.

In other words, Torakichi claimed there was nothing particularly Buddhist about his sitting or his chanting. Torakichi then claimed to know sixty or seventy different *mudra;* however, they were his master's style of *mudra*, not Buddhist *mudra*. He made the charge that the Buddhist use of *mudra* was random, undisciplined, and wrong, and he explained that *mudra* have no effect at all unless done correctly, that is, the way Torakichi's master taught Torakichi to do them.

This shows that Torakichi had learned something from his new master, Atsutane. His defense tactic was strikingly similar to Atsutane's favorite technique, which was to claim mastery of Buddhist practice, but also deny the Buddhist origins of that practice.

Atsutane's Own Buddhist Study and Practice

Torakichi's knowledge and practice of Buddhist ritual seemed to be controversial in *Senkyō ibun,* but his Buddhist and Shugendō experiences may have proven invaluable for Atsutane's own private religious research. Atsutane likes to present himself as a nativist who hates Buddhism because it is an inferior religion that originates in an inferior country. Nonetheless, Atsutane has a record of spending a great deal of time and effort in the study of Buddhism and in the practice of rituals that show Buddhist inspiration and influence.

In the preface to his premier work of anti-Buddhist discourse, *Laughing Discourse after Emerging from Meditation* (*Shutsujō shōgo*), Atsutane states that his purpose for studying Buddhist traditional stories is to point out that the Buddhist classics and doctrines as taught in Japan in his time did not come from the time of Shakyamuni's life. He claims that Buddhist history was a layered mixture of contradictory and self-serving teachings. Atsutane was not the first to make this claim; Tominaga Nakamoto had modeled this type of attack for him one hundred years earlier. However, Atsutane's criticisms are notable for their vitriolic intensity.

Despite this outward antagonism and hatred, in 1821 Atsutane compiled a work on Esoteric Buddhism called *Categories of Esoteric Doctrines and Rituals* (*Mippō shuji bunruikō*), which includes in its collection of Esoteric Buddhist rituals practices for the worship of *kami*. This is not a collection of rituals intended for criticism and ridicule. These rituals reveal a secret side of Atsutane's attitude toward Buddhist practice. In particular, the final ritual in this collection was very important to him. In typical Esoteric Buddhist fashion, this ritual calls for unification between the practitioner and the honzon, the central image or object of worship.

The name of this ritual is *Kuebiko saishiki*, and the explanation of the practice shows Atsutane's adherence to Esoteric Buddhist ritual structure. However, to first understand this ritual, a word or two must be said about Atsutane's theology. In Atsutane's Ancient Way, Musubi no kami is conceived of as the spiritual *kami* of creation. The Musubi no kami in the ancient Japanese histories are always described as formless creator spirits, and Atsutane also uses the term in that way. In his *Jeweled Sash* (*Tamadasuki*), Atsutane explains Kuebiko no mikoto as a universal *kami* who is the source of all souls.

In Atsutane's *Explanation of the Hidden and the Revealed* (*Yūkenben*), he explains that at death the body returns to its natural components while the soul remains unchanged. Furthermore, he claims that the individual soul is actually just a part of the universal soul. His theological debt on this point can be traced to a couple of possible different traditions, neither originating in Japan. However, what he recommends as a form of religious practice is the reunification of the individual soul to the world soul by a method that can be traced to a root Esoteric Buddhist/Indian model.

In *Kuebiko saishiki* the practitioner is instructed to set up a *honzon*. In Esoteric Buddhism this might typically be a Dainichi nyorai image or something that represents Dainichi nyorai. In Atsutane's ritual, Dainichi has been replaced by Musubi no kami. The Esoteric pattern would then call for offerings of several sorts, and this was also copied in Atsutane's ritual. In the Esoteric model, the climax of the ritual would occur after performing contemplation and meditations meant to produce an image of the intermediate being, an alter ego of Dainichi, Fudō myōō perhaps; then unification or identification with that intermediary would take place. In Atsutane's ritual, Fudō was replaced by Kuebiko no mikoto. While the Esoteric practitioner becomes a buddha in that very body, Atsutane's practitioner becomes a *kami* in that very body. The individual soul ritually achieves the goal of reuniting with the universal soul. In Atsutane's ritual, where the Buddhist would say "many buddhas," the Chinese character for buddha is simply replaced by the character for *kami*. In the spot where the text should say "becoming a buddha," it says "becoming a *kami*." The results and the goals of the ritual are written about as *kaji* and *rieki*, just what the Esoteric Buddhist practitioner would have been hoping for.[23]

The Shinto tradition does claim a long history of practitioners uniting with the *kami*, which we might be more used to associating with spirit possession, or even shamanistic practice. In modern Shinto terms, when this possession is seen to occur without artificial assistance, it is called *kishin*, and when it is induced it is called *chinkon*. Therefore, Atsutane's Kuebiko ritual could be categorized as a *chinkon* ritual, which could associate it with the so-called ancient Shinto tradition. However, the contents of his *Categories of Esoteric Doctrines and Rituals* are proof that he copied the ritual straight from an Esoteric Buddhist precedent and changed the buddhas into *kami*.

Categories of Esoteric Doctrines and Rituals contains more than a hundred more rituals, all coming from Esoteric Buddhist practice. Most of them are for defeating enemies, overcoming evil, or performing initiations. Many of the rituals in this collection contain references to or invocations of Daoist immortals, and many of them involve Kangiten or Shōten, which provides a link to Torakichi and his *sanjin* master. However, the attitude usually expressed toward Esoteric Buddhist rituals in *Senkyō ibun* is one of wariness. Atsutane readily recognized the power in these kinds of rituals, but he was afraid of their corrupting influences. Perhaps, as was explained by Torakichi, Atsutane agreed that those who held the proper reverence for the *kami* could practice them.

We know that Atsutane had published a daily morning ritual of *kami* worship he called the *Maichō shimpai shiki*, and he practiced this ritual devotedly every morning. Within the litany of the ritual is a passage that offers his worship and devotion to the very same Kuebiko no mikoto. Given the evidence of his devotion to spiritual studies and the occult, it seems likely that Atsutane himself carried out Esoteric Buddhist practice, at least in the form of the *Kuebiko saishiki*. A hanging scroll/*honzon* that depicts this *kami* is still preserved today within his archives.

Haga Noboru writes that while Atsutane was critical of Buddhism overall, and especially the more popular sects such as Nichiren Buddhism, he was relatively respectful of Zen and Shingon Buddhism, the latter being the source of his Esoteric Buddhist ritual collection. Haga goes on to suggest that these collected rituals, along with his *Maichō shimpai shiki*, may have been used for recruitment, especially around the time he was making his recruiting tours of the Kantō countryside before and after he met Torakichi.[24] The ambivalence and contradictions evident in both Atsutane's and Torakichi's attitudes toward Buddhism as expressed in *Senkyō ibun* probably reflect the true situation; that is, Buddhism was powerful and useful to both of them, so in truth neither of them could swear it off completely.

There is another interesting note on the connection between *Senkyō ibun* and Esoteric Buddhist practices. At one point in the text, Torakichi gives a particularly graphic description of a bizarre Esoteric ritual. It involves the statue of a naked woman with special emphasis on the genitalia. Dunking in feces and anointment by skulls filled with blood round out the description of the ritual, which is supposed to bring some sort of evil power to the practitioners.[25] Atsutane may have been an Esoteric practitioner in private, but what he records in *Senkyō ibun* about Esoteric rituals is quite negative. He usually makes Esoteric ritual, at least as practiced by Buddhists, sound much more like evil pornography than a blissful reunification with the universal soul.

Torakichi as Spirit Medium and Divine Child: Buddhist Precedents

One of Torakichi's special abilities and the one thing that set him apart from other religiously devoted teenage boys was his talent for spirit possession; he could intentionally cause spirits to possess him or his ritual assistants, or he could become spontaneously possessed. The exercise of these talents shows his debt to both the Buddhist and Daoist traditions,[26] but for the most part the possession rituals rely heavily on Buddhist images and practices. The following example has Torakichi describing a ritual he would commonly perform for people seeking his assistance.

After this, I [Atsutane] listened to what he [Torakichi] said he did when someone asked him to perform possession rituals. Acting as the visiting deity he recited the words for the purification of the six roots[27] and intoned the mantra for the Eleven-headed Kannon. After the possession ritual was over I asked, "Previously you said that the thing called Kannon does not really exist. And, didn't you say it was nothing more than a name attached to a statue someone made? In spite of that, you pray to and set up that Kannon as the visiting deity, which I find difficult to understand. What does it mean to have a nonexistent thing make a visitation?"

Torakichi said, "This is what my master said. The reason we perform possession rituals is that this is the way to help people who are at a total loss about what to do in a certain situation find the answer by asking a *kami*. Even though we are essentially inviting a *kami* in order to make a request, and the ultimate goal is to be graced by the presence of that *kami*, we, along with most of the other ritual specialists in the world, set up ritual images in the dual mandala style using Fudō, Kannon, and Marishiten. Nevertheless, as I stated earlier, these are just names attached to things that don't exist. Furthermore, because they are simply make-believe images they don't make visitations. However, there are many real demons, spirits, and ghosts prowling about in the world that do make visitations, and by doing so reveal their spiritual energies. This is the reason that those make-believe things are thought to exist.

Actually, I did not learn this technique from anyone else. One time I had someone play the spirit medium in fun and I mimicked the recitation of prayer and tried intoning various disconnected and meandering chants, and somehow unexpectedly that medium became possessed and revealed the presence of some spiritual energy. This surprised me and I asked my master about it and that's when he told me what I have just told you. After this happened and I figured out the secret of it, I would conduct the ritual and chant in ways that were appropriate to the supplicant using Fudō, Marishiten, or any other dual mandala-influenced mantras. Seven out of ten times there would be a visitation and something would happen that showed the presence of some spiritual energy. If ghosts or demons would make the visitation when it concerned someone who was sick I would pray saying that the spirit medium should raise the paper wand up to the left if the sickness would get better and up to the right if it would not. The prayer rituals are done for other people, which explains why the spiritual activities take a variety of different forms."

When I heard Torakichi explain it in this way, I praised what he had said. Then I read to him what I had written previously in the *Koshiden*, in particular the part about Kuebiko no *kami* who couldn't walk, but still knew everything there was to know about heaven and earth. This pleased Torakichi, who said, "What you told me makes me even more sure of the secret source of the power of the possession rituals [*kami*]."[28]

In other words, Torakichi openly admitted to repeatedly performing Buddhist rituals for divination purposes[29] at the request of laymen seeking spiritual assistance. In a roundabout way, he even strongly affirmed that they were spiritually effective. Of course, for Atsutane's benefit he also claimed that both he and his master did not believe in the reality of Buddhist deities and actually hoped for visitation from *kami* when they performed those rituals. Atsutane was satisfied with the answer and even brought up the deity mentioned in the previous section, to which Atsutane himself most likely performed his own Buddhist-influenced visitation rituals.

Torakichi was not only savvy about asking spirits for assistance, he was also quite knowledgeable about religious practices that employed spiritually powerful animals for personal gain, and he himself made the connection between such practices and the Buddhist tradition.[30] Once again, the following passage reveals how Torakichi's Esoteric *sanjin* knowledge is saturated with Buddhist influence:

I [Atsutane] said, "I have heard that Kōbō Daishi is still in this world and wandering through the provinces, particularly Shikoku, and in those various places, miracles are attributed to this Buddhist priest. Have you heard any of those stories in the Other World?"

Torakichi said, "I haven't heard about Kōbō Daishi doing those kinds of things. I have only heard that he had become a *tengu.*"

[Atsutane's] Note: Kōbō Daishi was the first to employ Heavenly Foxes.[31]

I asked, "Has your master spent time with Dōryō Gongen of Odawara Saijōji, Sanjakubō of Mt. Akiba, or Hōshōbō of Mt. Myōgi?"[32]

Torakichi said, "Those guys are real *tengu.* And besides, since they are strictly devoted Buddhists, their purposes are different than my master's, and he doesn't mix with them so I don't know much about them."

I asked, "I saw a certain thing in a work called [blank]. How much do you know about that? Also, according to that work, there are many people who have foxes doing their bidding. Have you heard anything about how they get them to work for them?"

Torakichi said, "The way to employ the fox is first to seek out a fox and ask its favor. Offer it a rat deep fried in sesame oil and gain its service by offering the oath, 'If you work for me I will periodically give these to you.' I hear that evil practices like this are continually being invented and then passed on to future generations in Buddhism where they modify these practices to get all sorts of creatures to do their bidding." [33]

Atsutane was also quite aware of certain Tantric Buddhist traditions that create a mystique surrounding certain "divine children." [34] There is even a genre of literature in Japan called *Chigo monogatari* that idealizes the male child used as a spirit medium and portrays him as endowed with qualities of spiritual power, beauty, and divinity. However, as Bernard Faure writes:

we may hesitate between reading these texts as Buddhist sermons or reading them as love stories. But this interpretive alternative may not be sufficient. We may also see them as a rather crude ideological cover-up for a kind of institutionalized prostitution or rape. [35]

This is clearly the way Atsutane was thinking of that particular tradition when he pondered the possible sexual implications of Torakichi's *tengu* abduction.

I [Atsutane] asked, "Isn't there homosexuality in the Other World?"
Torakichi said, "I don't know about other mountains, but there was none of that at the mountains I was on."
Actually I didn't personally ask about homosexuality. I had my student Moriya Inao privately ask Torakichi when he had gained his confidence. The reason I would ask this kind of question is that everyone knows that most of the people taken by *tengu* are young boys and if that *tengu* was actually a transformed Buddhist monk who was an evil sexual pervert while in this world, then people would immediately suspect that he might have been taken for that very reason. [36]

We can only assume that Atsutane would not have been so ready to believe this denial if Torakichi had claimed his master to be a Buddhist *tengu* and not an Ancient Way *sanjin*.

The fact that Torakichi was prone to spontaneous episodes of spirit possession himself clearly raised his stock in the eyes of the anti-Buddhist nativists. The following is an excerpt from *A Short Chronicle of the Divine*

Child's Possession Tales (*Shindō hyōdan ryakki*). This book focuses specifically on the spiritual and supernatural activities of Torakichi and, as argued
in a previous chapter, was produced to inspire talk of his strange powers
among Atsutane's extended circle of followers and potential followers.

> Then it was early evening on the fifth just a little past four in the after-
> noon I think. The divine child [Torakichi] was supposed to be playing as
> usual when the child Zennosuke I mentioned earlier came to me saying,
> "The divine child has fallen down over there and seems to be talking in
> his sleep."
>
> When I quickly went over there to look, the divine child appeared to
> be in a deep sleep, except his complexion was strange and his arms and
> legs were cold. Moreover, he was mumbling something. When I listened
> closely he seemed to be saying, "This is Sajima [Sajima was the name of
> the divine child's friend in the Other World]" and "return to the moun-
> tain." The divine child was mumbling other things, but I couldn't make
> them out, and I couldn't understand what he said.
>
> Unfortunately, that day the teacher [Atsutane] had gone over to Ban
> Nobutomo's, a person who was pursuing similar studies, and he hadn't
> yet returned. So there was quite a commotion as everyone in the house
> gathered round suggesting we do this and that. Just as I said, "Don't get
> excited; this is clearly a case of spirit possession," a fellow student named
> Shinkichi appeared and said, "This is unmistakably spirit possession, and
> we should let him rest here quietly." But the members of the household
> just made an even greater fuss suggesting all sorts of things.[37]

There is much more textual evidence in these works that shows that the
"divine child" tradition using the boy as spirit medium was reinvigorated
in Atsutane's nativist academy.

Sanjin as Ancient Way Medium and Savior of the People

To understand Atsutane's Ancient Way we should start from the most basic
premises, that the *kami* are all-important and everything is a result of the
actions of the *kami*. Unfortunately for Atsutane, the *kami* did not often
appear to inform the human world of the nature of their world. In Atsutane's view, the *kami* existing today lived the same way they had always
lived, yet knowledge of them that could be recovered from ancient texts
had severe limitations, and direct knowledge was virtually impossible.
Given that human knowledge of and contact with the *kami* was insuffi-
cient, there was a clear need for a medium. A being that could go back and

forth between the world of the *kami* and the world of the ordinary human would be the perfect source of information. Atsutane believed, or acted as if he believed, he had found that perfect source in Torakichi.

The knowledge of the *sanjin* could make up quite a bit for the paucity of human knowledge. Still, as stated earlier, Torakichi claimed that even the *sanjin* did not know everything about the *kami*, and their knowledge of the *kami* was similar to the human's knowledge of the *sanjin*. Nevertheless, Atsutane used the opportunity to find out everything he could about the *sanjin* so he could fill out his information about the Other World, the world shared by *sanjin* and *kami*. In other words, knowledge of the *sanjin* was not knowledge of the *kami*, but it was the next best thing.

As mentioned earlier, the *sanjin* occupied a position between *kami* and human. However, in one interesting speech from one interview, Torakichi inflated his claims about his master's importance.

> Then there are those like my master. Because they too live in the mountains, they are called *sanjin*. But actually they are living *kami* who have existed from a time when there was no Buddhism. They practice the Way of the Kami. They live in the mountains and guard the shrines for worship. They dispense the meritorious benefits of *kami* and sometimes they are worshiped together with the mountain *kami*. They accumulate billions and billions of years of life, continually burdened by the needs of the human world, so they never live peaceful and quiet existences.[38]

Judging from this claim, it seems that there are levels of *sanjin*, something like levels of bodhisattva. Some *sanjin* are equal to *kami*, but other *sanjin* are lower level. Despite this one-time claim of *kami* status, Torakichi and Atsutane, for the most part, hold that *sanjin* usually occupy a position between the *kami* and the human, where they were obligated and dedicated to bettering the human condition.

The *sanjin* helped the people of Japan at the most basic level. For example, they helped farmers grow crops:

> I [Atsutane] said, "I cannot understand why your master prays for rain at Mt. Ryūjin. In the Other World there aren't any rice paddies or dry fields, so nobody there suffers if there isn't any rain. Therefore, why make it rain?"
>
> Torakichi laughed and answered, "Only a human would think they need a special reason to do that. Certainly the *kami*, but also the *sanjin*, are not content when the world is in trouble. So of course it is important for him to pray for the human world." [39]

By this we see that in the minds of Atsutane and Torakichi, the *sanjin* acted as stewards for the human realm, entrusted with the responsibility of keeping it in proper working order.

Atsutane recorded in several places the assertion that *sanjin* were supernatural mediums whose purpose was to protect and better the lives of the people of Japan. He explained how they worked for the people, but he also had to explain how the people were supposed to get in touch with the *sanjin*. Previously we heard of how they were usually invisible and only showed themselves when they wanted to be seen. To demonstrate how people could contact the medium, Atsutane asked Torakichi the following:

> "When there is something a person wants to request or ask about from a *sanjin*, it seems he should climb up to a certain elevation, but then how does he send off the request and address the Other World?"
>
> Torakichi answered, "If a person speaks just normally or even in a loud voice, he still won't get through to them. However, if he prays just like it is a special prayer for the *kami* then it will reach them."
>
> I asked, "How can he know if his prayer was heard?"
>
> Torakichi answered, "He knows when the request is granted, or else he can get confirmation in a dream."
>
> I asked, "Isn't there some way a person can go to the mountains and meet them face to face when there is something he needs?"
>
> Torakichi replied, "A person cannot meet them face to face whenever he wishes, because they need to maintain the distinction between that realm and this realm." [40]

In other words, if one were able to meet the *sanjin* at will, this would reduce their mystique and they would become less special. They were to be treated like *kami*, even if they were not always on the same exalted level. They were not subject to human control or manipulation. Humans were left to trust in their good graces and pray to them with as much reverence as possible. However, Torakichi also warned that if worshiping the *sanjin* led to any decrease in the worship of the *kami*, such a cult could be subject to divine reprisals. Torakichi asserted that his master preferred only subdued occasional worship and did not seek multiple shrines dedicated only to him.

Toward the end of *Senkyō ibun*, Atsutane records Torakichi's summation of the relative merits of the worship of the Buddha versus the worship of the *kami*.

Someone asked Torakichi, "Why do you claim that the *kami* are noble and the buddhas are vile?"

Torakichi replied, "The fact that the *kami* are noble and the buddhas are vile is something that everyone should know without having to ask. Take a look at the world. It consists of heaven and earth and all the other things yet incomprehensible to us. The world moves through the four seasons. The rain falls and the wind blows. There are many different types of living creatures, humans, trees, grasses, birds, and beasts. Trees and grasses flower in the spring. In the fall there are seeds. These and all other matters are the workings of the *kami*. Everyone knows that heaven and earth were created by the *kami*.

Shaka was the first of the buddhas, but he was a human who appeared long after the *kami*. This my master told me. Shaka is nothing more than another creature created by the *kami*. *Kami* are the trunk and the buddhas are the branches.

Proof of this can be seen whenever there is a long drought or long extended heavy rains. We always end up praying to the *kami*. When we pray for rain or sunshine, we receive clear and obvious proof that the *kami* control rain, wind, droughts, and storms. This is due to the fact that rain, wind, drought, and storms are all the workings of the *kami* and all things on heaven and earth: humans, birds, and beasts were without exception created by the power of the *kami*.

Even though Buddhist priests and *yamabushi* read their sutras and pray for rain or the end to a drought, their technique of reading sutras to the buddhas never causes one drop of rain to fall. Rain falls after someone prays for visitation by *kami* and because of that we know that the *kami* are noble and the buddhas are vile."[41]

At one point Torakichi was asked about the origin of evil, in particular, if the source was the so-called *kami* of sickness and poverty. Torakichi did not point to *kami* as the source of evil. He said that twisted human souls became evil and performed evil deeds. These evil human souls were those twisted by evil teachings. He gave a specific example of souls that had been tricked into expecting to be reborn into a paradise. When the souls found out that such a place did not really exist, these disappointed souls turned resentful and worked to recruit and twist other human souls. Clearly he was here indirectly naming the Buddhist teachings as a source of evil in the world. Once again, Atsutane's Ancient Way was in part defined by its opposition to its Buddhist competitor.

This example of evil teachings led directly to a discussion on the evils of too many teachings. At one point a certain salon visitor criticized the Way of the Kami because of a lack of teachings. Torakichi answered the charge that native Japanese *kami* worship lacked a tradition of scholarship by claiming that scholarship always brought with it more bad than good. Torakichi asserted that scholarship never led to perfect understanding. On the contrary, he claimed that since most teachings were false assertions that led people into paths of evil, scholarship should be blamed for causing the world to be full of demons. Again in this section, Atsutane's Ancient Way was defined and defended by contrasting it with foreign religions and cultures.

Greed was another thing Torakichi claimed would bring evil into the world. He preached that rich people loved to hoard money, which caused problems for the poor people in the world. Torakichi even claimed the *kami* hated rich people. He went further to insist that people who were arrogant because they were either beautiful or talented were another related source of evil. Like the rich, they were haughty and self-indulgent and therefore they tended to enter paths of evil. This definition of evil made the *sanjin* a champion of the lower classes and revealed a populist tendency in Atsutane's reconception of native Japanese religion. However, this particular populist point was certainly not touted when Atsutane lobbied for the support of the rich and famous in the salons of Edo society.

Atsutane had Torakichi define evil so he could suggest another important function of his new religious hero. Several times in Atsutane's salon, Torakichi detailed the *sanjin*'s role in punishing evil. Atsutane opened the subject by relating his own story of a man who had secretly overheard two *sanjin* who happened to meet one night on board a riverboat. The man who overheard the conversation described the *sanjin* as unkempt men who looked as if they lived in the wild. He pretended to be sleeping as he listened in on their conversation (the *sanjin* of course knew he was listening but allowed it). One said he was starting out on a journey for a distant location but the other said he was on a mission of justice. It seemed that some shrine timber had been sold for use in the construction of a temple dedicated to Kannon. The *sanjin* said he was going to take care of that sacrilege, and later the man who had feigned sleep saw smoke rising in the distance from the torched construction site.

After this story, Torakichi, true to form, confirmed that *sanjin* did take on the role of righting wrongs and dispensing justice. Torakichi said that his master had often been involved in punishing the wicked. He claimed that his master sometimes rained fire down on those who deserved it. When asked what device or what kind of fire starter his master used, Torakichi laughed and claimed that his master could generate fire from his own body, and it was this flame that he cast down in retribution. He added that these acts of retribution were always done at the order of the *kami*.

Sanjin and Ancient Way Ritual

Atsutane was constantly questioning Torakichi concerning the ritual practices he had witnessed in the Other World. Torakichi spoke in detail of the annual calendar of festivals celebrated there.

> I [Atsutane] asked, "Do you throw beans on *setsubun*, skewer dried sardines on holly, put up pine and rope decorations at the New Year, make baths with iris petals on the fifth month seasonal festival and those kinds of things?"
>
> Torakichi said, "We don't set up any special pine at the New Year. But we do bow, pray, and make offerings to a living pine. I think these are related activities, but people would probably live longer if they prayed for long life to a pine tree every day and not just at the New Year."
>
> [. . .]
>
> I asked, "Is there a fixed yearly schedule of annual *kami* festivals starting with the New Year? Also, do they have a festival in July for all souls?"
>
> Torakichi said, "When it comes to our annual schedule of festivals from New Year's Eve to New Year's Day we celebrate the Toshikami [*kami* overseeing the abundance of the harvest], and on the first day of the horse in the second month we conduct the sacred rituals of rice planting. The person who acts as the *kami* of the rice field ties his hair up in an ancient men's hairstyle,[42] and we offer him deep-fried tofu. On the third day of the third month we celebrate Izanagi and Izanami no mikoto, and this is our celebration of the doll festival. The fifth day of the fifth month is when we celebrate Susanoo no mikoto. However, there is no celebration of the soul festival in the seventh month."
>
> [. . .]
>
> I asked, "On those festival days do you put sakaki branches, rice, and sake on the *kami* altar, and is there anything else you offer?"
>
> Torakichi said, "There are no offerings except water."
>
> When he saw the iron bells I had hanging in front of my *kami* altar, Torakichi said, "Those bells are true orthodox bells." So I asked him, "Are *sanjin* bells made of iron?"
>
> Torakichi said, "We also have brass ones, but they say the iron bells are the ancient style."
>
> I asked, "Do you ring bells in front of the altar, and also, do you hang them in front of the *kami* altar?"

Torakichi said, "We only hang *waniguchi* [large flat bells] in front of the altars."

I asked, "Do you make *mudras* in front of the *kami* altars?"

Torakichi said, "We practice Ryōbu Shinto over there, so we do make *mudras* in front of the *kami* altars. And also, we use the self-protection *mudra* methods practiced by *yamabushi*."

I asked, "If it's Ryōbu, you must burn the goma fire in front of the altar. Is the wood you use *nurude* [Japanese lacquer tree]?"

Torakichi said, "We use other wood too, but we will use *nurude* first."[43]

The collection of rituals that define the religious activities of the nativist *sanjin* consist mainly of seasonal rituals familiar to the common Japanese people. Typical of all of Torakichi's descriptions of the Other World, they outwardly intend to be anti-Buddhist but ultimately are unable to exclude all Buddhist influence. They are particularly tinged with Esoteric Buddhist images and practices that no doubt had infiltrated deeply into the far reaches of common Japanese religious practices. In the end, Torakichi's personal religious training before he met Atsutane, which had considerable Buddhist content, could not be completely removed from his portrayal of the ideal *sanjin* even in his self-conscious, cautious, nativist-directed conversations with Atsutane.

Torakichi sometimes talked of *sanjin* ritual prayers that were conducted in fulfillment of their roles as mediums between the *kami* and the common people. The *sanjin* usually fulfilled those roles attached to certain mountains as their primary places of worship and practice, but they were also involved in mountain pilgrimages which took them all around Japan. Certain mountains and certain times of years proved to be of special importance to *sanjin* practice. Although Torakichi's master was said to be one of the thirteen *tengu* of Mt. Iwama, Torakichi claimed that his master often traveled to other mountains both within Japan and beyond. Torakichi claimed that although his master was associated with the thirteen *tengu*, his primary residence was on Mt. Asama in Shinano Province and his second residence was on Mt. Tsukuba in Hitachi Province. Torakichi also claimed that in the past, Sugiyama had lived on various mountains in a number of provinces in China. In fact, all the *sanjin* were said to be mobile like this and to have multiple residences.

When *sanjin* circulated they usually carried a document from their primary mountain on which they collected the names of other *sanjin* they met on the various mountains they visited. This was the *sanjin* way of keeping track of each other's locations and was important for the completion of their philanthropic mission of passing on prayers to the proper *kami*. When Torakichi's master was not on his primary mountain, he could still be informed of the people praying there by *sanjin* who visited there and heard the supplicants' prayers.

Torakichi said that recently certain mountains had become well-known for the existence of *sanjin*. He added that there were *sanjin* on every mountain, just as there were *kami* on every mountain. Although *sanjin* could carry out their duties more easily if there were fewer pilgrims seeking their mediation, having the *sanjin* presence known was good because it increased the worship of the *kami*. Nevertheless, when a mountain became known for its *sanjin* and thus attracted more pilgrims with prayers, this caused a need for more *sanjin* to work on that mountain. Torakichi said that because of this, sometimes his master was forced to make difficult staffing decisions about where to send the *sanjin* under his command.

The circulation of mysterious documents in the mountains had also become publicly known, and a question concerning these was first brought to Torakichi by a visitor to Atsutane's salon. This visitor claimed to have seen an actual *sanjin* seal on Mt. Zōzu. Torakichi claimed to be happy with the recent increase in the notoriety of *sanjin* activities among the people of the seen world, yet he lamented the ever-increasing burden for *sanjin* who dedicated their nearly eternal lives to helping humans communicate their prayers to the *kami*. Torakichi claimed that sometimes the solution for a single human problem would require his master to fly back and forth from place to place for distances of hundreds of miles at a time.

Torakichi gave an example of how the seasonal needs for increased *sanjin* labor at certain mountains caused personal loss and inconvenience for his master. In the winter, it was Sugiyama Sanjin's habit to perform a month-long ritual of harsh ascetic practices. However, the previous winter he had answered the call of duty at another mountain and so had forgone the practices that built up merit and supernatural potency in him. About that Torakichi said,

> Last year from the third day of the last month to the third day of this New Year, for the thirty days of the cold weather season, my master stayed at Mt. Zōzu as part of his mountain circuit. As I said earlier, there are many things going on at that mountain and many people with prayers to perform there during the cold season. Since it is a time with a particularly large amount of prayer requests, every year during the cold season many *sanjin* from numerous mountains in various provinces gather there in order to give their assistance. Not only *sanjin*, but also *tengu* that transform into birds and beasts gather to render assistance. Lord Kompira [44] is held up as

the leader of all *sanjin* and *tengu*. But it's not the same at every mountain. Every year in the cold season many *sanjin* make the mountain circuit. However, Lord Kompira's *sanjin* do not leave their primary mountain to make the mountain circuit as the *sanjin* of other mountains do.[45]

Atsutane also seemed quite interested in what Torakichi had to say in elaboration of a ritual dance called the *Shichishōmai*, The Dance of the Seven Lives, which he claimed was practiced by *sanjin* in the mountains. There are detailed drawings made from Torakichi's description of this dance that show dozens of similarly costumed *sanjin* dancing in circles, accompanied by other similarly clad *sanjin* playing various musical instruments. Atsutane's keen interest in the dance lay in its revelation of sacred and celebratory elements of *sanjin* culture. Besides the various musical instruments described by Torakichi, this dance was one of the few examples of *sanjin* artistic expression.[46]

There was also another exchange of questions on the subject of supernatural music heard by travelers in the mountains and mariners at sea. In the short work about Torakichi's supernatural knowledge titled *A Record of the Dance of the Seven Lives* (*Shichishōmai no ki*), this supernatural music was explained in the following exchange.

Then a certain person asked, "They say in the mountains some kind of music can be heard, and there are similar cases of that out at sea. This kind of music seems to be commonly called the 'Tengu Beat.' But I've long held the suspicion that it isn't just *tengu* but also *kami* immortals [*sanjin*] that do that kind of thing. Have you ever been a part of or seen this kind of musical performance?"

Torakichi said, "Those people probably heard the playing of the dance music for the Dance of the Seven Lives also called the Dance of the Columns.[47] If it's that dance music, then I've seen it a number of times."[48]

I [Atsutane] asked, "I was thinking that this dance was maybe a form of recreation, but the description makes it sound like an extremely pious ritual. What is the reason for performing this?"

Torakichi said, "This dance makes the Kami of Heaven and Earth extremely happy. All the *kami* respond when this dance is performed. And in just the opposite way it repels all varieties of ghosts and demons better than anything. Therefore the dance is performed when the *sanjin* want to appease and receive some response from all the *kami* or when they want to purify the mountain on which they live by driving away all the evil influences from it. I have heard that the performance perfectly expresses the principle of music and has the power to reverse the evil spirit of the ghosts and demons and replace it with the spirit of good." [49]

The music of this dance was reportedly so beautiful and soothing that animals, birds, and fish were all compelled to gather round and listen. The performance of this musical dance by approximately seventy *sanjin* epitomized the *sanjin's* religious role of bringing harmony to the entire world by driving away evil and promoting good relations with the *kami* of the world.

Senkyō ibun is unique for the descriptions of the appearance and actions of the nativist *sanjin* contained within its pages. Atsutane deliberately used his interviews with Torakichi as a means of defining his native Japanese religious hero and making a statement about his important religious functions. The *sanjin,* in performance of his many official rituals as well as in his daily mediation between human and *kami*, kept the world running smoothly while being as unobtrusive as possible. Atsutane was anxious to reveal and have Torakichi verify that Japan and its people had always depended on this religious figure, whether they knew it or not, and should continue to do so ever more consciously in the future.

Although Atsutane hated Buddhism and seemed to take every opportunity to disparage its image among his fellow Japanese, this hatred was in fact inspired largely by jealousy. He could never bring himself to admit how much he and his country owed to the originally Indian tradition for its contribution to the splendor and magnificence of Japanese culture. The Buddhist tradition's continuing role in formulating the identity of Japan was so pervasive that Atsutane himself did not realize to what extent his own actions were determined by Buddhist influence—and let there be no doubt he was profoundly influenced by Buddhism.

Atsutane's difficult and embarrassing relationship with Buddhism made it all the more important for his new hero, the *sanjin,* to be able to successfully compete with all the more prominent religious heroes of East Asia, especially the Buddhist heroes. Ironically, Atsutane was forced to draw from that tradition once again in order to surpass it. As much as he might hate Buddhism as something inferior, he clearly borrowed heavily from it in fleshing out his nativist savior.

Thus far, we have seen how Atsutane used his new medium Torakichi to justify his cultural and religious appropriation from nearby Asian cultures. As much as Torakichi was meant to embody an anti-Chinese and anti-Buddhist critique, he, like Atsutane, retained and reinforced Chinese and Buddhist knowledge and practice. Atsutane was not able to distance himself from the very cultures he claimed to reject. In the following chapter we will see how Atsutane fared against non-Asian cultures. We will see how Torakichi, the medium from the Other World, could be used to appropriate technology from the West and claim it as verification of the superiority of the Japanese people, grasping with one hand while pushing away with the other.

CHAPTER 6

The Critique of the West and Defense of Native Knowledge and Ability

Atsutane's Ambivalence toward the West

Atsutane's attitude toward Western knowledge was one of respect, but he was also compelled to remind his audience that no matter how fine Western knowledge was, the Westerner's character and habits were bestial at best and they were therefore not to be admired or emulated. Nevertheless, he felt that Western knowledge and technology could and should be appropriated by the Japanese, using the pretext that this knowledge originated in Japan and the *kami* had brought it back demanding that it be repatriated.

Atsutane displayed contempt for Europeans as a race and furthered the opinion that they were an entirely different and inferior type of animal. In the following passage he describes the current state of knowledge concerning the differences between the Japanese and Dutch anatomies:

> Their eyes are really just like those of a dog. They are long from the waist downwards, and the slenderness of their legs makes them resemble animals. When they urinate they lift one leg, the way dogs do. Moreover, apparently because the backs of their feet do not reach the ground, they fasten wooden heels to their shoes, which make them look all the more like dogs. This may also explain why a Dutchman's penis appears to be cut short at the end, just like a dog's.[1]

Nevertheless, when speaking of their cultural achievements, he could be complimentary, as in the following:

> Having a patient and deliberate national style, they [the Dutch] deeply consider the very root of things. Because of that way of thinking, they have made various measuring devices. For instance, for seeing the sun, moon, and planets, they made the telescope and the helioscope. In order to know size and distance, they made things like the theodolite.[2] In conducting their studies they take five or ten years, even up to a lifetime. What

they have considered and measured, they pass on in writing, recording as much as they know. Their followers, descendants or students, for generations, continue to study this.[3]

In another place he writes:

It goes without saying how accomplished they are in astronomy and geography; people have also been amazed by the precision of their machines. They are particularly skilled in medicine and the preparation of drugs. It has doubtless been the will of the *kami* that European medical books have been brought here in ever-increasing numbers and have attracted wide attention.[4]

One particular reason he was not ambivalent toward Western knowledge was because he was impressed by its proven accuracy and efficacy. However, there was another reason for praising Western culture, as can be seen in this passage:

[Holland] is an excellent country; they do not use slippery statements based on conjecture like the Chinese. Because of that, when it comes to affairs they cannot figure out even after thinking about them exhaustively, they say that these affairs are beyond the understanding of humans and so are called God's[5] affairs. They say without the working of the gods of heaven[6] they cannot be figured out. They do not make hasty guesses.[7]

Here we can see that Atsutane had learned that praise of the West could also have the advantage of including a harsh criticism of other more familiar and traditional enemies. We can also see that what he is praising about the West in this passage is theologically consistent with his assertion of the ultimate superiority of the *kami*.

Atsutane's stated opinion was that the West held superiority in science that the Japanese *kami* had recently decided to bring back to Japan. He further recognized that this superior science could be good for the Japanese to learn. However, the above quotation that the *kami* had prompted the Europeans to bring the scientific knowledge to Japan came from an Atsutane work published in 1811. This pious assertion would later be dropped for something more suitable to his nativist agenda. In 1820 Atsutane met Torakichi and started his new supernatural inquiries into Japan's Other World. As a result of his new methods of investigation, Atsutane claimed to have discovered not only an addendum to his theology, but also a native

technological wizard and genius inventor. He discovered a way to argue
that native Japanese scientific knowledge did not have to take a back seat
to the technological wonders of the West.

Sanjin as Multitalented Multitasker

By 1822, in *Senkyō ibun*, Atsutane was to claim that he had found evidence
that people in the mountains, the *sanjin,* had knowledge and technology
that rivaled and was in fact superior to Western knowledge and technology. *Kami* did not need to bring Western knowledge in as he had claimed
earlier; it was already in Japan. Atsutane's writings also provide a glimpse
of early modern Western influence on Japanese religion, specifically Atsutane's brand of Ancient Way Shinto. The study of *Senkyō ibun* offers an
opportunity to move away from politically dominated analyses of Atsutane
and the West and toward one with a religious studies focus, for example,
one that highlights the *sanjin* as a Japanese religious culture hero who
responds to Western stimuli.

In *Senkyō ibun*, Torakichi describes the *sanjin* as being proficient
in many technologies. First of all, the *sanjin* were well-traveled and very
knowledgeable about world geography. In their mountain pilgrimages the
sanjin toured all the mountains of Japan, along with some famous mountains in China and India. Torakichi also claimed to have knowledge of several strange lands whose names he did not know. He said he had visited a
place he called the Island of Women, and another land where people wore
outfits that made them look like dogs. He even claimed to have visited
lands where people worshiped a man dying on a cross and pictures of a
mother and child.[8]

The *sanjin*'s penchant for travel also took him off the planet Earth,
which would have made the *sanjin* the ultimate authority on astronomy.
Even if the Copernican revolution was an important event in the West,
according to Torakichi, it was nothing new to the *sanjin*. Torakichi knew
the earth was round because he had seen it from outer space. He had traveled to the moon and declared that there actually were large holes that
went all the way through it. He had also visited the sun and had flown
around distant stars. He knew the different layers of the atmosphere and
also commented on the different temperatures of the celestial places he
had visited.

Torakichi described the *sanjin* as being trained in the martial arts.
He described them as proficient in hand-to-hand combat and said they
were experts with Japanese traditional weaponry; that is, swords, spears,

staves, and bows and arrows. In addition, he said the *sanjin* had firearms whose technology surpassed ordinary and currently known technology. One of these types of ballistic weapons was the long-range cannon, powered by "air" technology. Even though the *sanjin* were not usually found in armies, Torakichi claimed they were also well-versed in large-scale military strategy.

In addition to these skills, the *sanjin* were also supposed to be creative inventors. Torakichi described a wide variety of fantastic machinery found only in the mountains. Torakichi, when presented with some new type of machinery, could usually come up with some example of a similar if not a better device invented and used by the *sanjin*. The *sanjin* technology also included musical devices such as music boxes along with standard musical instruments.

For Atsutane, Torakichi's placement of these technologies in the hands of the *sanjin* in the mountains made them originally if not exclusively the property of the Japanese. As native Japanese technology, they supported the argument for Japanese superiority against all possible competitors. This impressive array of *sanjin* technology could have been used in an argument against China, but it would be a more appropriate answer to Western challenges to Japanese scientific and technological ability.

Earlier it was noted that Atsutane had two responses to Western influences. One was to appropriate it and justify the appropriation by claiming the technology to be originally Japanese. Atsutane's approval of Torakichi's tales of the technologically oriented *sanjin* is an example of the first response. The second response, which was to reject all contact, surfaced when Atsutane wrote about the *sanjin*'s military ability and his role in the military defense of the nation, which included avowed support of the current ruling government of Japan.

Astronomy and the *Sanjin*

Many Japanese intellectuals, not only nativists like Atsutane, recognized a knowledge gap between Japan and the West in most scientific fields. One of these fields was astronomy. Atsutane's acceptance of the superior Western astronomy is evident. He writes:

> Our great land is floating on a round object. Undeniable proof of this is the fact that if you take a boat east from here, you will eventually arrive from the west. That clearly proves the round earth theory." [9]

Elsewhere he writes:

> The heavenly sun rose up and was fixed squarely in position in the direct
> center of the great heavens. It stays in one place without moving to another.
> . . . This is the situation of the sun in the heavens. The earth floats in the
> great heavens and revolves to the right, far away from the heavenly sun in
> the center of the orbit. One revolution takes one year.[10]

After this passage he goes on to explain the earth's rotations and the phases
and revolution of the moon in a way quite similar, if not exactly the same,
to the way most people today might describe it.

Atsutane claims that heliocentric theory had become well-known
among the Japanese populace early in the eighteenth century. For this, he
credits a Japanese named Nishikawa Joken (1648–1724), who had been an
official in Nagasaki, where he had access to the latest in Dutch studies.

> The person who first brought the science of astronomy to this country and
> spread it publicly was Nagasaki's Nishikawa Kyūrinsai. Being a person
> of the Genroku period, before this time astronomy and the geography of
> all the foreign countries were completely unknown. The Japanese were
> immature in this aspect of sciences and no one knew about them, so he
> published *Questions on Astronomy Answered (Tenkei wakumon).*[11] In addi-
> tion to that he wrote *An Examination of Commerce Between China and
> the Barbarians (Kai tsūshōkō),*[12] about the customs of foreign countries,
> which he proceeded to make public. Besides this he has many other writ-
> ings. Due to these efforts the Japanese public came to learn many things
> about foreign countries.[13]

This was Atsutane's personal understanding of the popular introduction of heliocentric theory to Japan. Others would put it about a century
later, in 1796, when Shiba Kōkan published his *Dutch Astronomy (Oranda
tensetsu),* a manual with pictorial explication. Previous translations of
Dutch astronomy texts had been restricted to the Tokugawa government's
astronomy department.[14]

Although Atsutane accepted important aspects of Copernican theory,
much of it had to be reworked to fit the cosmogony he first wrote of in
The August Pillar of the Soul. In this work he presents a creation story
that has the world generated by Japanese *kami.* However, instead of the
flat universe, he presents one with three dimensions and three major
physical bodies: the sun, the earth, and the moon. He associates Japanese
mythological formations with these three bodies in an attempt to prove
that Western astronomy does not contradict traditional Japanese mythology but rather merely demands a new reading and interpretation of the

ancient texts. This new cosmogony also provided an opportunity to revise his theology and his theories on the ultimate destination of the soul.

Atsutane accepted some Western astronomy, first because it was proving irrefutable and becoming popular and second because it gave him a strong position from which to present new theological points. Some of the information he received from Torakichi simply confirmed the Western theory, but in a way that Westerners never could. That is to say, Torakichi claimed to have observed firsthand that the earth was round, having seen it from the distance of the moon and beyond. He also claimed to have seen the moon up close. The following exchange between Atsutane and Torakichi not only was supposed to trump Western scientific knowledge of the moon, but also their methods of investigation.

> Atsutane asked, "When you flew up to the stars, what did the moon look like?"
>
> Torakichi said, "As you approach the moon it gets bigger and bigger, and the cold air starts to really cut into you, so I thought it would be impossible to land there, but finally we were able to get a good look from a place about two *chō* square, where we landed, and it was unexpectedly warm. Anyway, in the places where the moon appears to be shining, there is something like the oceans we have on our land, and they appear to have mud mixed in with them. In the place where there is commonly thought to be a rabbit pounding *mochi*, there are two or three open holes. But then we left right away, so I don't know their shapes exactly."
>
> Atsutane said, "You said that the shiny part of the moon is like the sea we have here. I recall that Westerners have speculated that that was the case. However, I do not quite see how there could be holes in the place where the rabbit pounds *mochi*. I have heard that in that area, there are mountains like we have here."
>
> Torakichi laughed and said, "Your theory is flawed because it's based on information you found in a book. I don't know about books; I speak from seeing it up close. Even my master had said there were mountains there, but when we got close and looked, there really were two or three holes, and through those holes we could see the stars behind the moon." [15]

There was some controversy when Torakichi was asked about his firsthand experience with stars. Atsutane asked him what stars were, and Torakichi replied that they were actually vapor with a small solid core. He knew this because he and his master had flown through one, and he speculated that the Milky Way was a large number of small stars surrounded by water vapor that appeared as wispy white shards.

Atsutane had trouble with this explanation, so he had Torakichi tell this same story to a student he considered an expert on the makeup of the universe, Satō Nobuhiro. Nobuhiro explained his conviction that the substance of the star was the same as the substance of the earth; that is, a solidified thick heavy mud. Because of that, he insisted that it could not be penetrated any more than the earth could. Furthermore, Nobuhiro added, the light that appears to shine from stars does not come from them. Stars merely reflect the radiance of the sun. According to Nobuhiro, if one could see the earth from a distance, it would appear to shine like a star, because the reflective water vapor in the atmosphere causes all celestial bodies to shine. He claimed that the reflective quality of the earth's atmosphere could be proven by the fact that there is light in the morning and evening, even before the sun has risen and after it has set.

Nobuhiro's pronouncements were taken as hard scientific fact, but they did not seek to debunk Torakichi. Nobuhiro suggested that what they flew through was the water vapor atmosphere. Atsutane agreed this was reasonable, but thought another possible explanation might be that the supernatural powers of Torakichi's *sanjin* master may have included the ability to pass through stars.

Then Atsutane asked Torakichi if he had seen what the sun was made of. Torakichi claimed they had tried, but the intensity of the flames kept them away. Once Torakichi and his master climbed up to some high ground and looked at the sun through a telescope of sorts. He said that they saw electrical flashes shooting around, and flames dying out and then flaming up again.

Atsutane asked Torakichi if he had not spoken of the thirty-three heavens at Yoshishige's house, claiming they had specific colors that corresponded to them. This was another chance for Torakichi to deny any pro-Buddhist talk that Yoshishige attributed to him in his book *Heiji Daitō* and that other salon visitors also claimed to have heard from him. Torakichi immediately denied the suggestion that he had confirmed the existence of the thirty-three heavens, calling this just another Buddhist lie.

Torakichi claimed the high ground because of his actual experience of deep space, arguing that from that vantage point he certainly would have seen the thirty-three heavens had they existed. As for the colors, Torakichi claimed that when flying, if he spit, then through the spit the colors red, yellow, and blue, divided as in a prism, would be visible. Atsutane included a note to this story to affirm confirmation by Western scientific sources. He claimed that some of those Western sources also held that the three primary colors red, yellow, and blue could be seen in the sky.

Torakichi was once asked about the planets. He commented that the bright white star that shone just before the sun came out was mistakenly thought to be the Indian god Marishiten. Torakichi denied the existence of any such god. To confirm the justness of this dismissal, he described a common Marishiten practice that was thought to ward off evil, offering to perform it to show how ineffective it was.

Torakichi's talk of astronomy allowed him to articulate more on the importance of the sun in the grand scheme of things. Of course, the central importance of the sun as the great *kami* Amaterasu Omikami lay behind this cosmological explanation. To further aggrandize that *kami*, Torakichi claimed that all fire was originally the sun's fire, and he further asserted that all things, whether stone, metal, or wood, had fire within them. In other words, the energy source for all activities in the world was the fire of Amaterasu. Of course, a nativist variation of the ancient Chinese theory of the five phases can be seen at work here.

Torakichi also used that five phases theory to explain atmospheric phenomena. For example, he explained that thunder was the result of the interaction between the elements of fire and water in the sky. Torakichi claimed that in the summer, the sky held more of the fire element than usual, and when water-filled clouds surrounded the fire element, they would compress it and cause it to suddenly break out of the water element's confinement. This interaction during storms caused rain, or droplets of the water element, and lightning, or the compressed fire element breaking loose. These two formations were of course accompanied by the loud noise of the explosion of the fire element. Torakichi concluded that thunder was a necessary natural phenomenon, and although many people considered it to be evil, it actually contributed to the well-being of all the people.

If one were to change a few of the words of that description to something like positive and negative ions interacting in the sky during the summer, the explanation is not that absurdly different from things said today explaining thunder and lightning. However, Atsutane's follow-up question to the thunder explanation concerned a certain beast, the thunder beast,[16] which was said to land on earth with the lightning. Torakichi said he knew of this beast and had actually seen it from a vantage point above the storm. He claimed it was a wild and violent beast that loved riding the lightning. An interesting added detail was that the white variety of the thunder beast left something known as thunder dung wherever it landed.

When Torakichi was asked about the coloration of clouds, the conversation took a scientific turn back to something that might be considered pseudo-optics. Atsutane suggested the theory that clouds came in a variety of colors, namely, purple, red, blue, and black. This was not refuted by

Torakichi, but he could only explain two of the colors. Red, he said, was due to the reflection of the sun and black was due to the thickness of the clouds.

The next question moved to the reason for earthquakes. Torakichi did not claim to know the cause of earthquakes, but he made a point of denying the story of the giant catfish under the earth that shook his body in attempts to destroy the earth. After that he was asked about tidal activity and its causes. On this issue too Torakichi claimed ignorance, but still suggested that it was not the ocean, but rather the land that rose or sunk at certain times during the day and night.

The next question was about something like directional science, which could also be a general question about the cause of certain natural phenomena. Torakichi was asked if in the Other World the direction of the ox and tiger, northeast, was considered to be unlucky because it was the direction of the gate of demons. The follow-up question was if the other directional beliefs in the Other World were the same as those in this world. Torakichi's answer was that some were the same and some were different. In other words, some of this world's beliefs were right and some were wrong.

In summary, the questions in this exchange moved from the stars to the earth, from astronomy to seismology. However, scattered among these questions were queries concerning legendary creatures and traditional forms of divination. This whole complex of questions reveals Atsutane's type of nineteenth-century investigation into natural science. The investigation moved seamlessly back and forth from what the contemporary reader might see as the scientific to the pseudo-scientific and the mythological. Clear lines between different types of knowledge, and the validity of those types of knowledge, have not been drawn.

Geography and the *Sanjin*

In Atsutane's antiforeign arguments based on racist environmental determinist principles, he depended upon geographical information obtained from Western sources. He used the knowledge of geography he obtained from Nishikawa Joken, whom he cited as a Western authority, to denigrate China and India and their respective peoples. He claimed that China's vast geographical diversity had created many different peoples with varying temperaments within her borders. In addition, he claimed that China had been placed in a region easily accessible and thus easily invaded. Because of these geographical features, he concluded that China's land did not nurture a stable moral character, which was shown by the repeated changes in dynasties when rebellious subordinates overthrew their superiors. Accordingly, China's abundance of ethical and philosophical teachings existed because of its people's lack of inborn ethical character that, according to Atsutane, was actually caused by China's location in the world. In short, the inferior land had created inferior people.

India was also harshly criticized by Atsutane, again based on his pseudo-scientific environmental determinism:

> The darkies of the tropical countries like India are raised by nature. They grow up on their own, surviving on plants. Their lives are completely the same as that of birds and beasts.[17]

He further claimed that in Shakyamuni's time there were thousands of cases of unfilial sons and patricide. Therefore, if Shakyamuni was a prince among these kinds of people, he was no one to look up to.[18] Once again, Atsutane's conclusion was that inferior land had created inferior people.[19]

Japan, of course, received a different evaluation based on this pseudo-scientific environmental determinism.

> The capital in the center of Japan is thirty-some degrees from the equator. The eastern end of Japan is thirty-eight or thirty-nine degrees, and the western end is thirty-one or thirty-two degrees. This is why the climates of the four seasons are standard and harmonious. When comparing Japan to India and China, even though Japan is small, a country's value is not determined by size, but by the regularity of the four seasons. The people's inherent virtue determines their nobility or baseness. Because of this, if a country's land is extremely large, the character and customs of the people are many and varied, and therefore difficult to unify.
>
> The ruling line in China is often changing and in disarray, and it is difficult to stabilize for long periods of time. The size of Japan is neither too large nor too small. The customs and habits of the masses are shared and unified, so the people are easy to regulate and rule. This is why from the time of creation to the present day the Japanese imperial line has never changed. Of all the countries of the world, only Japan has been this way. Indeed, is this due to anything other than the divine wonder of our environment? . . . The quality of the naturally protective environment is the best in the world. . . . The masses of people are descendants of the *kami*, and their way is the inherited teachings of the *kami*. The people love the pure and untainted and appreciate the simple and unadorned. Their way is benevolent and brave, and their wisdom is self-sufficient. This is due to the inherent divine virtue of Japan.[20]

These conclusions are Atsutane's excerpted quotes from Joken, but in essence and practice, this is Atsutane's own explanation of national characters; in this case Atsutane chose to quote an authority rather than just give his own opinion. Moreover, the use of the authority in this case is meant to serve Atsutane's claim that these sentiments were originally the observations of Dutch explorers, not those of Japanese chauvinists. This claim is of course suspect.

Still, while this new Western knowledge was useful in belittling Neo-Confucians and Buddhists, in its unadulterated form it was also potentially dangerous to nativists. Therefore, Western knowledge had to be co-opted and controlled; it had to be used in specific ways. It could not be thrown out or ignored, but had to be tamed and twisted. As we saw above, Atsutane could twist this Western knowledge far enough so it could be used to defend nativism against Western-inspired criticism. For example, he claimed the ethically superior Japanese people had a naturally admirable character because the *kami* had placed them in the most favorable location. These conclusions of environmental determinism came equipped with Western geographical terminology and longitude and latitude demarcations. Western geographical science was being used to support Atsutane's attempt to divide the globe into parts that produced humans with superior and inferior traits.

Atsutane's recognition of the superiority of Western knowledge came with different strategies to alleviate this embarrassing concession. One strategy was to grant superior knowledge to the Westerner, but to attribute it to a flaw in their national character. For example, the reason people in the West were so knowledgeable about world geography was partly because their own lands were not satisfactory and could not support the people, forcing them to move into other people's territories. He further claimed that this exacerbated an inherent flaw in their character that predisposed them to act as greedy, violent thieves.

A second strategy used to counter apparent Western superiority in geography required the new, well-traveled *sanjin* to give evidence of a basic and original Japanese superiority. To this end, *Senkyō ibun* provided several examples of the *sanjin*'s travels to strange lands all over the globe. One of the first travels Torakichi related was, of course, in the company of the flying *sanjin*, his master Sugiyama. He claimed they flew north to a land Atsutane said was called the Land of Night. Torakichi called it Hot-suku no Ju no Kuni.[21] He went there in the summertime but even then the sun was very small, and it was very cold. Torakichi compared the amount of available sunlight to a solar eclipse where as much as 80 percent of the sunlight is blocked out. The nights were very long and the moon was not visible. The people there had dug many ditches in the earth and filled them with water to get some extra light from the reflection off the water.

Torakichi said the land seemed to be suitable for cereal agriculture, and he specifically mentioned wheat and rice. They had trees and grass, and they covered their pathways with straw. The people themselves were not quite the same as Japanese. They appeared generally thin and withered, tall with small heads. They had large noses and big mouths, but the strangest feature of all was that each of their limbs had two thumbs on it. He did not remember their clothing, but he remembered that they lived in caves, not houses.

Atsutane's geographical research taken from Western sources show the lands south of Japan to be too hot, leading to defects in the national characters of their inhabitants. This example of a visit to a northern land also confirmed that lands north of Japan were not as good as Japan. In this instance, the nights were too long, the climate was too cold, and the result was some kind of mutant human being. If not for the multiple-thumb description, the human in the northern land could resemble the Japanese opinion of what a European would look like.

Following that conversation, Atsutane inquired further about Torakichi's esoteric geographical knowledge.

Torakichi's description of the northern land was incomplete, he said, because he only stayed there a few days. After that, he and his master flew off to the Island of Women. The description of this land is particularly strange.

Torakichi said, "In the sea four hundred *ri* to the east of Japan there is the Island of Women. The inhabitants did not build houses; instead they lived in caves in the sides of the mountains. The openings were narrow but the interiors were quite large. They bent trees across the entryways and made roofs of seaweed over them to keep out the rain. They looked the same as Japanese women. They bound up their hair in bundles. They made their clothes from something that looked like the wrappings on sword handles and wore them in a closefitting fashion. For food they would dive into the sea to catch fish and gather seaweed. When they came out they shook their bodies and the water just seemed to slide off their clothes. I heard that the material for their clothes was impervious to flame. Also, they would gather thick bunches of seaweed the size of a human thigh, and then split those open to collect the slimy water from inside. They boiled that down to make a bracken *mochi*-like thing that they ate. Anyway, since it was the Island of Women, they craved men. When a man happened to paddle up they would attack him and eat him. In order to get pregnant they would hold bundles of bamboo grass in their hands and pray facing the west. Then the women would pair off and lay with each other. These acts [mating performances] occurred at fixed intervals. I lay hidden in that land for a whole ten days watching how they did things.[22]

When it came to imaginary geography, Torakichi could deny as well as confirm. Once he was asked if he had visited the mountain called Shumisen. Torakichi said his master told him it did not exist. The master said that if the Buddhist theory was correct and the mountain was actually eighty thousand *yujun*[23] high, then the base would have to be at least that if not bigger, and so it was impossible in all his travels that he had never seen it. Since Torakichi's master had taken him to the stars, he was certain that if it existed he would have seen it from that height. Torakichi and Atsutane used the *sanjin*'s superior geographical knowledge to disprove Buddhist cosmology.

Torakichi did not stop at attempting to discredit the story of the central Buddhist mountain; he also tried to discredit the ideas of Buddhist paradises and hells, which means he was attempting to use geography to disprove Buddhist soteriology.

> Torakichi laughed and said, "My master says that the things called hell and paradise are childlike fictions created to gain control over foolish people, particularly the stories about paradise which say there are ten trillion worlds[24] somewhere around the earth. I went way up in the sky with my master and we visited all the faraway places. We saw that the earth is round and it rotates, and nowhere nearby are the ten trillion worlds."[25]

Torakichi was asked the nature of his master's business when he visited "barbarian" nations, but he claimed ignorance of this. He did mention that his master often met with the residents of the barbarian lands and was able to communicate with them. Torakichi's stories of foreign and exotic travel also inspired stories of imaginary geography from his visitors that were sometimes equally fantastic but of course not backed up with firsthand visitation experience.

Sanjin Inventions

As mentioned at the beginning of this chapter, Atsutane could not help but admit that Western machinery had impressed the Japanese people. This is, of course, not to say that mechanical inventions came only from European sources. Nevertheless, Atsutane realized that the West was perceived to have an advantage in that specific field of scientific development. The interviews with Torakichi granted Atsutane the opportunity to provide evidence that would serve to counter that perceived advantage. Through Torakichi's stories, Atsutane learned that the native Japanese *sanjin* were very creative and had developed on their own a great many rare mechanical devices, some of which resembled Western mechanical devices and some of which were uniquely Japanese inventions.

On one occasion Atsutane brought in something that had magnetic properties. Torakichi rubbed the object with a nail and demonstrated that the nail then attracted iron filings. Atsutane asked Torakichi how magnetism worked. Torakichi's explanation came from Chinese philosophy, saying it was dependent upon *qi*, that is, basic vapor or spirit that was the essential energy of the universe. He explained that iron was endowed with the innate property of attracting objects. When the vapor or spirit that composed that property of attraction solidified, that solid object became a magnet that took the form of a stone (lodestone). He further claimed that the core of the earth was iron and that the vapor or spirit of that element had also solidified in great quantity in the north, where there were mountains of lodestone. Thus, magnets in compasses point north due to the massive lodestone mountains there.

Atsutane then asked if the *sanjin* used compasses when they flew.

> Torakichi said, "They always carry them and use them. Moreover, the compasses that were made in Japan were taken to distant lands, and now they are used all over the world. This fact is not common knowledge." [26]

In short, the compass was originally Japanese technology that was exported to foreign countries. It certainly did not originate in those countries no matter how expert and familiar the foreigners may have been with its uses. The theme here, prompted by Atsutane's leading questions and confirmed by Torakichi, was that there was no technology used in other lands that did not originate in Japan except for technology that developed in those lands to compensate for inferior character or physical nature.

The well water around Yoshishige's house in Tokyo was poor in quality, so he asked Torakichi how to dig a well that would produce an abundant flow of good pure water. Torakichi gave directions like a well-construction engineer. Atsutane recorded the detailed instructions for drilling through soft and hard surfaces and for building the supports for the sides. The explanation also included detailed pictures. Along with the engineering instructions, there were instructions for magical assistance in maintaining water flow and purity. Bits of crocodile skin and black powder were to be placed in the bottom of the well to ensure continuity of flow. A mirror was to be placed in the bottom for purification purposes. In addition, lacquered bowls weighted down with rock were also recommended for their powers of purification.

As we can see from these two examples, *sanjin* know-how covered a variety of technical fields. The compass served for exploration and navigation, while the well-digging techniques benefited the world by tending to the daily needs of the common person. Both of these types of know-how were regularly employed in Japanese human society. But there was another type of *sanjin* technology never before seen in Japanese or Western human society, but apparently used in the society of the *sanjin*.

Torakichi claimed there was a device in the Other World called a "Thought Releasing Platform." The complete drawing was unfortunately lost from the text, but a sketch of one of the parts remains. It was described as looking like a *go* board, with the major part of the structure made of hardwood. The legs were also like the legs of a *go* board, but each of the legs had a part made of glass that contained an oil and water mixture. In the box-like structure on top of the legs was a small *koto*. There was a dial on the side of the box that was to be spun with one's right hand, causing the *koto* to play.

Torakichi said he would climb in the box and sit on the wooden platform. With his left hand he would hold on to metal chains attached on the inside, and with his right hand he would turn the dial while blocking out all superfluous thoughts to concentrate on one thing. He was supposed to concentrate solely on the idea he was hoping to receive. No one else could turn the dial or there would be no benefit from the machine.

How this machine worked was impossible to understand or to explain. It was technology developed long ago in the Age of the Kami. Torakichi's master explained to him that the stored wisdom of the world was not yet completely known to the human world, and only by understanding the knowledge of antiquity could one comprehend the workings of this machinery. In other words, current Japanese, Chinese, Indian, or even Western science was not even close to coming up with the marvels created in the ancient times in Japan.

Not all the inventions from the Other World had purposes that were cerebral and exalted as did the "Thought Releasing Platform." Torakichi drew a picture of a metal machine used for making hot water. The machine had two valves and two poles as the only moving parts. The valves were adjusted and the poles were turned, and water was heated without any need for fire.

On one occasion Atsutane took Torakichi to visit Yamada Hiromaru, a collector of novelties who had expressed an interest in meeting Torakichi. Yamada was especially well-known for his collection of rare instruments, among them a novelty from the West called an *orugōru,* a mechanical music box from Holland. Upon examination Torakichi claimed that this was not the first time he had seen such a thing. He said that devices like this music box were made in the Other World. Yamada asked how it was made, and Torakichi said they put six flute pipes inside an iron box. They then put water in the box and when they boiled that water in the box, the flutes whistled.

This episode shows how versatile Torakichi was and how wide-ranging was his knowledge, and it also served to reinforce Atsutane's assertion that there was nothing the Westerner could make that did not have its counterpart or its original model somewhere in the Other World in Japan. The *sanjin* also made a variety of other musical instruments, but they were not objects for mere amusement such as the music box. They were things like flutes, drums, *koto,* and gongs that were to be used in sacred *kami* rituals.

The *Sanjin*'s Military Prowess and Responsibilities

Atsutane recorded that at the first showing of Torakichi at his house, Kunitomo Yoshimasa attended and was intent on asking Torakichi many questions. Kunitomo was associated with the Hirata School, but was best known as a gunsmith and an inventor. He was from Kunitomo Village in Ōmi Province, and for generations his family had worked for the bakufu. After seeing a Dutch model for an air-powered firearm, he designed something similar. He also built a reflecting telescope with which he was able to observe sunspots.

> At some point during that meeting he [Torakichi] was asked if they [the *tengu/sanjin*] had guns over there [in the Other World], and he said that they had the same kinds that we have here [in this world], both large ones and small ones, except they were decorated differently. Then Torakichi added that they also had air-powered rifles. I [Atsutane] and others who had recently been surprised by Kunitomo's work about air-powered projectiles[27] were even more surprised to learn of it. When I glanced over at Kunitomo I could see how excited he was. We both shared an interest in inquiring further about the guns of the immortals.[28]

After this Atsutane wrote how lucky it was for all of them that Kunitomo was there, because a certain expertise was needed to ask intelligent questions about these matters, and the conversation was over his head. If not for Kunitomo, Atsutane added, none of them would be aware of the guns in the immortal realm. Kunitomo asked detailed questions, and sketches of guns were made from the details he learned. The inhabitants of the Other World, whether one called them *sanjin* or *tengu*, were equipped with the latest in ballistic technology, at least the latest that the educated Japanese were knowledgeable of.

When Torakichi returned from the mountains and came to stay at Atsutane's house, Atsutane wrote that Kunitomo in particular was very pleased, since he had thought the boy might be gone for quite a long time, if not forever. He had not asked all the questions about the firearms of the Other World, so he was anxious for another chance to interview the boy. On their second meeting, Kunitomo brought his prototype of the air rifle with him to show to Torakichi. Atsutane wrote that they discussed firearms in the Other World again and Torakichi ended up sharing a lot of new information.

According to Torakichi, the *sanjin* were trained in modern military science and used advanced weaponry that equaled if not surpassed that of the Western nations, but they also retained native martial arts traditions. This was affirmed when Atsutane brought up the legend that the young Ushiwakamaru, Minamoto Yoshitsune, had learned martial arts from a *tengu* on Mt. Kurama, and he asked Torakichi if *sanjin* were not also trained in traditional martial arts. Torakichi explained that his specific group's training center was on Mt. Kaba. He said they were trained in sword fighting, staff fighting, and stone throwing. The training technique described by Torakichi was as amazing as it was unbelievable.

> Torakichi said, "When you first start to practice sword fighting, you put some beans in your mouth and blow them out one at a time, cutting them in two in the air with the long sword. After you cut a thousand beans, you start blowing them out two at a time, cutting both in half. Later on you would blow three or four out at a time and cut them all in half using two swords. After acquiring great skill by mastering this practice, you would actually put on armor and cross swords for real." [29]

For the staff-fighting practice, they would start by memorizing various forms until they had them down to perfection. Then they would train against an opponent. For the stone-throwing training, someone with a stone would face someone with a sword and try his best to hit the person holding the sword in the face, but the person with the sword could always block it. Torakichi saved himself from any martial arts demonstrations by saying he had only watched the martial arts training and learned a little stone throwing.

In addition, according to Torakichi, the *sanjin* in the Other World were skilled in the use of the bow and arrow. They used large bows and half-size bows. The construction of the bow and arrow was generally the same as it is in this world, but some of the arrows were hollowed out like pipes, while others had only two feathers. Another difference was that the *sanjin* did not usually practice with stationary targets. One person wore protective clothing and ran around erratically while the person with the bow and arrow tried to shoot him. Torakichi said that a successful hit with an arrow occurred only rarely, and fortunately for that unlucky *sanjin*, the practice arrow was blunted with a round nut. He added that if the *sanjin* were to use a stationary target, they would hit it one hundred times out of one hundred tries. Torakichi also explained and drew pictures of a variety of arrows used for hunting or fighting and added that sometimes for practice the swordsmen or staff fighters would face the bowmen and try to knock down the various flying projectiles.

Atsutane also brought up sumo wrestling as a martial art form. He had heard that in the past, veritable armies of wrestlers would fight each other. He also asked about *jūjutsu* and horseback riding, but Torakichi seemed to have reached the limit of his knowledge on these subjects. He simply stated that sumo, although amusing, was not to his knowledge a martial art of the Other World, and neither was *jūjutsu* or horseback riding. He suggested that anyone with a kind and good spirit was surely capable of riding any wild horse.

Atsutane asked if the swords in the Other World were single- or double-edged. Torakichi answered that they used both types. He added that his master always carried a sword, and this is depicted in some of the surviving drawings of Sugiyama. Torakichi said he secretly handled this sword once when his master had gone out on an errand. When his master returned unexpectedly, he discovered Torakichi with the sword and scolded him severely. Torakichi also affirmed that his master had many guns, but they were all noiseless because they used air power rather than firepower. *Senkyō ibun* contains a drawing of the gun with some sparse detail of the mechanisms.

On another occasion Kunitomo was over again, quizzing Torakichi about arms and the Other World.

Kunitomo Yoshimasa asked a question that had been posed to him saying, "Since the *sanjin* have such a variety of weapons and skill in the martial arts, it seems like they could help us out with our military preparations.

Should we not erect shrines to this Sugiyama Sanjin along the coastline and worship him as a *kami* of defense against attacks by foreign nations? What do you think?"[30]

Torakichi's response to this question revealed that part of the raison d'etre of the *sanjin* was to do just such a thing.

Torakichi said, "It does not matter to them in the Other World whether or not anyone prays to them for that, because they would defend the populace in the event of any attack by a foreign nation anyway. They have thoroughly studied the weapons, tactics, and even large-scale campaign strategy needed to ward off attackers and drive them back. Anyway, I was instructed when I came down from the mountains to be secretive and deceptive, so I cannot give details about my master's name and whereabouts. Therefore I cannot divulge any information about how to pray to and worship him."[31]

According to this claim, the *kami* who saved Japan from Mongol invaders in the thirteenth century had modified their tactics and turned over the defense of Japan to their official go-betweens, the *sanjin*. Torakichi clearly contended that the *sanjin* took it as their duty to defend the Japanese nation from foreign invaders.

Although the *sanjin* were committed to serving and protecting the Japanese populace, they were not a revolutionary force protecting the masses from oppressive government.

[The *sanjin*] revere the emperor and the shogun just like humans revere *kami*. [Torakichi's] master claims it is only natural that the shogun should be revered, because the shogun has been commissioned to pacify all the lands, and rule and bless the people of this world. In this way they are similar to the *kami*. Like them, the *kami* by nature cannot help but protect the people of the world. The more reverence they receive, the more their authority grows and the better they protect the world. The *sanjin* are placed between *kami* and humans. They conduct the business of the *kami* and therefore can do nothing other than revere the lord [emperor] who reigns over the world.[32]

The *sanjin* were committed to saving the Japanese from the non-Japanese, but as a military force they would not stand against the powers that be. Atsutane and Torakichi, along with the *sanjin*, were not willing to get involved in a debate concerning domestic politics. As for international politics, Torakichi did not concern himself much with the question of Western invasion; he seemed confident the situation was in good hands.

In addition, according to Torakichi, in times of internal strife the emperor and shogun were both protected by these spiritual guardians.

> When the land is filled with strife, *sanjin* and *tengu* perform austerities and pray to the august *kami* of the Way of Heaven. In times of emergency, it goes without saying that they leave Nikkō and the other mountains to protect and patrol the Imperial Palace and Edo Castle.[33]

The *sanjin* had enough Buddhists and sinophiles to fight without acting as social reformers or angering the government. That also seemed to be Atsutane's sentiment, although he eventually did anger the Tokugawa authorities enough to earn censorship and exile.

From Defense of Japan to Defense of Japanese Superiority

In 1807, early in Atsutane's career and a year after he had been officially recognized as a student in Norinaga's academy, he edited a work he titled *White Waves of the Kuriles: Maps Appended* (*Chishima no shiranami: fuchizu*). This work, as the first line in the preface declared, was written in direct and immediate response to threats of Western contact and encroachment upon Japanese soil.

> This book was written because last year in 1806 Russians suddenly came to the islands of Ezo [Hokkaidō] with hostile intentions. After that, barbarians called the English came rudely and uninvited to Tsukushi's Nagasaki.[34]

Atsutane continued on to say that the work was a collection of data and stories from a variety of informants, including people who had firsthand information about the aforementioned events and therefore important information about this new enemy. Atsutane and fellow scholar Yashiro Hirokata both felt this information should be passed on immediately to all their students, primarily to dispel the false rumors and misinformation that had been circulating about the incidents and the Westerners themselves. Atsutane wanted to tell the true story, complete with illustrations and maps. His insistence upon clarifying the situation suggests that many people were shaken by this contact and that the images of the Westerners and their power had grown quite menacing. Atsutane used the incidents as an opportunity to repeat the *kokugaku* line about Japanese superiority.

However, in regard to national defense, this early work stands in sharp contrast to what he would write fifteen years later in *Senkyō ibun.*

Atsutane stated that this was not the first time these barbarian incursions had happened. As far back as the Genbun period (1736–1741) there had been reports of ships menacing the coast of Sendai. But even before that, foreigners had occasionally dared to breach the shores of Japan. Atsutane emphasized the futility of such acts, noting that either the armies of the emperor, or the *kami,* acting as a divine wind, had always destroyed the invaders. For Atsutane it was imperative that the readers understand that all such attempts by any and all foreign nations were foolhardy and would end up in disaster for them. Note, however, that in 1807, the infallible defenders of Japan were specified as either Japanese soldiers or Japanese *kami.*

Despite the confidence in victory, Atsutane did not suggest that foreign incursions should be belittled or ignored as harmless. On the contrary, he believed that there could be real harm in suffering these visitations. To back up his fears, he offered precedent to remind his readers of the looming danger of foreign contact.

When Oharida[35] first sent the envoy to the Tang dynasty in the august spirit of the *kami,* and people were allowed to learn about the ways of that country, numerous people developed a longing to study those things, and so there came to be a lot of intercourse between the two countries. As a result, the teachings of Buddhism were established here and spread throughout the country. We ended up degrading our own country's noble majesty on our own. Eventually, scholarship and letters came to be emphasized while bravery was neglected. We came to like all the shiny and decorative accoutrements of culture, and the rough trappings of the warrior were put away. Contact made Japan feminine.

After that, we could not discern the trunk from the branches. Even our writing system was changed. We strayed from the ancient laws. We praised all foreign practices and trinkets. Especially recently because of Dutch studies, great numbers of people have become enamored of the red-haired people. That sort of thing is unbearably filthy and degrading. Whenever I hear of people who have strayed from what is good and true, I am both angered and saddened.[36]

Atsutane went on to say that although the armies of the emperor could beat all comers, there had been times when infiltration occurred and evil influences gained the upper hand over the superior Japanese way. The prime example of this, he claimed, was Japan's entire medieval period.

During that time, power fell into the hands of debased groups who could not fathom the difference between the nobility of Japan and the baseness of China and India. These groups continued to corrupt Japan until the Tokugawa leadership during the Kan'ei period (1624–1644) finally corrected the situation by implementing a policy of strict isolation from foreign contact.

This was the first step in the process of reducing the corrupting influences of foreign ideas and restoring Japan to its native greatness. Atsutane optimistically looked forward to the day when the emperor would send off his own ships to contact foreign shores. In a show of rhetorical swagger he even suggested that the Japanese people should plan for that eventuality by planting trees that could be used to build the ships necessary to fulfill Japan's destiny. His work *White Waves of the Kuriles: Maps Appended* was to be secretly transmitted to future generations as a source of information about the barbarians who would one day be contacted by the ships of Japan.

The preface to Atsutane's treatise on national defense/offense in 1807 was a confident document, stating that not only would the potential Western invaders be easily repelled, they themselves would eventually be subject to invasion. This document was purportedly not a sourcebook for information to be used for the defense of Japan, but actually information to be used for the expansion of Japan. Of course, that arrogant stance may have been in part necessary braggadocio. There does seem to have been sufficient concern that stories of the power of Western military technology had put a scare into the Japanese public. Certainly the Western nations had demonstrated superior naval power and had gained secure and embarrassing footholds in India while pressuring China to agree to Europe-friendly trade agreements. These two Asian civilizations, which had impressed the Japanese for centuries, were proving helpless and vulnerable in the face of Western power. The strength and quantity of Atsutane's protestations against these Western nations attest to his own considerable estimation of their powers.

Whatever the motivation for *White Waves of the Kuriles: Maps Appended*, the forces mentioned to be used in the defense of Japan were both human armies and the *kami*, specifically in the form of the typhoon winds that had saved Japan during the Mongol invasions more than five hundred years before. There was no mention of a *sanjin* army with air rifle technology, devoted to the defense of Japan against foreign enemies. The *sanjin* army was, of course, a later development, another convenient usage of the new medium discovered by Atsutane's ethnographic research into the Other World.

We have seen that Atsutane felt threatened by the West due to its military incursions. However, he spent much more time and attention defending Japan from the damage already inflicted by internal proponents of Western knowledge. The role of the *sanjin* military in defending Japan's borders was minor and incidental. The more important role of the *sanjin* was to prove to the Japanese people as a whole that they were actually superior, in spite of Western evidence to the contrary.

Western knowledge had already raised some questions about the nativist proposition of Japanese superiority. About this Atsutane writes:

> Those who pursue the newly inaugurated Dutch studies learn a great deal about the manners of foreign countries. However, sometimes during their studies, their intentions change and blindly they start to favor the ways of the Western countries. For example, they will say that Russia is a large country with intelligent people. In addition, when talking about explosives, they claim that Russians have created wondrous cannon and projectiles. They say that with one shot those cannon can completely demolish fortress walls a hundred *ri* away. A small country like Japan would be smashed into powder. Those people say ignorant things like that.[37]

In another place Atsutane writes:

> This generation of scholars is seriously drowned in confusion about foreign theories and is unaware of the noble accomplishments of our country. Even on the rare occasion when they hear the true theories, their wills become perverse, and they are unable to believe them. They go to extremes to refute and destroy those true theories. Furthermore, the scholars attracted by foreign theories are always saying that our country is very small; in addition, they say that Japan's development is retarded.[38]

Here we can see that the two most common arguments concerning the inferiority of Japan stemmed from its small size and its lower level of technological development. These arguments seem to be an obvious if superficial way of evaluating Japan's position in the world. In other words, these simple facts were very annoying to Atsutane and very effective in hampering the acceptance of nativist teachings of superiority.

Atsutane defended his school and his conception of Japan against these galling arguments in the following ways. Concerning size, he writes:

> Even though they try to slander Japan, saying over and over that it is a small country, not only among countries but also in all things, the nobil-

ity or baseness, and the beauty or ugliness of things are not dependent on size. A large stone of several *jō* is not as valuable as a jewel of one square *sun*. Furthermore, even though beasts such as cows, horses, and elephants are bigger, they are not superior to people. No matter how large it is, an inferior country is an inferior country. No matter how small and narrow it is, a superior country is a superior country.[39]

Another argument pointed out that although America and Russia were large, there were vast uninhabitable portions. Once again, Atsutane was promoting the environmental determinist theory that good land creates good people.

In defense of the criticism of the slow development of Japanese civilization, his argument once again came from an animal comparison; it sounded like it was based on the principles of pseudo-zoology.

Immediately after they are born, birds and beasts pick up grain and insects to eat. In the same manner, only two or three months after they are born, they have sex and can do almost any other thing they need to by themselves. The fact is that they are all lower creatures, and comparatively speaking, humans are certainly slow developing. Yet, this is the basis for why humans are better than beasts.[40]

This was coupled with Atsutane's argument that Japan as the primal land was permeated with the earth's vital spirit, the *qi*,[41] and the rest of the world was not. Japan was therefore animated by breath; it was a living organism. The rest of the countries in the world were merely coagulated mud and brine. Therefore, as a superior spiritual organism, Japan's development should be expected to be slower than its base counterparts.

We should recognize here that in defending Japan against charges of backwardness and late development, Atsutane had admitted it was true. Being a late bloomer does not exactly support his other claims that all advanced and superior cultural developments started in Japan and were reimported. His stance on these issues was, at the very least, a confusing one. His ultimate point was always that Japan was superior. If it came first, then it was superior because it came first. If it came last, then it was superior because it came last.

Another interesting attempt to use Western knowledge to support his claim for Japanese superiority occurred when Atsutane performed a zealous overreading of Englebert Kaempferer's[42] experiences in Japan. According to Atsutane's interpretation, this "objective" Western traveler had recorded a true account of Japan, which included praise for the character and intelligence of the Japanese people. Perhaps even more important, this traveler to many lands had proclaimed Japan to be superior to all others. The conclusions of other Western writers concerning Japan are not brought up by Atsutane, for they are not all favorable. In particular, Atsutane denounced as lies any Western stories of successful incursions onto Japanese soil and successful skirmishes with Japanese people. Once again, Atsutane's strategy for Western knowledge was to take that which would support his claims for Japan and reject that which would not. He had a clear desire to use Western things, but only those that could be put in service to his ideology and beliefs about the divinity of the land of Japan.

In *Senkyō ibun*, Atsutane confronted Western culture, but not always to discredit it. Atsutane supported a belief in the efficacy of Western knowledge, and he asked Torakichi to speak about it in order to allow the *sanjin* to appropriate that knowledge. He invited his expert on modern ballistic weapons, Kunitomo Yoshimasa, to interview Torakichi, which resulted in the *sanjin* being armed with heavy cannon and smaller firearms. He invited his expert on astronomy, Satō Nobuhirō, to interview Torakichi, which resulted in the *sanjin* becoming recognized as the first space travelers. In short, the *tengu* medium and the ethnographic method once again enabled the *sanjin* to overcome the common criticisms of Japanese inferiority so vexing to Atsutane.

The Medium Is the Message

Spiritual Extension and Material Amputation

I chose the Marshall McLuhan reference in the title of this chapter to emphasize the focus of this particular study, which is the importance of the medium in Atsutane's message.[1] That message in *Senkyō ibun* is ultimately no different than Atsutane's standard offering, which he usually delivered through a textual medium. Its import was, of course, that the Japanese people are essentially different and superior to all other human beings in the world. This study has sought to examine the packaging of that message in a new delivery system, as described in the text of *Senkyō ibun*.

The key to the new system was a supernatural Shinto medium. The whole exotic episode, where Atsutane performed as a carnival sideshow barker touting his Tengu Boy oddity, was an elaborate presentation staged to introduce the theological innovation called the *sanjin*. This was to be the Shinto hero, holy man, and religious medium who could show the Japanese people that they no longer needed to look outside of native Japanese culture for a champion in whom they could take pride. However, this choice of a spiritual medium had consequences for the redefinition of Japanese identity. The new medium suggested that the best signifiers of Japanese identity were not in the material world, but rather in the spiritual world.

In McLuhan's *Understanding Media: The Extensions of Man*, he states that every extension of humanity that new technologies afford demands an amputation. For example, the introduction of the automobile had consequences for walking, and the introduction of the television had consequences for one-on-one human interaction. In Atsutane's case, extensions were introduced specifically to encourage the accompanying amputations. For example, the adoption of supernatural *tengu* knowledge was supposed to cast doubt on human knowledge, and the emphasis on a spiritual standard for evaluating Japanese worth was meant to discourage a valuation of Japanese achievement based on historical, cultural, and technological accomplishment.

Atsutane was disappointed by what historical sources, the representatives of human knowledge, said about Japanese culture. In addition, he was disappointed by the results of comparing Japanese cultural achievements with those of China, India, and the West. He was looking for a way out of these standard ways of evaluating Japanese culture and was intent upon finding a method to establish convincingly the superiority of things Japanese, once and for all. This overwhelming desire prompted his move to a spiritual methodology.

Atsutane's spiritual method succeeded in finding Japanese superiority in the Other World, an unseen realm. He had also hoped to establish recognition of Japanese ownership of the cultural accomplishments of foreign cultures in this world, but this had proven impossible. After all his efforts, the only lasting effect of Atsutane's discourse on Japanese superiority and unique Japanese cultural identity exists in lingering present-day ideas of a Japanese spirituality shrouded in mystery. Atsutane was not the only thinker who tried to place the essence of Japan in a spiritual dimension, but he was among the first.

The self-orientalized image of the Japanese as a mysterious people with a vast spiritual depth beyond the comprehension of foreigners did not begin in the Meiji period with Nitobe Inazo's (1862–1966) *Bushido: The Soul of Japan.* Nor was the spirit of Zen as explained by Suzuki Daisetsu (1870–1933) the first religious spirit equated with the essence of Japan. Generations before those two men, so important to the creation of an illusion of essential Japanese identity, Hirata Atsutane began to construct a powerful image of the Japanese spirit that still lingers in many hearts and minds inside and outside Japan.

A Review of the *Sanjin*'s Development

Any actual discovery in the nineteenth century of a new "ancient" type of mountain practitioner devoted to Shinto would have been extremely serendipitous. Religious men had been living and practicing in the mountains of Japan for more than a thousand years, and it is highly unlikely that a secret Shinto sect would have been able to keep itself hidden for so long. It is much more plausible to conclude that Atsutane was renaming a group that was already there. In other words, he attempted to invent a new identity for certain Japanese mountain practitioners.

The stories about the *sanjin* in *Senkyō ibun* argue for the recognition of a palpable, independent identity for a Japanese native religion, culture, and community. They attempt to establish a culture hero in the form of the *sanjin,* a devotee of the Ancient Way. In their roundabout and haphazard way they define what the *sanjin* is and does and also how the *sanjin* is different, better, and independent in origin from "foreign" religious practitioners and practices that had come to dominate nineteenth-century Japanese religion.

The stories attempt to establish the new nativist culture hero first by the discovery of a living human medium, one who could transmit Atsutane's message and disguise that it had originated from Atsutane himself. This medium was to be seen as bringing a true message from an actual place inside Japan that still preserved the unadulterated culture of ancient Japan. The existence of the medium himself was to lend credence to Atsutane's new idea of Japanese cultural identity.

Torakichi's appearance and his claim to have lived in the mountains with *tengu/sanjin* were not invented or planned by Atsutane, but the idea that the *sanjin* could be depended on to defend Atsutane's beliefs about the Other World started with Atsutane. Atsutane's choice to cast the *sanjin* as his human medium, to be featured as his method of explicating a culturally unadulterated Japan, is rooted in the history of the Japanese nativist movement itself.

Nativism: From Philology to Anthropology of the Imaginary

The nativist movement in the Tokugawa period was deeply concerned with discovering the so-called "true essence" of Japan in the ancient past before it came into contact with foreign cultures. Ironically, however, Tokugawa nativism was in part inspired by an intellectual movement begun in China during the Ming dynasty that asserted that Song dynasty Neo-Confucianism actually stood as an impediment to the correct understanding of the ancient Chinese classics. This inspired an Ancient Learning movement based on renewed readings of the ancient texts devoid of annotation and commentary that were seen to be dependent on particular concerns of particular historical moments. The great Zhu Xi's commentaries on the classics lost their aura of universality and truth and were recognized as being limited by both time and place. These limitations made them potentially inappropriate for any contemporary understanding and certainly robbed them of their prior air of absolute and universal authority.

This movement in China contributed to a later but similar Japanese movement whose best representatives, Ogyū Sorai and Itō Jinsai, founded schools which defined the Japanese version of Ancient Learning. These schools emphasized the importance of philological method. Varieties of philological methods were employed, but what they all shared was a call to read original texts. The method, in its most general understanding, insisted on ancient written text as the only reliable source for understanding ancient ideas and truths. Yet even that limitation allowed for many different ways to understand and interpret those ancient texts.

Japanese nativism started with the shift of focus from classical Chinese texts to the most ancient Japanese texts. Many scholars see the first nativist to be Keichū, the Shingon priest who was recruited to work on an analysis of the *Manyōshū*, which had become unreadable by the seventeenth century. He was also thought to have worked on the *Kojiki*, but there is no extant work of his that can verify this. One of Keichū's methods of philological investigation of the ancient Japanese language was to compare texts of supposedly similar age and use passages from similar texts to help fill in gaps in understanding. There were other methods of textual interpretation that stretched the reliability of philological method. For example, a common Neo-Confucian technique was to evaluate the significance of specific texts based on how they fulfilled certain ethical requirements. In other words, moral rectitude was seen as implying textual accuracy. Nevertheless, scholarship of Atsutane's time in the Tokugawa period had come to focus on textual analysis of various degrees of reliability.

Atsutane, in *Jeweled Sash* (*Tamadasuki*),[2] recognized Kada Azumamaro as the founder of *kokugaku*, crediting him with the submission of the petition to the shogun for the establishment of an academy for the expressed purpose of studying Japanese classics. The authorship of the petition has been called into question, yet Kada is still recognized as a nativist scholar, although for some his standing was lessened by his continued reliance on Neo-Confucian ethical ideas and concerns. Atsutane left Keichū out of his genealogy of *kokugaku* because Keichū did not emphasize Japanese superiority. In addition, as important as he was for the development of *kokugaku* and the work of both Kamo no Mabuchi and Motoori Norinaga, Keichū was a Shingon priest. Atsutane asserted that Japanese nativism required a stance concerning the identity of Japan, its culture, and its people that stood in contrast to the identity of other cultures and peoples of the world. For Atsutane, nativism meant defining Japanese culture and community, not just studying the principles of ancient poetry in order to compose poetry in the manner of the ancients. His brand of nativism was not about aesthetics, but about metaphysics and ontology. Atsutane's nativism was, in fact, specifically called something different, *kodōgaku*, or Studies of the Ancient Way, a fundamentally religious concern.

With that concern foremost in Atsutane's mind, a philological method that did not speak to metaphysical and ontological questions became secondary to results. When history and philology failed to produce the answers or to provide the opportunity for finding those answers, Atsutane showed that he was not averse to abandoning them. Like Western explorers in the Age of Discovery, Atsutane had speculated about a New World, something yet undiscovered. When he heard that Torakichi claimed to have lived in that world, he sought to explore it and study it as a foreign culture. Just as Western scholars did when they went in search of answers about foreign cultures, Atsutane went armed with an interview technique aimed at producing an anthropological study of the unknown land and culture.

In this case, the object of the anthropologist's observation was, in reality, the cultural imagination of his Japanese anthropologist self. From numerous examples of Western anthropological studies, we have already learned to be suspicious of the anthropologist's own contributions to his study of the unknown.[3] Even with the knowledge of the need for reflexivity, the ethnographer shapes the stories of his informant. Atsutane's case is even more dubious, first because he lacks that reflexivity, and second because the informant is a particularly strange boy with a troubled past and neurotic, sometimes psychotic difficulties.[4] Nevertheless, as in the case of other ethnographies, the informant's stories are often manipulated by the questions to produce the responses expected by the anthropologist.

Since Atsutane was collecting stories of the community and the culture of *sanjin,* the mountain dwellers of Japan, this work can be seen as a forerunner of *minzokugaku,* or Japanese folklore studies, which also emphasized a similar project, the recovery of an ideal rural Japanese culture. Origuchi Shinobu, a scholar often associated with that movement but who proclaimed himself to actually be in search of a new *kokugaku,* or nativism, eagerly admitted admiring and being greatly influenced by Atsutane.[5] Origuchi claimed that although his predecessor, the renowned Yanagita Kunio, did not acknowledge such close ties to Atsutane, Yanagita nonetheless was walking in the same footsteps as Atsutane.[6] Other scholars have also convincingly argued this claim.[7]

Atsutane, as an ethnographer of the imaginary, endeavored to craft a description of the supernatural inhabitants of the Other World upon which his whole Ancient Way cosmology was based. More important than the location, which is actually the same as this seen world of Japan, were the usually unseen inhabitants of that Other World, especially those unseen inhabitants he claimed served as mediums between human beings and *kami.* One major function of *Senkyō ibun* was to establish that *sanjin* did exist and to describe their abilities and functions. If Atsutane's stated purpose of *The August Pillar of the Soul* was to provide comfort and confidence for the people of Japan that this life would not be followed by a fall into a defiled and unpleasant existence, then it follows that the goal of *Senkyō ibun* was to establish a culture hero whose primary reason for existence was to render the Japanese comfort, assistance, and protection until they reached that Other World. Atsutane was not satisfied with having his followers and fellow believers longing for the good life in the next world; he also empowered them to ask the *kami* for wealth, health, and security in this world.

What also must have served to reinforce Atsutane's theological claim made through his supernatural medium Torakichi was the popularity of mountain pilgrimage in the Tokugawa period and the development of a rural religious quasi-professional who made or supplemented his living by guiding pilgrims and enabling their mountain worship. In essence, these new guides acted as mediums for the pilgrims, assisting in the actualization of prayer and devotion. Of course, these guides were not clearly Shinto, Buddhist, or Shugendō in affiliation, and this was not a requirement of popular religion. However, these guides for mountain pilgrimage became living proof that there were religious professionals living in the mountains whose purpose in life was seemingly to assist pilgrims in performing their prayers and devotions.[8]

Atsutane's identification and near reification of *sanjin* brought the Other World closer to the seen or revealed world by providing a bridge between them. It also emphasized the need for religious attention, mediation, and practice. Therefore, in a practical sense, the discovery of the religious importance of the *sanjin* made Atsutane more important by associating his teachings with popular religious practice. In sum, the *sanjin* was a theological development that made the world a better place for believers in the Ancient Way, but it also had the potential to make the world a better place for Atsutane.

Historical and Religious Mediation

The great innovation of *Senkyō ibun* was its use of a spirit medium. Above all, Torakichi's arrival allowed Atsutane to claim superiority over practitioners of philological methods that relied upon ancient written texts. The extant histories had proven to be difficult for him to use because they did not back up his Ancient Way theology. Therefore, he was forced to be actively involved in the writing of new history. His philological method was to collect the oldest Japanese works available and use the parts of each that agreed with his first principle of truth; that is, Japan was the Land of the Kami, firstborn and superior to all other lands. Starting from this premise, he analyzed the ancient histories to show how they had been corrupted by the inclusion of foreign ideas. His philological work was undertaken in great part to show how existing history that based the authority of text on its antiquity was a deliberate set of lies pieced together by proponents of foreign cultures. In fact, a great deal of Atsutane's historical work was undertaken to directly debunk accepted histories. The best example of this is his work on Buddhism, *Laughing Discourse after Emerging from Meditation* (*Shutsujō shōgo*), in which he took up where Tominaga Nakamoto left off in a wholehearted attempt to discredit a millennium of Buddhist scholarship. In the preface to *Laughing Discourse after Emerging from Meditation,* a student who recorded the lecture writes:

> This is the outline of *Shutsujō shōgo* [*Laughing Discourse after Emerging from Meditation*]. Part One of the lecture begins by covering the land and customs of the country of India. The first traditional histories of this country are not from Shaka's lifetime. Furthermore, not even one section or volume of any of the various Buddhist teachings can honestly be attributed to Shaka. Every last one of them is a fictional argument or story recorded by those who came after him. Next he [Atsutane] explains the facts concerning the Buddhist law's transmission through China to Japan. After that he deals with the origins of the various sects in Japan. Following that he reveals the original meaning of the Buddhist law and various different ways in which it has been interpreted throughout time. Actually, the master's revered master [Norinaga] repeatedly lectured on the malicious and presumptuous thoughts and intentions of the proponents of Chinese studies. However, he had very little to say about the Buddhist law.[9]

Atsutane was clearly trying to undermine the authority of the pro-Buddhist discourse in Japan in the same way Norinaga had attempted to undermine pro-Chinese discourse a half-century before him.

The medium from the Other World was to help Atsutane in his effort to rewrite history. From *The August Pillar of the Soul* we know that the theological importance of Atsutane's Other World was not so much that it was inhabited by *kami* and demons, but that it was seen to be the destination of all Japanese people after their deaths, and it would have to have been that destination since the creation of the world. The soul in this soteriology was eternal and this eternal soul retained a personality and a consciousness, that is, if the soul had been able to avoid evil dissipation. According to Atsutane, this meant that souls with consciousness and memory existed in that Other World. On top of that, we learned from *Senkyō ibun* that certain *kami*-like humans, the highest level of *sanjin*, had been alive since the beginning of time. Therefore, according to Atsutane, the problem of history could only be resolved by communication with the Other World, and communication with the Other World could only be undertaken with the help of a capable medium. Torakichi himself did not know the true history of Japan, but he claimed to have access to beings that did.

To lend credence to the implication that the true history of Japan was alive in the Other World, Atsutane recorded Torakichi's claim that one could meet famous historical personages in that world. One guest at one of Atsutane's Torakichi interview parties told the story of a samurai who had been spirited away to the Other World, only to meet a living historical figure from Japan's Sengoku period (1467–1568). Torakichi suggests that this occurrence should be seen as commonplace when he says:

> Needless to say, the hidden realm is full of ancient figures such as he, who look as if they are still living today. I have not met any of them, but listening to my master's stories it seems that even the ancestor of the shogunal house, the Kami of Nikkō [Tokugawa Ieyasu] is there right now along with Yoshitsune, Tametomo, and other such people.[10]

In other words, true history lay in the Other World. The key to the past continued to exist in a parallel dimension. Therefore, the best way to study the past would be to make contact with the Other World. Since this was something the common person was not able to do, the medium became the only conduit to the truth of history.

Torakichi was only one of the mediums discovered in *Senkyō ibun*. Another medium was the *sanjin* himself. Atsutane adopted Torakichi's Shugendō ascetic master as the perfect example of this "new" Ancient Way religious virtuoso. He then placed this newly discovered Japanese religious culture hero in a place between *kami* and the common person. The *sanjin*'s religious role as medium was to ensure that the prayers of the devoted were heard by the *kami*. However, in addition to the *sanjin*'s scholastic and pious functions, Atsutane's new Ancient Way medium also performed other functions consistent with Atsutane's religious and political purposes.

Sanjin as Defense of Japanese Superiority

The picture of the *sanjin* transmitted in *Senkyō ibun* was not merely based on Torakichi's description of his master. The *sanjin* was enhanced by all the questions and answers about the special and different features of the Other World. Torakichi's imagination and Atsutane's array of experts, whose questions covered a variety of fields of knowledge, combined to produce a composite and multicultural superman. Atsutane's basic rule for deciding Japanese ownership of cultural achievement was based on a simple principle: Japanese superiority was to be accepted as *a priori*. If there was some cultural artifact that was clearly recognized as being superior in quality, then that artifact's origin was necessarily Japanese. Torakichi acted in complicity by never letting the *sanjin* appear to be lacking in any comparison of knowledge or ability. His motivation for acting this way is not perfectly clear, but his statements show that his *sanjin* never took a back seat to any competitor. The result of Atsutane's *a priori* and Torakichi's feisty defenses created a hero more or less defined by a refusal to admit inferiority.

By Atsutane's era, the idea of cultural dependence on China had become distasteful to many people for whom the Chinese Neo-Confucian and Ancient Learning movements held little attraction. Moreover, those whose political, social, and economic power depended on the strength of Chinese discourse were at odds with each other as differing Chinese-based discourses came into competition. The Buddhist establishment, on the other hand, was learning it had to fear its own history, as a more positivistic style of historiography had begun to question contradictions in Buddhist texts. While those popular discourses were facing difficulties, a Western discourse of science and technology was growing in support, bolstered by a domestic information revolution. Although evidence of a nativist Japanese consciousness has been documented centuries before in the Tokugawa period, nativist activity was clearly spurred on by the internal intellectual turmoil, the steady influx of Western ideas, and the ready access to information of all sorts.

It should be noted that Atsutane's discourse generally appealed to a wider cross-section of people than did most of his competitors' discourses. Buddhism, which had originally been the technology of the nobility, or at least the ruling classes, had in the Tokugawa period become a part of the ruling bureaucracy, working for and with permission of the ruling shoguns. Chinese philosophy had become important as a sign of ruling pretension, and it was used to justify status and power, especially for the warrior class, but also for the emergent merchant class. Atsutane claimed to shun both Buddhism and Chinese philosophy as means to power, partly because he recognized them both to be discourses people adopted simply for the power they afforded. Although born into the samurai class and later adopted into another samurai family, Atsutane's economic and social dealings were not strictly limited by class boundaries, and his ideas do not reflect an emphasis on the importance of such categories. His rhetoric was intended to unite the people of Japan into appreciating all members of the society as equally special, all potentially *kami*.

Atsutane felt that Japan was under attack from within, prompting statements such as the following:

> All those people who maliciously perform foreign studies do so to spread bad foreign doctrines. From early on, Buddhists have only praised India because that country was the homeland of the Buddha and therefore the country they valued most. They call Japan the Country of the Lost Millet Grain. They annoyingly say things like we were a country created when one millet grain floated east out to sea. The Confucianists praise the land of Han as the Country of the Sages. They slander Japan in comparisons to China, calling it a tiny land and the country of eastern barbarians.[11]

Senkyō ibun is the work in which Atsutane found a multipurpose medium to defend his country against such slander by lovers of India and China. Not coincidentally, Torakichi's listeners also learned that among this new *sanjin* medium's many fine qualities, he was particularly able to answer Western challenges to nativist claims of Japanese superiority. The *sanjin*'s presentation as savior and source of pride for the people of Japan even against the new Western menace should be appreciated as another of Atsutane's innovations.

Oda Nobunaga had effectively employed firearms and European military tactics in Japan at least two hundred years earlier. Atsutane's *sanjin* also studied these military tactics and large-scale military strategy with firearms. However, a *sanjin* had the superhuman ability to fly at incredible speeds to distant planets. He could separate into as many multiple, identical, and fully functional bodies as he desired. Beyond that, carrying no weaponry other than the fan he used to steer while in flight, he was known to rain down fire on the wicked whom the *kami* wished to punish. These powers would certainly have made the *sanjin* army invincible against even the most advanced twenty-first-century Western military technology. In other words, *sanjin* had no need for Western-style firearms and strategies, yet he possessed and practiced them anyway. This would indicate that Atsutane was simply intent on laying claim to any and all technology that might be recognized as superior.

In fact, Atsutane's *sanjin* was not unique and did very little that could be considered new. His characteristics resembled and sometimes directly copied those of his foreign counterparts. Still, there is no exact way of telling whether his special powers were based on Chinese, Indian, or even

Western models. Stories of supernatural beings with these powers were common in Japan. They were brought in centuries before from foreign lands accompanying foreign religious traditions. However, Atsutane's *sanjin* was able to compete with and surpass the Buddhist bodhisattva and the Chinese immortal because he was specifically designed to be an improvement upon them.

Atsutane's teachings claimed that all superior culture had originated in Japan, a claim that was challenged by everyday Japanese material reality. In *Senkyō ibun* Atsutane was able to defend his claim by introducing the unseen repository of that superior culture. He could then make the additional claim that this superior culture still remained in Japan, watched over by *sanjin* in the Other World. Therefore, it was ultimately important for Atsutane that the *sanjin*'s superiority in all things be demonstrated in story after story.

Atsutane's medium, Torakichi, had the ability to take information he had recently heard and turn it into his own. Torakichi's detractors within *Senkyō ibun* said that what Torakichi learned at one salon would later become something he claimed to have learned in the mountains. Torakichi also had a habit of claiming that almost anything he was shown he had seen earlier in an altered form in the mountains. This was fortuitous for Atsutane, since his teachings and his new methodology relied heavily on a medium with Torakichi's particular talents. For his efforts in displaying his talents as a medium, Torakichi became a well-taken-care-of celebrity. In other words, this collaboration between Atsutane and Torakichi benefited both of them.

Atsutane did not have to go so far as to provide scripts for Torakichi's performances. Torakichi had a large repertoire of stories, some he created and some he borrowed. He also showed an exceptional sensitivity toward his audience and had a knack for tailoring the story to his audience, thinking on his feet and embellishing as he went. As long as Torakichi was successful in this, Atsutane merely chose not to doubt him, as long as not doubting him served his theoretical positions and strengthened his nativist discourse.

Atsutane as the Ethnographer and Ritual Medium

Atsutane and Torakichi's relationship should be seen as that of ethnographer and informant. From this starting point we can evaluate how much liability each holds for the contents of the stories and to what extent either of them believed in the actuality of the narrated events. Even if we suspend our disbelief and attempt to put ourselves in the mindset and a cultural context where men fly faster than the speed of sound and two human beings can fit into a four-inch-diameter pot, we should still wonder whether both Atsutane and Torakichi believed Torakichi's stories had really happened.

On Torakichi's part, there is abundant evidence in *Senkyō ibun* that should cast suspicion on his honesty. For Atsutane's part, most of the scholars who write of his relationship with Torakichi contend that he believed in Torakichi's tales of the Other World. However, the evidence from the text makes it clear that Atsutane only encouraged and elicited testimony about the Other World that supported his own theories. When Torakichi's stories strayed from Atsutane's expectations, he either rejected or revised them.

Furthermore, the evidence is solid that many of Torakichi's words about the Other World and the *sanjin* were stimulated by or copied from Atsutane's ideas. In short, Atsutane manipulated the medium to create the story of a *sanjin* in order to give a "verifiable" supernatural identity of superiority to Japanese people. In addition, at times Torakichi did nothing more than parrot Atsutane's Other World eschatology to those who questioned him, making Atsutane's words into a true description of the natural laws of that Other World. Yet even arriving at this conclusion, if we recall Crapanzano's discussion of certain Western ethnographers, Atsutane's misrepresentation of Torakichi's stories and Torakichi's pandering to his ethnographer and audience would fit them both squarely within the tradition of Western ethnography.

However, there is another way of understanding this dynamic between Atsutane and Torakichi. The relationship can be understood from a religious studies perspective, and there is a traditional Japanese ritual precedent that may help us understand the relative contributions of the two individuals of this *sanjin*-creating process. Atsutane, as the author of *Senkyō ibun* and the manager and director who set up and staged Torakichi's performances, can also be understood to have been performing as a traditional Japanese ritual specialist. The ancient Japanese technique of inducing possession of a human medium by a *kami* required a ritual specialist called a *saniwa*, who acted as a second medium to interpret the speech of the possessed first medium. In this ritual dynamic, the *saniwa* had the power because it was he who determined the meaning of the words of the possessed medium, even though he did not produce them. Atsutane and Torakichi did not actually perform this specifc ritual, although Torakichi claimed that he had and could do so again. My point is that this two-medium process was something practiced and respected even in the late

Tokugawa period, and Atsutane and Torakichi were playing roles similar to these in their interactions. In other words, even though Torakichi was doing most of the talking, Atsutane's role was to let his audience know what Torakichi really meant to say.

As Atsutane himself recorded in *Senkyō ibun*, his work as the promoter did not always go smoothly, and Torakichi as a medium was occasionally reported to be unconvincing. However, those passages that point to controversy or show public distrust of Torakichi are not simply evidence of the honesty of Atsutane the author; they also serve another function. They work to disguise Atsutane's *saniwa*-like manipulation by suggesting that Atsutane's record has not been purposefully edited to correct Torakichi's "errors." Opposition to Torakichi also served to support Atsutane's assertions that detractors of the Ancient Way were constantly working to undermine him. Ultimately, Torakichi the medium stood, and still stands, as a buffer protecting Atsutane from the full force of public and scholarly criticism. To this day, there are scholars who absolve Atsutane for any inaccuracies in the storytelling and would much rather blame Torakichi for manipulating Atsutane. This conclusion seems to ignore the obvious power relationship.

Atsutane may not have been putting words directly into Torakichi's mouth, but in those cases when Torakichi asserted something Atsutane found disagreeable, Torakichi would backpedal to positions that supported what he knew to be Atsutane's position on a pure Ancient Way. There is clear manipulation of the informant throughout *Senkyō ibun*, but even so, it is not simply a fictionalized account put together to support Atsutane's theological and cosmological assertions. In the final analysis, *Senkyō ibun* is both an example of bad, or at least immature, scientific method and a record of a relationship that echoes a classical Japanese ritual process in which Torakichi acted as spirit medium to Atsutane's intrepretive *saniwa* role.

Revisiting Atsutane Scholarship

Senkyō ibun is supposedly well-known, yet lengthy discussion of it in Western literature is confined to Carmen Blacker's solitary English-language analysis. This perhaps points us to the reasons for its relative neglect by Western scholars. The bulk of the subject matter of *Senkyō ibun* is labeled supernatural, that is, belonging to the world of the imaginary. The work is therefore considered to belong to the genre of the folk tale with the content categorized as superstition. The result has been that Atsutane is made to appear as an irrational and eccentric collector of oddities, another victim of the power of superstitious thought in the nineteenth century, and Carmen Blacker frames her analysis accordingly. However, the Blacker quote that opened this study acknowledges that *Senkyō ibun* and Atsutane did not fit into that category as neatly as she would have liked. Blacker recognizes a "matter of fact" quality and "disenchantment" in these stories and speculates that it was those very qualities that actually pleased Atsutane. The point is that Atsutane, while clearly a predecessor of Yanagita Kunio's folklore studies, was not collecting folk tales. He was, in his mind, collecting scientific evidence of the factual reality of the Other World.

Senkyō ibun is therefore not a collection of folk tales, but an ethnographer's logbook, something that could stand as an example of Atsutane's idea of a scientific record. As an anthropological ethnographer, Atsutane submitted his visitor from a "foreign land" to public questioning by some of the top minds of his times. Atsutane was intent on recording what he believed to be factual evidence to be held up to public scrutiny.

Atsutane knew that more people were beginning to doubt the existence of *tengu*, demons, monsters, and ghosts. He was also acutely aware of the power of Western scientific method and often used Western knowledge himself to discredit and ridicule the unscientific minds of his opponents and detractors. Just as Buddhists of that period were refitting ancient Indian Buddhist models of the universe to conform to Western Copernican theory,[12] Atsutane began modernizing the Japanese world of spirits and monsters. Science may have been calling Japan out of Weber's "enchanted garden," but Atsutane sought to keep Japan in the garden by disenchanting it, by making the incredible credible. Atsutane's new direction, which included these accommodations and accessions to some of the demands of Western discourse, caused Blacker's dissatisfaction with Atsutane's *Senkyō ibun* "folk tale collection."

The failure to recognize the serious religious importance of *Senkyō ibun* causes the reader to overlook the book's focus on a new category of Japanese religious medium first defined therein. This medium, the *sanjin*, was not solely Atsutane's invention, rather it was discovered and renamed by Atsutane to remedy an eschatological shortcoming and to compete with the religious virtuosi of other traditions within Japan. To compete successfully on the stage of world religion, the supposedly indigenous *sanjin* was endowed with political, religious, cultural, domestic, and international importance.

Atsutane used *Senkyō ibun* and Torakichi to introduce a religious innovation in the so-called indigenous Japanese tradition that, if accepted, would shore up his overall re-presentation of Japanese cultural identity.

He was attempting to produce a Japanese identity that would support his vision of a central role for Japan and the Japanese in the greater world. The *sanjin* was offered up as both a superman and a savior who would comfort and serve both the common Japanese person and the greater cultural community of Japan, which he was intent upon redefining.

The Aftermath of *Senkyō ibun:* The Measure of Atsutane's Success

This study can also serve as an example of how a minority religious movement in Japan began to build itself into a formidable force in national politics. In achieving this meteoric rise, Atsutane engaged in a great contest involving multiple discourses. Religious symbols and figures were used as weapons, and those that proved weaker were traded in for stronger ones. Some time-tested doctrines proved more inviolable than others, but in the end, principles, traditions, and doctrines often succumbed to the necessity for change in order to survive. *Senkyō ibun* provides us with some insight into this contest for the ownership and invention of "nineteenth-century indigenous" Japanese religion.

The pages of *Senkyō ibun* show us specifically how Atsutane faces the challenge of countering three powerful discourses that held the upper hand over his so-called native Japanese offering. We can see him attempt to undermine their power by appropriating what he considers best in them for native Japanese religion. He denies their claims of authority and rejects their theories of knowledge. He does all this by exploiting newly popularized doubts about historicity and promoting a new avenue to ultimate truth available only to the practitioner of native Japanese religion. In addition, he attempts to locate a visible figure from Japanese popular religion, give him super powers, and make him into Japan's ancient super religious hero.

In hindsight, Atsutane's maneuverings, revealed in *Senkyō ibun* and in his other methods of self-promotion, clearly had an effect. The enrollment at his school increased dramatically. He received support from all classes of society. He made friends in important places. He attracted so many Shinto priests to his school that he caused consternation among the Shinto powers that be, the Yoshida and Shirakawa families, and provoked them into vying for his services. Atsutane's *sanjin* did not become the culture hero of native Japanese religion, but this numinous mountain man evolved into a notion of a spiritually charged mysterious stranger who appears out of nowhere to threaten or bless Japanese communities. In addition, the mystical bent of Atsutane's studies continues to have an acknowledged effect in Japanese occult religious circles today.

After Atsutane's death in exile, the Hirata School expanded rapidly under the guidance of his adopted son Kanetane and moved on to dominance in Japanese religious politics in the early Meiji period, but not long after that its power and political clout faded away. The school's strongest proponents moved from government politics to academic politics and, as a result, lost most of their relevance. Fragmented Atsutane-like nationalist ideas continue in Japan into the twenty-first century, as does Western fear of lingering Japanese nationalism. This causes suspicion of Atsutane studies to remain, but not enough to preclude further studies of Atsutane's mystical and occult proclivities, where his continuing value to religious studies lies.

In an ironic twist, Atsutane orientalized the Japanese people before any Western nations had a secure foothold in Japan and could start doing their own work on that project. The "true" Japanese of Atsutane's inspired imagination were exalted and exotic. The Japanese people he met in his contemporary reality were mere shrunken versions of the former divine selves he so admired. In *Essence of the Ancient Way* he writes:

> The numinous qualities of the ancient times disappeared and the ordinary people of today came into being. I will try to explain the conditions of ancient times by comparing them to things we are familiar with today. Our ancestors who first built their houses in Japan were big men, exactly the height of the sumo wrestlers Shakagatake [13] and Tanikaze, [14] seven to eight feet tall with a shoulder span over three feet wide. The span of their hands was larger than a half sheet of writing paper. Their shoes were two feet long. They were so strong they could pick up their mothers in four- or five-foot-square bathtubs filled with water, and carry the whole thing around easily. [15]

Atsutane seemed to want the Japanese people to feel inferior to their "true" selves, which existed only in his imagination. It could only be small comfort to "the ordinary people of today" that this imaginary world, in which they could never measure up, was supposedly once home to the most fabulous civilization the world had ever known.

In Atsutane's version of reality, the Japanese had the option of joining colonial India and China, which was fast moving in India's colonial direction. That is, the Japanese had the choice of thinking of themselves as members of civilizations whose present populations were sad reflections of what they had once been. However, in the Japanese case, their greatness was to be found in a mythical age, something that existed only in a supernatural Other World. Atsutane's purpose may have been to make the Japanese stop adoring foreign cultures and value themselves and their own land and cultural achievements, yet his claim that the achievements of foreign cultures were originally Japanese subtly reinforced the underlying notion that Japan was a Johnny-come-lately nation whose culture was imported from abroad. Atsutane's consolation argument was that Japan was the best imitator in the world and always improved on what it imitated:

> When foreign-made things are brought to Japan, we can greatly improve them with one glance, no matter what they may be. The fact that we can do that is indeed a feature of Japanese superiority. Everything I do is undoubtedly done better than any foreigner could. This is our innate national character because we are from the Land of the Kami.[16]

Atsutane's recognition of this great talent was, in so many words, recognition that ultimate creativity lay elsewhere, and his pronouncement reads like a booby prize for "Most Creative Imitator." In one sense, his work contributed to the pathology of a national inferiority complex, with all the lingering self-loathing and self-destructive aftereffects.

Postscript: What of Torakichi?

After *Senkyō ibun* and the other short works written at about the same time, information about Torakichi becomes scarcer and scarcer. After the events of 1820, Torakichi was mentioned from time to time in the Ibukinoya diaries, which recorded that in the fourth month of 1821, Atsutane, Torakichi, and some other academy students went on a research trip to Mt. Asama in Shinano Province to visit Sugiyama Sanjin's home base. After that, Torakichi's name appeared a few times every year in reports of some outing or other in which he participated. In 1825, after Atsutane left on another tour of present-day Chiba, Torakichi was reported to have left Atsutane's home, it seems without permission, but in 1826 it was reported that he returned.

Torakichi was still at Atsutane's home the next year but there was apparently nothing noteworthy about which to write. The most interesting and the last news concerning Torakichi to appear in the diaries was recorded in 1828. Torakichi was again absent from the academy, and while there had been some expectation that he would become a physician, news was received that he had shaved his head and taken the tonsure. It is also recorded that he reappeared later that year verifying the news that he had become a Buddhist monk.

There is another story, recorded in Kamata Tōji's work, of a Torakichi sighting after he left Atsutane's academy. This story reported that Tora-kichi was sighted sitting in the high chair overlooking the entrance to a public bath, the establishment being appropriately named "Hot Waters of the *Tengu*." [17] Either way, Torakichi had left his *sanjin* studies far behind him and had reverted to his *tengu* beginnings.

Notes

All Japanese-language works are published in Tokyo unless otherwise indicated.

Introduction

1. See Donald Keene, *The Japanese Discovery of Europe, 1720–1830* (Stanford, Calif.: Stanford University Press, 1952 and 1969); Donald Keene, *Some Japanese Portraits* (Tokyo: Kodansha International, 1978); Carmen Blacker, "Supernatural Abductions in Japanese Folklore," *Asian Folklore Studies,* vol. XXVI-2 (1967): 111–147; or Carmen Blacker, *The Catalpa Bow: A Study of Shamanistic Practices in Japan* (London: George Allen and Unwin, 1975).

2. I am using nativism as a general rubric that includes the Tokugawa Japanese *kokugaku* movement. *Kokugaku* is a specific term designating a number of different schools in Japan during the Tokugawa period that held in common a focus on Japanese antiquity.

3. These are the *amatsukami,* a distinct classification of Shinto *kami* most often associated with creation myths.

4. Hirata Atsutane, "Kodō taii," in *HAZ,* vol. 1, 22. This work is particularly valuable when studying Atsutane's claims for Japanese superiority, and it provides a general overview of his basic polemic, as the title, *Essence of the Ancient Way,* would suggest.

5. The various types of Chinese studies will be explained in detail elsewhere.

6. The most common image of the *tengu* today would be the long-nosed, red-faced, supernatural trickster who is usually dressed like a *yamabushi.* Some versions might even be winged and have birdlike facial features. The Chinese characters literally mean "dog from the heavens," and in the ancient Chinese *Records of the Historian (Shi ji)* (first century BCE), and the ancient Japanese *Chronicle of Japan (Nihon shoki)* (720 CE), the word appears to refer to a type of shooting star that was said to be a kind of dog when it landed on earth. By the Heian period, as evidenced by the word's usage in the *Tale of Genji (Genji monogatari),* it had come to mean a supernatural trickster living

in the mountains. We can see by the early twelfth century *Tales of Time Now Past* (*Konjaku monogatarishu*) that the word had developed an association with deluded Buddhist priests who worshiped *tengu* and eventually turned into them. The Kamakura period saw a clear association of *tengu* with wicked Buddhist priests, with even the most eminent monks depicted as corrupt bird-like *tengu* in the well-known *Tengu zōshi* from 1296 (see Wakabayashi Haruko, "Tengu zōshi ni miru Kamakura bukkyō no ma to *tengu*," in *Emaki ni chūsei o yomu*, ed. Gomi Fumihiko and Fujiwara Yoshiaki (Yoshikawa Kobunkan, 1995)). From that time on, *tengu* came to be more closely associated with *yamabushi* and their practices. Eventually in popular religion *tengu* even came to be recognized as mountain *kami*. Atsutane's specific descriptions and ideas concerning *tengu* will be explained in detail in the next chapter. For more on the fascinating history of *tengu*, see Komatsu Kazuhiko, ed., *Tengu to Yamamba*, in *Kaii no minzokugaku* 5 (Kawade Shobo Shinsha, 2000); or Chigiri Kōsai, *Tengu no kenkyū* (Hara Shobō, 1975).

7. Although supernatural has proven to be a particularly problematic term, culturally and temporally determined as it is, I beg my readers' indulgence on this issue. I trust they will be aware that many Japanese of this time period, in particular Atsutane, believed in the existence of *tengu* and other such creatures not found in our daily experiences, and therefore might have considered them to be more natural than supernatural. I use the term with the sensibility of a twenty-first-century American who does not believe in ghosts but who has a healthy fear of them under the proper circumstances.

8. This intellectual movement, founded by Yanagita Kunio (1875–1962), is a "new nativism," an attempt to glorify rural Japanese culture spurred on by fears of urbanization in the late nineteenth and twentieth centuries. It has been criticized for attempting to create an essential image of Japan based on stereotypes of agricultural communities.

9. This association of Atsutane with emperor worship is certainly not without basis, but it is by no means his defining life's work. In fact his thoughts about the centrality of the emperor were understood to be directed at political objectives within Japan, not toward an image of Japan on the world stage. The circumstances surrounding his exile to the countryside bear this out. In 1840 he was ordered to leave Edo and stop publishing. Early the next year he returned to his home province of Dewa where he died two years later, devastated that he had fallen from eminence and could no longer be active in Edo. Atsutane's enemies had reported his allegedly subversive writings to the bakufu, who had problems with the "politically subversive" *Questions about the Great Way* (*Taidō wakumon*), in which Atsutane asserted that loyalty to the emperor was more important than loyalty to one's lord. The bakufu saw this

idea as a threat to Tokugawa power, which it eventually was, but not ultimately due to Atsutane's influence. Atsutane's problems with the Tokugawa bakufu started in 1836, when they objected to the circulation of *Thoughts on the Great Japanese Nation* (*Daifusōkokukō*), which likewise pleased the emperor but displeased the shogun. However, what finally brought on the exile was *Almanac of the Eternal Imperial Dynasty* (*Tenchō mukyūreki*), which apparently did not appropriately value the shogunal house. *Senkyō ibun*, written more than a decade earlier, is not controversial in that respect; it claims that its heroes, the *sanjin*, are loyal to both the emperor and the shogun.

10. Blacker, "Supernatural Abductions in Japanese Folklore."

11. Ibid., 146–147.

12. Kamata Tōji, *Hirata Atsutane no shinkai fiirudowāku* (Sakuhinsha, 2002).

13. Atsutane started his nativist activities after Norinaga died. However, he claimed to have met Norinaga in a dream, where Norinaga recognized him as his true disciple. Atsutane considered this dream to be an actual (in my world supernatural) event that meant he was recognized as a true disciple.

14. One term Atsutane commonly used for this world was *kakuriyo*, hidden or unseen world, used in contrast to *utsushiyo*, or seen world. Another term he often used for this world was *yūmeikai*. In fact Atsutane used many other variant terms to refer to the same thing. I am using the term Other World as the generic name for Atsutane's supernatural world of the afterlife.

15. Hirata Kanetane (1799–1880), the leader of the Hirata School after Atsutane's death in 1843, married Atsutane's daughter and was adopted as his heir in 1824. He later became a tutor to Emperor Meiji and a member of the Jingikan, the short-lived early Meiji Shinto Bureau.

16. Around this time he wrote three other works focused on supernatural topics: *Kokon yōmikō*, *Katsugoro saisei kibun*, and *Inō mononokeroku*. See Harold Bolitho, "Metempsychosis Hijacked: The Curious Case of Katsugoro," *Harvard Journal of Asiatic Studies* LXII, 2 (December 2002): 389–414, for a summary and analysis of Atsutane's interest in a boy who claimed to remember his previous life.

17. Koyasu Nobukuni, *Hirata Atsutane no sekai* (Perikansha, 2001).

18. An early case of Stockholm syndrome, perhaps.

19. E. M. Satow, "The Revival of Pure Shinto," *TASJ*, III, pt. L (Yokohama, 1875).

20. William Aston, Shinto, *The Way of the Gods* (London: Longmans Green, 1905), 4.

21. A few studies were undertaken in German before World War II. In a 1936 essay titled "Hirata Atsutane, ein geistiger Kämpfer für Japans Frei-

heit," Atsutane was portrayed as a Japanese freedom fighter and leader of the *kokugaku* nationalist movement for a Shinto revival. See Horst Hammitzsch, "Hirata Atsutane: ein geistiger Kämpfer für Japans," *Mitteilngen der deutschen Gesellschaft für Natur und Völkerkunde Ostasiens,* vol. XXVIII, pt. E (5), (1936): 1–27. A couple more German essays on Japanese and Chinese studies appeared in 1939. These were not specifically about Atsutane, though he was recognized. See Heinrich Dumoulin, "Die Entwicklung der *Kokugaku,*" *Monumenta Nipponica* 2, 1 (1939): 140–160. Also see Horst Hammitzsch, "Kangaku und *Kokugaku*: Ein Beitrag zur Geistegeschichte der Tokugawa Zeit," *Monumenta Nipponica* 2, 1 (1939): 1–23. In 1939 there was also a German translation of Atsutane's *Taido wakumon,* one of the texts that offended the bakufu and helped get Atsutane censored and exiled back to Akita in his twilight years. See Wilhelm Schiffer, trans., "Taidō wakumon (Es fragte einer nach dem Grossen Weg), *Monumenta Nipponica* 2, 1 (1939): 212–236.

22. Donald Keene, "Hirata Atsutane and Western Learning," *T'oung Pao* XLII, 5 (1954): 353–380. This was later included in Keene, *The Japanese Discovery of Europe.*

23. Donald Keene's writing on the subject in the late 1970s has five or six pages devoted to Atsutane's *Senkyō ibun,* but it has little to add to what Keene had already explained about the subject in the 1950s and 60s. It is in some ways a call for more attention to *Senkyō ibun,* as Keene describes it as "constantly absorbing reading" and "an unforgettable glimpse of a seldom-revealed side to life in the Japanese intellectual world at the end of the Kinsei period." Keene, *Some Japanese Portraits,* 151.

24. In the 1960s David Earl wrote about Atsutane in relation to nationalism and emperor worship. See David Magarey Earl, *Emperor and Nation in Japan: Political Thinkers of the Tokugawa Period* (Seattle: University of Washington Press, 1964). Also in the late 1960s Walter Odronic produced the only complete translation in English of an Atsutane work, *Essence of the Ancient Way* (*Kodō taii*). (Atsutane and *kokugaku,* of course, are associated with the Shinto religion, in particular *fukko shinto,* Restoration Shinto, or *koshinto,* Ancient Shinto. However, Atsutane himself did not refer to his way as such. His teachings in his own time were called *kogaku,* Ancient Learning, or *kodōgaku,* Ancient Way Studies, and he referred to them as *kodō,* or the Ancient Way, which is what I prefer to use.) See Walter John Odronic, "Kodo taii (An Outline of the Ancient Way)" (Ph.D. diss., University of Pennsylvania, 1967). Half of Atsutane's career was covered in Peter Nosco's dissertation, which was later published as a monograph on Japanese nativism minus the Atsutane study. See Peter Nosco, *Remembering Paradise: Nativism and Nostalgia in Eighteenth-Century Japan* (Cambridge, Mass.: Council of East Asian Studies, Harvard Univer-

sity, 1990). In the 1980s Richard Devine wrote about Atsutane's use of Christian sources. See Richard Devine, "Hirata Atsutane and Christian Sources," *Monumenta Nipponica* 36, 1 (1981): 37–54. This is a subject also brought up by Keene, but which was first recognized by the Japanese scholar Muraoka Tsunetsugu in the first half of the twentieth century. See Muraoka Tsunetsugu, "Hirata Atsutane no shingaku ni okeru yasukyō no eikyō," in Muraoka Tsunetsugu, *Zōtei nihon shisōshi kenkyū* (Iwanami Shoten, 1940).

25. In the early 1980s Jennifer Robertson studied Atsutane's relationship and contribution to grassroots nativism. See Jennifer Robertson, "Sexy Rice: Plant Gender, Farm Manuals, and Grass-Roots Nativism," *Monumenta Nipponica* 36, 3 (1984): 233–260. In 1988 H. D. Harootunian wrote a complex study of nativist discourse. H. D. Harootunian, *Things Seen and Unseen* (Chicago: University of Chicago Press, 1988). This contribution to the study dealt with some of the larger issues of Atsutane's new discourse that will also be touched upon herein. In the 1990s Anne Walthall addressed some important social dimensions of nativism and the Hirata School. Anne Walthall, "Off With Their Heads! The Hirata Disciples and the Ashikaga Shoguns," *Monumenta Nipponica* 50, 2 (1995): 137–170; and Anne Walthall, *The Weak Body of a Useless Woman: Matsuo Taseko and the Meiji Restoration* (Chicago: University of Chicago Press, 1998). Susan Burns' book on *kokugaku* published in 2003 contains occasional mention of Atsutane and his influence but is focused on previously overlooked *kokugaku* scholars whose dates overlap Atsutane's. Susan L. Burns, *Before the Nation: Kokugaku and the Imagining of Community in Early Modern Japan* (Durham, N.C.: Duke University Press, 2003).

26. Atsutane and Torakichi's relationship is touched upon in a couple pages of Harold Bolitho's interesting articles about Katsugoro and metempsychosis from 2002 and 2004, but the depths of *Senkyō ibun* are left unexplored. See Bolitho, "Metempsychosis Hijacked," as well as Harold Bolitho, "Tidings from the Twilight Zone," in *Practicing the Afterlife: Perspectives from Japan,* ed. Susanne Formanek and William R. LaFleur, 261–282 (Vienna: Austrian Academy of Sciences, 2004).

27. Mark McNally, "Phantom History: Hirata Atsutane and Tokugawa Nativism" (Ph.D. diss., University of California Los Angeles, 1998).

28. Mark McNally, *Proving the Way, Conflict and Practice in the History of Japanese Nativism* (Cambridge, Mass.: Harvard University Press, 2005).

29. Susanne Formanek and William R. LaFleur, eds. *Practicing the Afterlife: Perspectives from Japan* (Vienna: Austrian Academy of Sciences, 2004).

30. Not recognizing the importance of the category of *"sanjin"* means one cannot see how important it was for Atsutane to have this term "naturally" come out of Torakichi's mouth. See chapter 3.

31. This term is of course quite broad and is used here to mean the Confucian studies developed in the Song dynasty and which is most commonly associated with Zhu Xi (1130–1200). Atsutane used terms such as *rigaku, shushigaku,* and *sōgaku* when referring to the work and ideas of its Tokugawa period representatives in Japan, in particular, adherents of the Hayashi and Ansai schools of Neo-Confucianism.

32. This is the *kogaku* movement of Ogyū Sorai and Itō Jinsai, to be discussed in detail in the next chapter.

33. Arthur Waley, *The Way and Its Power: A Study of the Tao Te Ching and Its Place in Chinese Thought* (New York: Houghton Mifflin, 1935), 193.

34. See Gerald Figal, *Civilization and Monsters: Spirits of Modernity in Meiji Japan* (Durham, N.C.: Duke University Press, 1999), 217, for more on this modern Japanese tendency to seek superiority in "intangible otherworldliness."

Chapter 1: Constructing Japanese Identity: *Senkyō ibun*

1. Some eminent scholars of Daoism feel the term "immortal" used for this combination of characters is inaccurate and misleading in describing the ancient Chinese practitioners; they prefer the term "transcendent." My choice to stay with "immortal" is not to show disagreement with these scholars, but is simply due to the weight of history and the fact that Blacker started the discussion using that term.

2. H. D. Harootunian, *Things Seen and Unseen* (Chicago: University of Chicago Press, 1988), 153.

3. For example, for a summary of Atsutane's conclusions about India and its people, see Hirata Atsutane, "Shutsujō shōgo," in *HAZ,* vol. 1.

4. James Clifford, "Introduction: Partial Truths," in *Writing Culture, The Poetics and Politics of Ethnography,* ed. James Clifford and George E. Marcus, 23–24 (London: University of California Press, 1986).

5. Michel de Montaigne, *The Complete Essays of Montaigne,* trans. Donald Frame (Stanford, Calif.: Stanford University Press, 1958).

6. Charles de Secondat Montesquieu, *Persian Letters,* trans. C. J. Betts (New York: Penguin Books, 1993).

7. Again see Clifford, "Introduction: Partial Truths," 23.

8. See Maruyama Masao, *Studies in the Intellectual History of Tokugawa Japan,* trans. Mikiso Hane (Princeton, N.J.: Princeton University Press, 1974).

9. See the conclusion in Herman Ooms, *Tokugawa Ideology: Early Constructs, 1570–1680* (Princeton, N.J.: Princeton University Press, 1985).

10. See Richard Rubinger, *Private Academies of Tokugawa Japan* (Princeton, N.J.: Princeton University Press, 1982).

11. Marius B. Jansen, *The Making of Modern Japan* (Cambridge, Mass., and London: The Belknap Press of Harvard University, 2000), 210.

12. In 1604 Tokugawa Ieyasu implemented this system partly as an anti-Christianity guarantee.

13. The Portuguese first arrived in Japan in 1542, so Western studies began sometime in the sixteenth century. There was also Russian contact with Japan, and there are documents that show that Atsutane attempted to decipher some Russian language sources.

14. Mary Elizabeth Berry, *Japan in Print: Information and Nation in the Early Modern Period* (Berkeley: University of California Press, 2006).

15. An example of this would be the *Wakan sansai zue*, Japan's first encyclopedia, written in 105 volumes and published in 1712 by a physician from Osaka, Terajima Ryōan, in imitation of the Ming Chinese encyclopedia titled *Sansai zue*.

16. See Laura Hostetler, *Qing Colonial Enterprise: Ethnography and Cartography in Early Modern China* (Chicago: University of Chicago Press, 2001). This work shows how Chinese in the Qing in pursuit of imperial ambitions were also emphasizing empirical science in their cartographic and ethnographic activities.

17. See Michael Dylan Foster, "Morphologies of Mystery: Yōkai and Discourses of the Supernatural in Japan, 1666–1999" (Ph.D. diss., Stanford University, 2003). Also, Gerald Figal, *Civilization and Monsters: Spirits of Modernity in Meiji Japan* (Durham, N.C.: Duke University Press, 1999).

18. The eighth Tokugawa shogun ruled from 1714 to 1745 and was an advocate of Western learning.

19. Jansen, *The Making of Modern Japan*, 266.

20. Atsutane's intellectual movement, *kokugaku*, is sometimes referred to in modern scholarship as nativism, ethnic nativism, Tokugawa nativism, or national learning. A summary of the background of Atsutane's *kokugaku* follows, and whenever any of the various favorite terms of contemporary scholarship mentioned above should arise, they can be taken as functionally synonymous unless otherwise indicated. It is also important to keep in mind one important point from McNally's *Proving the Way, Conflict and Practice in the History of Japanese Nativism* (Cambridge, Mass.: Harvard University Press, 2005); that is, during the Tokugawa period what scholars today refer to as *kokugaku* was not a distinct school of nativism with a unified intellectual continuity.

21. Current scholarship questions whether Kada no Azumamaro actually authored this document, but the story grew and was widely believed as the foundation story of *kokugaku*.

22. This, quite simply put, is an acute awareness, appreciation, and sensitivity to emotional qualities of life.

23. This was written in 1805 and used as one of the "writing samples" he used to apply to the Suzunoya. It was not published at that time and was later revised in 1820 and given a slightly different title, where it fits well as the starting line for his writings concerning the supernatural, which took off in that year.

24. See James Ketelaar, *Of Heretics and Martyrs in Meiji Japan* (Princeton, N.J.: Princeton University Press, 1990), 19–36.

25. Tominaga was the scholar who wrote *Shutsujō kōgo,* a book that criticized the way Buddhist histories had been written up to that time and specifically called into question the many historical claims made by would-be historians within the Buddhist tradition. It, of course, served as the inspiration for Atsutane's similarly named anti-Buddhist critique.

26. In 1686 the Japanese government banned Christian books, and people found in possession of them could be crucified. Atsutane's work pertaining to these banned books were marked "not to be seen by others." Keene suggested that Atsutane's Mito school connections might have given him access to their Christian collection.

27. Matteo Ricci was the most famous of the early Jesuit missionaries to China. He wrote these works in Chinese. The first is a dialogue concerning the attributes of God, and the second is a record of conversations with Chinese officials on a variety of subjects. Both are anti-Buddhist in nature. Didacus de Pantoja was Ricci's companion and also wrote in Chinese. His work concerns the seven deadly sins.

28. Atsutane's claims for a creator deity, the paradisical afterlife, and the trinity of gods are sometimes attributed to his knowledge of Christianity. However, Indian traditions, Buddhism included, could have been the source for these ideas.

29. For the difference between a *Rangaku* scholar's and Atsutane's appreciation of Western science, see Donald Keene, *The Japanese Discovery of Europe 1730–1820* (Stanford, Calif.: Stanford University Press, 1952 and 1969), 157–158.

30. *A Supplement to the Senkyō ibun* (*Senkyō ibun furoku*), *A Record of the Dance of the Seven Lives* (*Shichishōmai no ki*), an Other Worldly ritual dance taught by Torakichi. There is another work about Torakichi, which records much of the same information but has extra stories of his possession experiences, called *A Short Chronicle of the Divine Child's Possession Tales* (*Shindō hyōdan ryakki*).

31. See Hori Ichirō, *Folk Religion: Continuity and Change,* ed. Joseph Kitagawa and Alan L. Miller (Chicago: University of Chicago Press, 1968), particularly chapter IV, "Mountains and Their Importance for the Idea of the Other World."

32. Torakichi too had nothing good to say about *miko*, traditional female *kami* cult mediums. There is a story from *Senkyō ibun* where Torakichi proudly and publicly exposed as a fraud a *miko* who had been performing a divination ritual.

33. Shugendō is a Japanese mountain religion. The participants are called either *yamabushi* or *shugenja*. They practice asceticism in the mountains in order to develop spiritual power. The practices are a mixture of Buddhism, Shinto, Taoism, and popular religion.

34. In a postscript to *Shichishōmai no ki* in Hirata Atsutane, *Senkyō ibun* (*gendaigoyaku*), trans. Yamamoto Hiroshi (Hachiman Shoten, 1997), 262.

35. See Hirata Atsutane, "Zoku shintō taii," in *HAZ*, vol. 1.

36. The Yoshida and the Shirakawa families, which together controlled the licensing of approximately 90 percent of the Shinto priests during Atsutane's time, competed against each other to employ Atsutane, and both of them did at different times. It was not so much that they were impressed with Atsutane's teachings, which were radically different than their own standard ones, rather they were alarmed by his popularity among Shinto priests and were afraid of losing their membership to his influence.

37. Carlos Castaneda, *The Teachings of Don Juan; a Yaqui Way of Knowledge* (New York: Ballantine Books, 1969).

38. Richard De Mille, *Castaneda's Journey: The Power and the Allegory* (Santa Barbara, Calif.: Capra Press, 1976). De Mille's work goes a long way toward debunking Castaneda's supernatural claims.

39. Clifford, "Introduction: Partial Truths," 4.

40. Ibid., 3.

41. A great example of a surrealist corrupting an ethnographic enterprise and blending literature with anthropology can be seen in Michel Leiris, *L'Afrique fantôme* (Paris: Gallimard, 1981).

42. Clifford, "Introduction: Partial Truths," 6.

43. Vincent Crapanzano, "Hermes' Dilemma: The Masking of Subversion in Ethnographic Description," in *Writing Culture, The Poetics and Politics of Ethnography*, ed. James Clifford and George E. Marcus, 51–76 (London: University of California Press, 1986).

44. Ibid., 76.

45. Yashiro Hirokata (1758–1841) was a scholar of *wagaku*, Japanese studies, and a prolific writer. He was a coeditor of the *Gunshō ruiju* and was Atsutane's most influential friend within elite intellectual and political circles.

46. Yamazaki Yoshishige (1796–1856), from an Edo drug merchant family, was a collector of antiquities and a student of *kokugaku*. He had formerly been Atsutane's student and then had become a student of Edo school *kokugaku*, an Edo literary brand of *kokugaku*, under the tutelage of Oyamada Tomokiyo

(1783–1847), with whom Atsutane also kept company. He is mentioned in many of Takizawa Bakin's (1767–1848) works due to their close friendship, and he himself authored a number of works including the *Heiji Daitō,* which was about his talks with Torakichi.

47. Ban Nobutomo (1773–1846) was a fellow *kokugaku* scholar and a friend until their falling out.

48. The Kalavinka bird appears in chapter seven of the Lotus Sutra, among other places. It was supposed to live either in the Pure Land or in the Himalayas and was recognized as having the most beautiful singing voice of any and all birds. Its voice is a metaphor for the Buddha's voice.

49. Hirata Atsutane, "Senkyō ibun," in *HAZ,* vol. 3, 1.

50. Wallace Martin, *Recent Theories of Narrative* (Ithaca, N.Y., and London: Cornell University Press, 1986), 23. Martin went on to qualify the statement for the anthropologist analyzing several similar tales, but the qualification clearly does not apply in this case. Furthermore, Martin conflates the story told by the informant with the story told by the anthropologist, with no thought that the anthropologist has added his own transcending story.

51. Ge Hong was a Daoist master who practiced alchemy and longevity techniques. His writing greatly influenced Atsutane, who later would claim that these Chinese ideas were developed by the *kami* of Japan and exported to China.

52. Gérard Genette, *Narrative Discourse: An Essay in Method,* trans. Jane E. Lewin (Ithaca, N.Y.: Cornell University Press, 1980), 227, on narrative levels, with terminology too complex to explain herein.

53. Ibid., 256.

54. John J. Winkler, *Auctor & Actor: A Narratological Reading of Apuleius' Golden Ass* (Berkeley and Los Angeles: University of California Press, 1985), 75.

Chapter 2: The Medium Finds a Promoter: Torakichi and Atsutane

1. The Edo-based *kokugaku* scholar Oyamada Tomokiyo (1783–1847) describes the many visitors and social activities at his house in *Yōshorō Nikki,* in *Kinsei bungei sōsho* (Kokusho Kankōkai, 1912), 208–391. *Senkyō ibun* also shows similar social activity and distinguished visitors who come to see Torakichi. Tomokiyo himself was mentioned in *Senkyō ibun* as part of Atsutane and Torakichi's social circle. For recent work on aesthetic group activities during the Tokugawa period, see Eiko Ikegami, *Bonds of Civility: Aesthetic Networks and the Political Origins of Japanese Culture* (Cambridge, UK; New York: Cambridge University Press, 2005).

2. Another story described him as a tobacco seller.

3. Atsutane lived in Edo in the Yamanote district at Yushima Tenjin, not far from the modern-day Tokyo University at Hongō. Yoshishige lived approximately a mile away. Torakichi's family also lived in the same vicinity, but Yoshishige lived in a large gated house and Torakichi's family lived in a single room. Yashiro lived about half a mile away from Yoshishige. Many of the *kokugaku* scholars lived in the vicinity or in the nearby Shitamachi district. This provided a center for the salon society but did not limit the guest list to people who lived in the area. People from all over Japan dropped into the center of Edo to hear the latest discussions or to see attractions such as Torakichi.

4. Haga Noboru, "Kaisetsu (2)" in *SHAZ geppō* 2, vol. 9, 9.

5. Hirata Atsutane, "Senkyō ibun," in *HAZ*, vol. 3, 3.

6. This is Yoshishige's record of his talks with Torakichi. *Heiji* is derived from a Torakichi alias, so the title would mean something like *Responses from Torakichi*. In *Senkyō ibun*, Torakichi denied the contents of Yoshishige's version. Torakichi claimed that Yoshishige's writings made him seem fond of Buddhism, which he had to disavow for Atsutane.

7. He actually wrote "seven years," but he was counting by the old standard Japanese age counting system, which adds an extra year.

8. He was told by the strange diviner to do a practice that required him to hold a flame in his hand for as long as he could stand it. He was understandably resentful when he found out he had been tricked.

9. This story is taken directly from Chinese literature. Sire Gourd and the Immortal's Heaven found in his gourd were also legendary in Japan. Drawings of this kind of tale decorated gourds, silks, and even game pieces in this era of the nineteenth century. It is likely that Torakichi heard the story somewhere or saw it, or both (see Chigiri Kōsai, *Sennin no kenkyū* [Tairiku Shobō, 1976], 520). Although Torakichi was illiterate, early versions of this story can be found in *Biographies of Immortals* (*Shinsenden*) from fourth-century China and also *Later Han Writings* (*Gokansho*) from fifth-century China, which both contain the story of the Daoist student Fei Changfang, who saw Sire Gourd, an exiled immortal, selling medicines and later climbing into his gourd. Sire Gourd then invited Fei Changfang to join him in the gourd, which contained an immortal's heaven. The name of this legendary character was brought up as a topic of conversation in *Senkyō ibun*, but there was no elaboration on the subject. In addition, in his work *Biography of Master Ge Hong* (*Kassenōden*), Atsutane mentioned this Fei Changfang and Ge Hong's *Shinsenden*, one of the earliest sources of the story. Still, this never seemed to have been a reason to doubt Torakichi; rather, it seemed to be held in his favor. For more on this story, see Rolf Stein, *The World in Miniature* (Stanford, Calif.: Stanford Uni-

versity Press, 1990), or Robert Ford Campany, *To Live as Long as Heaven and Earth: A Translation and Study of Ge Hong's Traditions of Divine Transcendents* (Berkeley: University of California Press, 2002).

10. At this point Torakichi had not yet been urged by Atsutane to clarify the difference between *tengu* and *sanjin*. That important distinction will be detailed in the following chapter.

11. Torakichi told a story of his *sanjin* master dressing up and handing out talismans to screaming and laughing children who would follow him around. The master wore a mask and called himself the "Wai Wai Tennō." Not knowing who this was at first, Torakichi got caught up in the fun, then found himself lost and alone at dusk with his master. The master walked him home and at that time they accidentally ran into Torakichi's father, who had come out to look for him and who thanked the master profusely for bringing the boy back. Torakichi's father asked the master's name but received a false one, and when he tried to find him the next day to give a thank-you gift, he found he had been lied to. Torakichi's description of his family is not flattering, especially where it concerns caring about Torakichi's whereabouts. Another question this story brings up is why this man was recruiting children. Could this be true concern for the children's safety and true belief that talismans given away to them for free would help keep them from harm? The other possibilities are ominous.

12. He was actually sent to work at two different temples while still a child. One was a Zen-affiliated temple and the other was Nichiren-affiliated. The particular school of Buddhism did not seem to be an issue, and Torakichi's mother was characterized as being partial to Pure Land practice. Torakichi also claimed to have been the student of a master of Hiruko (sometimes read Ebisu) Shinto. Hiruko refers to the first child of the creator pair Izanagi and Izanami, who was cast adrift in a reed boat. Later this rejected child was conflated with Ebisu, one of the Seven Gods of Good Fortune.

13. This seems to be an exceptionally harsh and guaranteed fatal version of a Shugendō ritual.

14. Hirata Atsutane, "Senkyō ibun," in *HAZ*, vol. 3, 148.

15. Torakichi was quite fond of playing hide and seek, and the visitors and members of Atsutane's household played this game with him for hours, and then again the next day.

16. Atsutane wrote at least three different versions of his daily prayer ritual *Maichō shimpai shiki*. The second was written in the 1820s after he met Torakichi and has a verse dedicated to Torakichi's *sanjin* master, but the ones prior to and after it do not. There was also a *honzon* scroll with a portrait of Torakichi's *sanjin* master, which may have been used so that Atsutane could fulfill his promise.

17. Hirata Atsutane, "Senkyō ibun," in *HAZ*, vol. 3, 23.

18. Ibid., 22.

19. See Kamata Tōji, "The Disfiguring of Nativism: Hirata Atsutane and Orikuchi Shinobu," in *Shinto in History: Ways of the Kami*, ed. John Breen and Mark Teeuwen (Honolulu: University of Hawai'i Press, 2000), 308.

20. One of Sugiyama's fellow *sanjin* who seemed to be second in charge was referred to as Koromei. He was also supposedly quite old and had special powers and knowledge.

21. Besides the obligatory copy to the Ise shrine library and others like it, these books were published for just the reserved number of people that the author thought would be interested in them.

22. See Jennifer Robertson, "Sexy Rice: Plant Gender, Farm Manuals, and Grass-Roots Nativism," *Monumenta Nipponica* 36, 3(1984): 233–260.

23. See Richard Rubinger, *Private Academies of Tokugawa Japan* (Princeton, N.J.: Princeton University Press, 1982).

24. Haruniwa was the oldest son and had a reputation as an exceptionally gifted scholar; however, he went completely blind in his middle age, prompting Norinaga to formally adopt Ohira.

25. Murata Harumi was a *kokugaku* scholar and poet who came out of Kamo no Mabuchi's school. He and Katō Chikage (1735–1808) were the most prominent members of the Edo-based faction (Edo-ha) of literary nativists.

26. This was an Edo *kokugaku* scholar of the Suzunoya school, older than Atsutane and Nobutomo, who argued back and forth with Edo school's Murata Harumi about the nature of nativism. Harumi had been critical of Norinaga's teachings, and Makuni ended up harshly criticizing Harumi for betraying nativism by privileging Chinese sources over Japanese sources.

27. See Mark McNally, *Proving the Way, Conflict and Practice in the History of Japanese Nativism* (Cambridge, Mass: Harvard University Press, 2005). This work gives detailed information of the various nativist sects forming throughout Japan at this time.

28. Fiction writer and Ukiyoe artist.

29. Comic fiction writer.

30. Popular Edo fiction writer.

31. See Eiko Ikegami, *Bonds of Civility*, for a complex history of the social life of Tokugawa Japan highlighting the details of aesthetic group activities.

32. Atsutane was born in 1776 in the city of Kubota in Dewa Province, where he was known as Owada Masakichi. He was the fourth son of Owada Sachitane, a samurai who served the Satake family of Akita. He left home for Edo because of strained family relations and arrived in Edo where he is said to have had a difficult but colorful life before being adopted by the Hirata family and changing his name.

33. Yamaga Sokō (1622–1685) was a founder of a Confucian school of

Ancient Learning, rejecting Zhu Xi and Wang Yangming's Neo-Confucianism while emphasizing the study of proper warrior conduct.

34. Yamazaki Chōemon, formerly Ginjirō, also known as the Aburachō, or the oil boss, took the first part of Atsutane's name to show his affiliation with the master.

35. The first name for Atsutane's school was Masugenoya, or Simple Reed Hut. In the pivotal year for Atsutane's career, 1816, the name was changed to Ibukinoya. This is a reference to the divine purifying wind written of in the earliest histories and was inspired by the mystical tugboat whistle noise created by the stone flute he claimed he was divinely inspired to find on his trip to Chiba in that year.

36. This is expressed in Tahara Tsuguo's biography of Atsutane, and it is not merely cynical commentary on Tahara's part, seeing how Atsutane's fortunes changed dramatically after that year.

37. Yoshida Shinto, also called Yuiitsu Shinto, was primarily a Neo-Confucian hybrid, but it also retained Buddhist elements. Shirakawa Shinto was more influenced by Shingon Buddhism. Both of these types of "foreign"-influenced Shinto were not to Atsutane's liking, therefore he must have seen it as an opportunity to purge the Shinto establishment of all foreign elements. However, we know that he brought in a few foreign elements of his own, which he of course did not recognize as foreign.

38. This woman was actually the daughter of a tofu merchant from Atsutoshi's town. She had been previously adopted by Atsutoshi. Her original name is unknown. Her first name was changed to Orise, the name of Atsutane's beloved first wife. Atsutane also had a short-lived second marriage that was dissolved.

39. As *Daikaku* in *Senkyō ibun* this is a "stellar" honorific derived from ancient Chinese astronomy. However, it is more often written with different Chinese characters meaning ocean.

40. Hirata Atsutane, "Senkyō ibun," in *HAZ*, vol. 3, 41.

41. Hanawa was a brilliant student of *kokugaku* who studied under Kamo no Mabuchi in Edo. He lost his sight when he was seven years old and so had to rely on what must have been a remarkable memory. He is credited as being the editor of the *Gunsho ruijū* with his friend Yashiro's assistance. He also worked on the editing for the *Zoku gunsho ruijū* and has other scholarly credits to his name.

42. See Watanabe Kinzō, *Hirata Atsutane kenkyū* (Rokko Shobō, 1942), 286–306.

43. See ibid., 260, for the rejection letter that characterizes Atsutane as a strange man harboring delusions.

44. Hirata Atsutane, "Senkyō ibun," in *HAZ*, vol. 3, 1.

45. Satō Nobuhiro (1769–1850) was a late Edo expert in agriculture, economics, and Dutch studies.

46. Kunitomo Yoshimasa (1778–1840) was an inventor who mass-produced guns and developed his own air-powered rifle from a Dutch model. He also built his own reflecting telescope and undertook regular observations of the sun.

47. Hirata Atsutane, "Senkyō ibun," in *HAZ*, vol. 3, 12.

48. Ibid.

49. Some of these people have interesting historical credits, some have little more than their family names or business to distinguish them, and others can only be identified as Atsutane's students, which was enough to get their names listed in the official record.

50. Hirata Atsutane, "Senkyō ibun," in *HAZ*, vol. 3, 32.

51. James Clifford provides a handy list in James Clifford and George E. Marcus, eds. *Writing Culture: The Poetics and Politics of Ethnography* (Berkeley: University of California Press, 1986). They are Camille Lacoste-Dujardin, *Dialogue des femmes en ethnologie* (Paris: Maspero, 1977); Vincent Crapanzano, *Tuhami: Portrait of a Moroccan* (Chicago: University of Chicago Press, 1980); Marjorie Shostak, *Nisa: The Life and Words of a !Kung Woman* (Cambridge, Mass.: Harvard University Press, 1981); Fatima Mernissi, *Le Maroc raconté par ses femmes* (Rabat: Société marocaine des éditeurs réunis, 1984).

Chapter 3: Manipulating the Medium: Separating the *Sanjin* from the *Tengu*

1. See Donald L. Philippi, trans., *Kojiki. Translated with an Introduction and Notes* (University of Tokyo Press, 1968), 134.

2. Oe Kenzaburō, in his Nobel Prize acceptance speech, mentioned that one of his ancestors claimed to have been present at an interview with Torakichi and even had a copy of this iron-eating beast's picture, which had been drawn by Torakichi himself.

3. Strangely enough, this story of glowing wood led to a practical joke on the *Tengu* Boy, instigated by one of Atsutane's students who made the claim that masturbating in the dark would lead to an illumination of sorts. Torakichi did not find this to be true. On the subject of sex, women were off limits in the Other World, and Torakichi also denied that there was ever any homosexuality among *sanjin*.

4. This picture is not included in the *zenshū*, but there are pictures of Torakichi's demons in Aramata Hiroshi and Maita Katsuyasu, eds. *Chi no nettowaaku no senkakusha, Hirata Atsutane* (Heibonsha, 2004).

5. Hirata Atsutane, "Senkyō ibun," in *HAZ*, vol. 3, 151.

6. Ibid., 151–152.

7. This is presented as another name for Mt. Atago. Mt. Atago as a site for *tengu* activity is well-storied in Japanese cultural history. For an extensive history of this connection, see Komatsu Kazuhiko, ed., *Tengu to yamamba in Kaii no minzokugaku* 5 (Kawade Shobō Shinsha, 2000).

8. Haga Noboru, "Kaisetsu (2)," in *SHAZ geppō* 2, vol. 9, 9.

9. Hirata Atsutane, "Kokon yomikō," in *SHAZ*, vol. 9, 77.

10. Hirata Atsutane, *Tama no mihashira,* ed. Koyasu Nobukuni (Iwanami Shoten, 1998), 194 n. 4.

11. Origuchi Shinobu was certainly an expert on Atsutane, but he was admittedly biased in Atsutane's favor. When speaking of *Thoughts on Supernatural Beings of Past and Present,* Origuchi did not believe that Atsutane's association of Buddhist priests with *tengu* should be attributed in any way to prejudice on Atsutane's part. Origuchi pointed out that Buddhists had been called *tengu* regularly, at least starting from the end of the medieval period. He also pointed out that even Kōbō Daishi and Dengyō Daishi had been called *tengu*. Nevertheless, the fact that the association of *tengu* with Buddhism did not start with Atsutane does not put him in a neutral objective camp. He enjoyed the association of famous Buddhists with reportedly evil supernatural beings. See *OSZ*, vol. 20, 429.

12. Hirata Atsutane, "Kokon yomikō," in *SHAZ*, vol. 9, 78.

13. This Atsutane bias was continued and reinforced by a slightly later imitator of the ethnography of the Other World style. Haga Noboru, in *Yanagita Kunio to Hirata Atsutane* (Kōseisha, 1997), 178–179, provides a list of actual historical figures separated out into *sanjin* and *tengu* in that later work.

14. At one point Torakichi said that they sold talismans when they needed money for new clothes. He also told another story that they were never really worried about money, because whenever they did need it, the elder *sanjin* would mysteriously go somewhere and come back with all they needed. There was also the story of a magic stone that located lost money.

15. Better-known citations come from Guan Zi, seventh century BCE, and Xun Xi, third century BCE.

16. For example, Hiraga Gennai, the eighteenth-century artist and inventor, is also known by the sobriquet Fūrai *Sanjin*.

17. See Yanagita Kunio, "Sanmin no seikatsu" and "Tōno monogatari," in *Teihon Yanagita Kunio shū*, vol. 4 (Chikuma Shobō, 1969).

18. Torakichi modified this characterization in another interview that will be discussed in chapter 5.

19. Koyasu Nobukuni compares this to orientalist depictions of Asian culture in that some of the questions seem to suggest that the questioner doubted

the common humanity of the members of the other culture; for example, "Do you sleep, do you dream, and do you like music?"

20. Torakichi's explanation for why his master goes by the Buddhist title of *Sōjō*, which would translate as Buddhist bishop, was that the characters (as well as he could remember characters, which was not very well) were different and that his master's alias should probably be pronounced slightly differently, as *sōshō*.

21. Bourdieu's *habitus* might be helpful in considering Torakichi's storytelling talents and habits. "The *habitus* is a spontaneity without consciousness or will, opposed as much to the mechanical necessity of things without history in mechanistic theories as it is to the reflexive freedom of subjects 'without inertia' in rationalist theories." Pierre Bourdieu, *The Logic of Practice* (Stanford, Calif.: Stanford University Press, 1980), 56.

22. In this very interesting passage, Torakichi is also instructed by his *sanjin* master not to reveal the master's real name but to call him Sugiyama. This certainly makes one wonder if Atsutane was given another name, perhaps Takane, which he used in his daily rituals, but which he himself never would admit to knowing. Atsutane shared a Daoist-like belief in the power of names and naming and perhaps he considered this too powerful a secret to record. See Hirata Atsutane, "Senkyō ibun," in *HAZ*, vol. 3, 8–9.

23. These are three types of suffering from Buddhist teachings that usually are thought to afflict the *nagas*, or dragons of Buddhism.

24. Hirata Atsutane, "Senkyō ibun," in *HAZ*, vol. 3, 140.

25. Ibid., 131.

26. Ibid., 81–82.

27. Chigiri Kōsai, an expert in *sennin* and *tengu* studies, surmised that the choice of *sanjin* over *sōjō* for Sugiyama's title was due simply to Atsutane's hatred of Buddhism. It is my contention, of course, that Atsutane had more grandiose plans for the *sanjin* appellation. See Chigiri Kōsai, *Tengu no kenkyū* (Hara Shobō, 1975), 208–236.

28. Hirata Atsutane. *Tama no mihashira*, ed. Koyasu Nobukuni (Iwanami Shoten, 1998), 171, 172.

29. Ibid., 194.

30. Hirata Atsutane, "Senkyō ibun," in *HAZ*, vol. 3, 98.

31. Koyasu Nobukuni suggested he may have been a yin yang master, but Watanabe Kinzō characterized him as a relatively well-known Buddhist scholar, which would seem likely from the context. For more on divination and mountain *kami*, see Yoshino Hiroko, *Yama no kami: Eki, gogyō to nihon genshi hebi shinkō* (Jinbun Shoin, 1989).

32. Hirata Atsutane, "Senkyō ibun," in *HAZ*, vol. 3, 94.

33. Ibid., 35.

34. See Kamata Tōji, "The Disfiguring of Nativism: Hirata Atsutane and Origuchi Shinobu," in *Shinto in History: Ways of the Kami*, ed. John Breen and Mark Teeuwen (Honolulu: University of Hawai'i Press, 2000), 301.

35. See Donald Keene, *The Japanese Discovery of Europe, 1720–1830* (Stanford, Calif.: Stanford University Press, 1952 and 1969); or Donald Keene, *Some Japanese Portraits* (Tokyo: Kodansha International, 1978).

36. For McNally's analysis of their "working" relationship, see Mark McNally, *Proving the Way, Conflict and Practice in the History of Japanese Nativism* (Cambridge, Mass.: Harvard University Press, 2005), 196–197.

37. This recorded lecture took place in 1943 at Kokugakuin University at a ceremony commemorating the hundredth anniversary of Atsutane's passing.

38. See Origuchi Shinobu, "Hirata kokugaku no dentō," in *OSZ*, vol. 20, 440.

39. This derisive title *sanshi*, Mountain Master, pops up time and again after Atsutane's promotion of the Torakichi episode.

40. This flute is the inspiration for the name of his school, and the story is that he found it on one of his recruiting trips to Chiba at a possible ancient *kami* worship site. He wrote about it in a work called *The Heavenly Stone Flute* (*Ame no ishibue*).

41. Hirata Atsutane, "Senkyō ibun," in *HAZ*, vol. 3, 40–41.

42. Ibid., 42.

43. Ibid., 42.

44. Ibid., 41.

45. The *Senkyō ibun* record clearly contradicts this statement. Atsutane merely wanted to publicize his findings without appearing to be anxious to take advantage of this publicity bonanza.

46. Hirata Atsutane, "Shindō hyōdan ryakki," in *HAZ*, vol. 3, 11.

Chapter 4: The Critique of China and Defense of Native Culture

1. His onetime good friend and fellow Edo Suzunoya *kokugaku* scholar Ban Nobutomo, for one, disagreed with him on this point. On top of this, Norinaga's theories on the ancient Japanese and their language celebrated the lack of written representation.

2. These three formless *kami* of creation, who were self-created, came to be grouped together in the Edo period by nativists in response to Christian theories of the trinity. See *Shinto jiten*.

3. Hirata Atsutane, "Kodō taii," in *HAZ*, vol. 1, 28. In some small defense of Atsutane on the issue of Christian influence, his pique at Shakyamuni's conflation of Brahma and Indra and his own polytheistic multiplication of heavenly

kami make his heavenly deities more Indian than Christian. Iyanaga Nobumi has written convincingly about Atsutane's interest in relating Indian/Hindu and native Japanese deities. Furthermore, Atsutane's afterworld "heaven" is spatially coexistent with the world of the living, and in Atsutane's own opinion, it was preferable to be alive than to be a spirit in heaven. So according to Atsutane, Earth is a better place than Heaven, which is certainly not a Christian position.

4. This is the first part, which contains stories only about *kami*. The Japanese had not yet "devolved" into humans.

5. *The Book of the Prince of Huai nan* (*Huai nan zi*) is from the second century BCE and *Cycles of Threes and Fives* (*San wu li ji*) is from the third century CE and is not extant except for quotations in later texts. Both texts contain examples of Chinese cosmological models.

6. Hirata Atsutane, "Kodō taii," in *HAZ*, vol. 1, 19.

7. Ibid., 24.

8. Eternally Standing Deity of Earth is the first *kami* to appear in the *Nihongi*, but the sixth in the *Kojiki*.

9. This *kami* is also called Toyo kuni nushi in the *Nihongi*, which makes him the Lord of the Abundant Country.

10. These are variant names for the underworld, or Root Country. For Atsutane this underworld was not within the earth, but was the moon, which he believed at creation was a round mass under the earth.

11. Hirata Atsutane, "Kodō taii," in *HAZ*, vol. 1, 34.

12. Hattori Nakatsune (1756–1824). For more on this little-known figure's heliocentric theory and the in-house *kokugaku* debate it triggered, see Mark McNally, *Proving the Way, Conflict and Practice in the History of Japanese Nativism* (Cambridge, Mass.: Harvard University Press, 2005).

13. Even this "innovative" idea was appropriated from among the Japancentric theorizing of Yoshida Shinto scholars.

14. Hirata Atsutane, "Kodō taii," in *HAZ*, vol. 1, 42.

15. Ibid., 6.

16. See *NST*, vol. 19.

17. Ibid.

18. A special algorithm is needed to come up with sixteen generations; that is, the four paired generations times two, added to the three unpaired generations of heavenly *kami* plus the five generations of earthly *kami* all added together equal sixteen.

19. For more on medieval Japanese Shinto/Buddhist syncretic cosmologies, see Mark Teeuwen, *Watarai Shinto: An Intellectual History of the Outer Shrine in Ise* (Leiden: CNWS Publications, the Research School CNWS, Leiden University, the Netherlands, 1996).

20. *kunitsukami.*

21. The three sources are heaven, earth, and man. Their harmonious relationship is often depicted by the Chinese character for king.

22. Hirata Atsutane, "Kodō taii," in *HAZ*, vol. 1, 44.

23. There are of course stories of Chinese immortals, Jp. *sennin*, who selflessly serve others, but Torakichi seemed unaware of that. This difference also sounds suspiciously like a Mahayana Buddhist criticism of Hinayana arhats.

24. See Tahara Tsuguo, *Hirata Atsutane. Jinbutsu sōsho*, no. 111 (Yoshikawa Kobunkan, 1963), 228–229.

25. Their titles are: *A Compilation of the Teachings of the Divine Immortals* (*Shinsen kyōkahen*); *A Compilation for Introduction into the Divine Immortals* (*Shinsen dōinhen*); *A Compilation of the Potions of the Divine Immortals* (*Shinsen fukuyakuhen*); *A Compilation for Directing Qi* (*Shinsen gyokihen*); *A Compilation of the Techniques of the Divine Immortals* (*Shinsen hōjutsuhen*); *A Compilation on the Mastery of the Divine Immortals* (*Shinsen saihōhen*); *and The Essential Methods of Becoming a Divine Immortal* (*Shinsen shiyōhō*).

26. Some scholars might prefer that he be referred to as "proto-Daoist."

27. Hirata Atsutane, "Kassenōden," in *SHAZ*, vol. 14, 411.

28. This is Ch. yangsheng, called by Robinet "nourishing the vital principle." To see Robinet's detailed definition, see Isabelle Robinet, *Taoism: Growth of a Religion*, trans. Phyllis Brooks (Stanford, Calif.: Stanford University Press, 1997), 91.

29. This is a reference to the Tang period story of Chunyu Yong's trip to the ant kingdom in a drunken reverie.

30. Hirata Atsutane, "Senkyō ibun," in *HAZ*, vol. 3, 65–66.

31. Present-day western Shizuoka Province.

32. This is a reference to "complex systems of body divination and theories of fetal endowment" important in early Chinese religion. See Robert Ford Campany, *To Live as Long as Heaven and Earth: A Translation and Study of Ge Hong's Traditions of Divine Transcendents* (Berkeley: University of California Press, 2002), 140.

33. Hirata Atsutane, "Senkyō ibun," in *HAZ*, vol. 3, 70.

34. Ibid., 159.

35. For details on these, see Fabrizio Pregadio, "The Elixirs of Immortality," in *Daoism Handbook*, ed. Livia Kohn, 165–195 (Leiden: E. J. Brill, 2000).

36. Hirata Atsutane, "Senkyō ibun," in *HAZ*, vol. 3, 159–160.

37. Tōun was a Tokugawa period (1603–1867) masterless samurai from Edo who was said to have been abducted by *tengu* and taken to Mt. Kompira. See Chigiri Kōsai, *Tengu no kenkyū* (Hara Shobō, 1975), 424.

38. Atsutane is here conflating *tengu* with *sanjin,* on this occasion accommodating Torakichi's preference to do so.

39. Illusions of fire blamed on foxes thought to be playing tricks on humans.

40. Hirata Atsutane, "Senkyō ibun," in *HAZ,* vol. 3, 63–64.

41. He is also called Great Sanjin.

42. Onion, garlic, leek, absinthe, mustard.

43. Hirata Atsutane, "Senkyō ibun," in *HAZ,* vol. 3, 137–138.

44. Ibid., 105–106.

45. William Aston, Nihongi: *Chronicles of Japan from the Earliest Times to A.D. 697* (Rutland, Vt.: Charles E. Tuttle, 1972), 59–60.

46. See Michel Strickmann, *Chinese Magical Medicine,* ed. Bernard Faure (Stanford, Calif.: Stanford University Press, 2002), particularly chapter one on "Disease and Taoist Law," the ideas of which are echoed by Edward L. Davis in *Society and the Supernatural in Song China* (Honolulu: University of Hawai'i Press, 2001). In brief, illness was considered to be a spiritual matter caused usually by some moral failing on the part of the sufferer or some part of his or her extended family.

47. Atsutane was not exactly in line with Ge Hong or other ancient Chinese physicians concerning the causes of illness. For example, he did not hold to the idea of destroying the "three corpses" who longed to be released from the body and so conspired against a person's health. What he did share was the belief that spiritual agents caused illness and these agents answered to higher spiritual powers.

48. Again, the above-mentioned works by Strickmann and Davis expound on the belief that illness-causing demons obey their superiors. For further study of the bureaucratic model in Daoism, see also Robert Hymes, *Way and Byway: Taoism, Local Religion, and Models of Divinity in Sung and Modern China* (Berkeley: University of California Press, 2002).

49. Hirata Atsutane, "Senkyō ibun," in *HAZ,* vol. 3, 94.

50. See Hirata Atsutane, "Shizu no iwaya," in *SHAZ,* vol. 14. Hakuin's description of the technique is unmistakably Daoist in origin.

51. A very specific type of Japanese demon, not the ones described by Torakichi in chapter 3 of this book.

52. Hirata Atsutane, "Senkyō ibun," in *HAZ,* vol. 3, 61–62.

53. An inflammation of the urinary tract sometimes sexually transmitted.

54. *Momme* = 3.75 grams, *gō* = 1.8 liters, *shaku* = .18 liters

55. For vomiting (emetic).

56. Hirata Atsutane, "Senkyō ibun," in *HAZ,* vol. 3, 64–65.

57. A distilled spirit.

58. Possibly red and blistered in appearance.

59. Hirata Atsutane, "Senkyō ibun," in *HAZ*, vol. 3, 72.

60. This is a type of ignition device made of cattails, used in this case to cauterize.

61. This is a type of crow with a white patch on its back.

62. A type of labiate grass.

63. Hirata Atsutane, "Senkyō ibun," in *HAZ*, vol. 3, 67–68.

64. Ibid., 68.

65. Ibid.

66. Ibid.

67. Ibid., 69.

68. *Kushigaki* are sweet persimmons skewered, peeled, and dried.

69. Hirata Atsutane, "Senkyō ibun," in *HAZ*, vol. 3, 69.

70. Ibid., 160.

71. These are plants commonly used in Chinese medicine. The first is a laxative, the second is for coughs, the sweats, and chest pains, and the third is a form of sedative.

72. Hirata Atsutane, "Senkyō ibun," in *HAZ*, vol. 3, 69.

73. Snake impregnation is a theme from ancient times recorded in ancient histories and in Heian and medieval period story collections.

74. Hirata Atsutane, "Senkyō ibun," in *HAZ*, vol. 3, 68–69.

75. Ibid., 158–159.

76. Possibly red with cinnabar pigment.

77. "Fox teabags," a mushroom/fungus.

78. An evergreen of the cypress family.

79. Japanese-style Chinese name for carrot.

80. A plant with long, thin, green, curving fruit that resembles a snake.

81. This is another name for jimsonweed or locoweed.

82. Having disinfectant qualities perhaps.

83. *Daiō* (great yellow), a popular plant long used in Asian medicine, especially for its laxative qualities.

84. A calculus commonly formed in the stomachs of ruminants, but also occurring much less frequently, as in the case here, in other types of mammals. It has long been considered to have magical curative properties.

85. Hirata Atsutane, "Senkyō ibun," in *HAZ*, vol. 3, 109–110.

86. Ibid., 160.

87. For lists of Chinese pharmacopeias, see Strickmann, *Chinese Magical Medicine;* Campany, *To Live as Long as Heaven and Earth;* and also James R. Ware, trans. *Alchemy, Medicine, Religion in the China of A.D. 320: The Nei P'ien of Ko Hung (Pao-p'u tzu)* (Cambridge, Mass.: The M.I.T. Press, 1966).

88. Unlike Norinaga, Atsutane worked from a variety of texts and picked out one story line from them that he felt made the most sense and of course supported his fundamental beliefs about the Japanese land and people. The history he reconstructed, which was in a sense his tribute to Norinaga's *Kojiki-den*, he called *Reconstituted Ancient History* (*Koshi seibun*).

89. Susan L. Burns, *Before the Nation: Kokugaku and the Imagining of Community in Early Modern Japan* (Durham, N.C.: Duke University Press, 2003), 105.

90. The following and more detailed historical information on *jindai moji* can be found in Kokugakuin's *Shinto jiten*.

91. The Tachibana family's Kikke Shinto and Yamazaki Ansai's Suika Shinto came to overlap in the eighteenth century through leading practitioners receiving the secret transmission from both traditions.

92. The words of the edict, hi fu mi yo i mu na ya ko to mo chi ro ra ne shi ki ru yu i tsu ku nu so o ta ha ha ku me ka u wo he ni sa ri he te no ma su a se e ho ke re, were used as a chant for placating spirits and could be lined up and converted to the *iroha*.

93. Buddhism, Confucianism, and Shinto.

94. See Hirata Atsutane, "Kanna hifumiden," in *SHAZ*, vol. 14, 191.

95. The *kuji* is a nine-letter phrase used by Japanese mountain practitioners and ancient Daoists, among others, to repel enemies by expressing the idea that powerful armies were arrayed against them. The *Seimei kuji* is the *kuji* said to have been created by the Heian period yin yang master Abe no Seimei.

96. Hirata Atsutane, "Senkyō ibun," in *HAZ*, vol. 3, 102.

97. This first character has been often translated as ogre, just as *tengu* has been often translated as goblin, but the images do not translate that conveniently.

98. In his famous answer to the question of how to serve these supernatural beings, Confucius avoids the issue by berating the questioner for not yet knowing how to serve the living.

99. Hirata Atsutane, "Zoku shintō taii," in *HAZ*, vol. 1, 102.

100. Cheng Hao (1032–1085) and Cheng Yi (1033–1107).

101. Hirata Atsutane, "Zoku shintō taii," in *HAZ*, vol. 1, 102.

102. Ibid., 104.

103. Ibid., 109.

104. Ibid., 113.

105. Ibid.

106. Hirata Atsutane, "Senkyō ibun," in *HAZ*, vol. 3, 100.

107. Ibid., 99–100.

Chapter 5: The Critique of Buddhism and Defense of Native Religion

1. Hirata Atsutane, "Shutsujō shōgo," in *HAZ*, vol. 1, 2.

2. Hirata Atsutane, "Senkyō ibun," in *HAZ*, vol. 3, 33.

3. Ibid., 183.

4. Torakichi was not exactly wrong when he pointed out misogyny in Japanese Buddhism. There is an extensive tradition of excluding women from sacred places, much the same way as demons are excluded. On the other hand, Torakichi seemed to one-up even Buddhist misogyny by claiming that articles worn by women warded off the normal run-of-the-mill demon. In addition, he claimed that leaving a home by passing through the legs of a woman was another sure-fire way to keep demons away. Hori Ichirō, in *Japanese Journal of Religious Studies* 2/4 (December 1975): 233, wrote of the talismanic power of women's possessions using some of Yanagita's classic research, and for more on Buddhist nyonin kekkai practices, see Bernard Faure, *The Power of Denial: Buddhism, Purity, and Gender* (Princeton, N.J., and Oxford: Princeton University Press, 2003), especially chapter seven, "Crossing the Line."

5. Hirata Atsutane, "Senkyō ibun," in *HAZ*, vol. 3, 69–70.

6. The *Naga*, a dragon people, are of course bestial guardians of Buddhism.

7. See Edward Conze, trans., *Buddhist Scriptures* (New York: Penguin Books, 1959).

8. Ancient Indian cosmology produced the idea of a *kalpa* where the human lifespan was eighty thousand years, but then after a long slow decline it gradually degraded to one hundred years. For more on Indian cosmology, see W. Randolph Kloetzli, *Buddhist Cosmology: Science and Theology in the Images of Motion and Light* (Delhi: Motilal Banarsidass Publishers, 1989).

9. Ibid., 82--83. Of course Chinese cults of immortality are also probable sources of influence.

10. See Robert Ford Campany, *To Live as Long as Heaven and Earth: A Translation and Study of Ge Hong's Traditions of Divine Transcendents* (Berkeley: University of California Press, 2002).

11. I say supersonic because the flights to distant places could take place in the wink of an eye.

12. Torakichi claimed to have flown to deep space with his master's assistance, and on one such trip he saw that the moon actually had large holes straight through it, which accounted for the dark splotches that can occasionally be seen from the earth.

13. Some Chinese immortals also have this ability to make multiples of themselves. Ge Hong in particular writes of several immortals possessing "the Way of body division."

14. In fact, buddhas or bodhisattvas were not the only Buddhists who had special powers. Any good meditation master was expected to be able to do nearly everything Atsutane's *sanjin* could do. See Carl Bielefeldt. "Disarming the Superpowers: The abhijñâ in Eisai and Dōgen," in *Dōgen zenji kenkyū ronshū*, ed. Daihonzan Eiheiji Daionki Kyoku (Fukui-ken: Eiheiji, 2002).

15. Hirata Atsutane, "Senkyō ibun," in *HAZ*, vol. 3, 69.

16. Ibid.

17. This must have been a convenient story when Atsutane and Torakichi visited Mt. Asama together in search of Other World inhabitants.

18. Hirata Atsutane, "Senkyō ibun," in *HAZ*, vol. 3, 136–137.

19. Burton Watson, trans., *The Lotus Sutra* (New York: Columbia University Press, 1993).

20. One spiritual penetration (power) has to do with physical powers and covers flying, invisibility, multiple bodies, shaking the earth, shooting fire and water, and even space travel. Two more account for special sight and hearing, and another gives mind-reading ability. The problematic two are knowledge of past lives and knowledge of the extinction of all defilements, which do not fit Atsutane's religious program.

21. Buddhist *shumisen*, world altar.

22. Hirata Atsutane, "Senkyō ibun," in *HAZ*, vol. 3, 179–180.

23. For a more detailed analysis of this ritual, see Kamata Tōji, *Hirata Atsutane no shinkai fiirudowaaku* (Sakuhinsha, 2002), 226–253.

24. See Haga Noboru, "Kaisetsu (12)," in *SHAZ geppō* 14, vol. 11, 12.

25. See James Sanford, "The Abominable Tachikawa Skull Ritual," *Monumenta Nipponica* 46, 4 (1991): 1–20.

26. See Edward L. Davis, *Society and the Supernatural in Song China* (Honolulu: University of Hawai'i Press, 2001), particularly chapter 5, "The Daoist Ritual Master and Child-Mediums."

27. The five sense organs and the mind.

28. Hirata Atsutane, "Senkyō ibun," in *HAZ*, vol. 3, 180.

29. For information on the use of child mediums by Tantric Buddhist ritual specialists, see Michel Strickmann. *Chinese Magical Medicine*, ed. Bernard Faure (Stanford, Calif.: Stanford University Press, 2002), particularly the chapter titled "The Genealogy of Spirit Possession."

30. See Strickmann, *Chinese Magical Medicine*, this time the chapter on "Tantrists, Foxes, and Shamans."

31. This is one of the five types of foxes explained elsewhere in the text by Torakichi.

32. These are three famous Buddhist priests Atsutane knew were reputed *tengu*.

33. Hirata Atsutane, "Senkyō ibun," in *HAZ*, vol. 3, 83.

34. See Irene Hong-Hong Lin, "Traversing Boundaries: The Demonic Child in the Medieval Japanese Religious Imaginaire" (Ph.D. diss., Stanford University, 2001).

35. Bernard Faure, *The Red Thread: Buddhist Approaches to Sexuality* (Princeton, N.J.: Princeton University Press, 1998), 265.

36. Hirata Atsutane, "Senkyō ibun," in *HAZ*, vol. 3, 158.

37. Hirata Atsutane, "Shindō hyōdan ryakki," in *HAZ*, vol. 3, 14–15.

38. Hirata Atsutane, "Senkyō ibun," in *HAZ*, vol. 3, 82.

39. Ibid., 133.

40. Ibid., 157.

41. Ibid., 184–185.

42. *Mizura* or *bizura*. This is a Nara period young male's hairstyle parted in the middle and tied in two bundles hanging down in front of the ears.

43. Hirata Atsutane, "Senkyō ibun," in *HAZ*, vol. 3, 160.

44. Kompira is identified here as the leader of the *sanjin*, but he is also the *kami* famous for maritime protection, among other things. He is sometimes known as Zōzusan Kompira Daigongen, and by that name is considered a transformation of the Indian god known in Sanskrit as Kumbhira. This god was worshiped as the guardian god of Mount Vipula in Rajagrha, which was on the Buddha's pilgrimage circuit. Since this mountain resembles an elephant's head, it is called Zōzusan (Mt. Elephant Head) in Japanese. It is more than a little ironic that this Indian and Buddhist-related god should be identified as the lord of the native Japanese *sanjin*. For short *suijaku* histories, see Matsunami Kōdō, *Essentials of Buddhist Images*, trans. Wilburn Hansen (Tokyo: Omega-Com, Inc., 2005).

45. Hirata Atsutane, "Senkyō ibun," in *HAZ*, vol. 3, 54.

46. A separate work titled *A Record of the Dance of Seven Lives* (*Shichishō-mai no ki*) contains a detailed account of Torakichi's description of this *sanjin* ritual.

47. Probably because several columns are erected to perform the dance according to Torakichi's own detailed description.

48. Hirata Atsutane, *Senkyō ibun* (*gendaigoyaku*), trans. Yamamoto Hiroshi (Hachiman Shoten, 1997), 254.

49. Ibid., 261.

Chapter 6: The Critique of the West and Defense of Native Knowledge and Ability

1. In Donald Keene, *The Japanese Discovery of Europe, 1720–1830* (Stanford, Calif.: Stanford University Press, 1952 and 1969), 170.

2. A surveying instrument.

3. Hirata Atsutane, "Kōdō taii," in *HAZ*, vol. 1, 53.

4. In Keene, *The Japanese Discovery of Europe*, 160 n.13.

5. Here he uses three characters that mean "Lord Who Created Things," but the *furigana* says *Gotto*.

6. This is *Amatsukami*. The conflation of the Western God and Japanese *kami*, of course, is not a problem for Atsutane here.

7. Hirata Atsutane, "Kōdō taii," in *HAZ*, vol. 1, 53.

8. Torakichi said his master told him that the crucifix and the mother and child symbols were from an evil religion, and his master would spit on them if he saw them.

9. Hirata Atsutane, "Kōdō taii," in *HAZ*, vol. 1, 53.

10. Ibid., 41.

11. This is actually a translation with commentary of a Chinese work by You Ziliu in 1675.

12. *An Examination of Commerce Between China and the Barbarians* (*Kai tsūshōkō*) was published in 1695 and contains information about China, the Far East, Europe, and the Americas.

13. Hirata Atsutane, "Kōdō taii," in *HAZ*, vol. 1, 54.

14. See Okada Masahiko, "Vision and Reality: Buddhist Cosmographic Discourse in Nineteenth-Century Japan" (Ph.D. diss., Stanford University, 1997), 21.

15. Hirata Atsutane, "Senkyō ibun," in *HAZ*, vol. 3, 171.

16. Atsutane also expressed interest in this creature in his *Thoughts on Supernatural Beings of Past and Present*.

17. Hirata Atsutane, "Kōdō taii," in *HAZ*, vol. 1, 63.

18. See James E. Ketelaar, *Of Heretics and Martyrs in Meiji Japan: Buddhism and its Persecution* (Princeton, N.J.: Princeton University Press, 1990), 31, and also Atsutane's *Laughing Discourse after Emerging from Meditation* for more insults of India and Indians.

19. Atsutane's view on *kunigara*, or national character, was that every nation had a different type of nature, like a personality. The land was the major determinant, but the people and their human nature were all woven together inseparably in determining type.

20. Hirata Atsutane, "Kōdō taii," in *HAZ*, vol. 1, 54–55.

21. Okhotsk?

22. Hirata Atsutane, "Senkyō ibun," in *HAZ*, vol. 3, 56–57.

23. This is from the Sanskrit *yojana* and is approximately forty *ri*, or a little less than one hundred miles.

24. Here he is again refuting traditional Buddhist cosmology. See W. Randolph Kloetzli, *Buddhist Cosmology: Science and Theology in the Images of Motion and Light* (Delhi: Motilal Banarsidass Publishers, 1989).

25. Hirata Atsutane, "Senkyō ibun," in *HAZ*, vol. 3, 166.

26. Ibid.

27. Atsutane gives a precise citation for the text, which I have omitted.

28. Hirata Atsutane, "Senkyō ibun," in *HAZ*, vol. 3, 20.

29. Ibid., 142.

30. Ibid., 75.

31. Ibid.

32. Ibid.

33. Ibid., 74.

34. Hirata Atsutane, "Chishima no shiranami: fuchizu," in *SHAZ*, supp. vol. 5, 1.

35. This was the name of Empress Suiko's palace, which is being used to refer to her government, or Shōtoku Taishi's regency.

36. Hirata Atsutane, "Chishima no shiranami: fuchizu," in *SHAZ*, supp. vol. 5, 2.

37. Hirata Atsutane, "Kodō taii," in *HAZ*, vol. 1, 64.

38. Ibid., 42–43.

39. Ibid., 43. This is close to a word-for-word repetition of his master Motoori Norinaga's argument.

40. Ibid., 48. In addition to these examples he gave two examples from Japanese history. He pointed out that Oda Nobunaga was called the Idiot Lord until sometime in his twenties because of his meekness and incompetence. He also noted that Ōishi Kuranosuke was called stupid until he was about twenty and started to show his prowess.

41. This is an idea Atsutane would have noticed came from early Chinese philosophy; however, we can guess his explanation for why it only appears to be of Chinese origin.

42. Englebert Kaempferer was a German physician who worked for the Dutch in Nagasaki. He was in Japan from 1690–1692 and his book is called *History of Japan*. There are also parts of this work that are not flattering to the Japanese. Atsutane has again been selective with his Western sources.

Conclusion: The Medium Is the Message

1. The phrase and concept "medium is the message" is an important one in McLuhan's 1964 work *Understanding Media: The Extensions of Man*. In 1967 he followed up with the more remarkable title *The Medium Is the Massage*. The "message" variation is more appropriate to this paper, along with its reminder of the importance of misremembering in writing culture.

2. This work is a detailed explanation of Atsutane's morning ritual, but it

also includes Atsutane's version of the development of nativism. In it he makes a claim for rightful succession as the leading scholar following Norinaga.

3. See James Clifford and George Marcus, eds., *Writing Culture: The Poetics and Politics of Ethnography* (Berkeley: University of California Press, 1986).

4. Atsutane and others documented possession behavior and also some violent temper tantrums.

5. See Origuchi Shinobu, "Hirata *kokugaku* no dentō," in *OSZ*, vol. 20.

6. Blacker made a connection between Atsutane and Yanagita on exactly the same point; namely, the study of the abduction of women and children by "mountain men," pronounced in Japanese as either *yamabito* or *sanjin*. See Yanagita Kunio, "Yama no jinsei," in *Teihon Yanagita Kunio shu*, vol. 4 (Chikuma Shobō, 1969), p. 77. Also, see another version of the story in Yanagita's *Tōno monogatari*, in *Teihon Yanagita Kunio shu*, vol. 4 (Chikuma Shobō, 1969).

7. For one, see Haga Noboru, *Yanagita Kunio to Hirata Atsutane* (Kōseisha, 1997).

8. See Helen Hardacre, *Religion and Society in Nineteenth-Century Japan: A Study of the Southern Kantō Region, Using Late Edo and Early Meiji Gazetteers* (Ann Arbor: Center for Japanese Studies, The University of Michigan, 2002).

9. Hirata Atsutane, "Shutsujō shōgo," in *HAZ*, vol. 1, 1.

10. Hirata Atsutane, "Senkyō ibun," in *HAZ*, vol. 3, 74.

11. Hirata Atsutane, "Kodō taii," in *HAZ*, vol. 1, 64. Atsutane's responses to these kinds of attacks often just parrot Norinaga's responses to similar attacks.

12. See Okada Masahiko, "Vision and Reality: Buddhist Cosmographic Discourse in Nineteenth-Century Japan" (Ph.D. diss., Stanford University, 1997).

13. See Walter John Odronic, "Kodo taii (An Outline of the Ancient Way)" (Ph.D. diss., University of Pennsylvania, 1967), 174.

14. Ibid.

15. Hirata Atsutane, "Kodō taii," in *HAZ*, vol. 1, 48–49.

16. Hirata Atsutane, "Kodō taii," in *HAZ*, vol. 1, 44.

17. Kamata Tōji, *Hirata Atsutane no shinkai fiirudowaaku* (Sakuhinsha, 2002), 138.

Bibliography

Hirata Atsutane zenshū	= *HAZ*
Kōhon Kamo no Mabuchi zenshū	= *KKNMZ*
Nihon shisō taikei	= *NST*
Origuchi Shinobu zenshū	= *OSZ*
Shinshū Hirata Atsutane zenshū	= *SHAZ*
Transactions of the Asiatic Society of Japan	= *TASJ*

Primary Sources

All Japanese-language works are published in Tokyo unless otherwise indicated.

Ban Nobutomo. *Ban Nobutomo zenshū*. Edited by Kawase Kazuma. Perikan-sha, 1979.

Gunsho ruijū. Compiled by Hanawa Hokiichi (1779–1819). 24 vols. Naigai shoseki, 1928–1937.

Hayashi Dōshun. "Honchō jinjakō." In *Kaizō bunko*, daiichibu, dai 243 hen. Kaizōsha, 1942.

Hayashi Razan. "Shintō denju." In *NST* 39. Iwanami Shoten, 1972.

Hirata Atsutane zenshū. Edited by Muromatsu Iwao, 15 vols. Itchido, 1911–1918.

Hirata Atsutane. "Chishima no shiranami." In *SHAZ*, supp. vol. 5.

———. "Kanna hifumiden." In *SHAZ*, vol. 14.

———. "Kassenōden." In *SHAZ*, vol. 14.

———. "Kodō taii." In *HAZ*, vol. 1.

———. "Kokon yomikō." In *SHAZ*, vol. 9.

———. "Senkyō ibun." In *HAZ*, vol. 3.

———. *Senkyō ibun · Katsugorō saisei kibun*. Edited by Koyasu Nobukuni. Iwanami Shoten, 2000.

———. *Senkyō ibun (gendaigoyaku)*. Translated by Yamamoto Hiroshi. Hachi-man Shoten, 1997.

———. "Shichishōmai." In *SHAZ*, vol. 15.

———. "Shindō hyōdan ryakki." In *HAZ*, vol. 3.

———. "Shizu no iwaya." In *SHAZ*, vol. 14.

———. "Shutsujō shōgo." In *HAZ*, vol. 1.

———. *Tama no mihashira*. Edited by Koyasu Nobukuni. Iwanami Shoten, 1998.

———. "Tama no mihashira." Edited by Tahara Tsuguo, Saeki Arikiyo, and Haga Noboru. *NST 50*. Iwanami Shoten, 1973.

———. "Zoku shintō taii." In *HAZ*, vol. 1.

Hirata Kanetane, ed. "Kiyosōhansho." In *SHAZ*, supp. vol. 5.

"Huai-Nan-tzu." In *Kambun taikei*. Vol. XX. Fuzambe, 1910–1916.

Izumi Makuni. "Meidōsho." In *Kokugaku undō no shisō*, edited by Haga Noboru and Matsumoto Sannosuke. *NST 51*. Iwanami Shoten, 1971.

Kada no Azumamaro. "Sōgakkōkei." *NST 39*. Iwanami Shoten, 1972.

Kamo no Mabuchi. "Go'ikō." *NST 39*. Iwanami Shoten, 1972.

———. "Ka'ikō." *KKNMZ*, shisō-hen. Kobundō, 1942.

———. "Kokuikō." *NST 39*. Iwanami Shoten, 1972.

———. "Manabi no agetsurai." *KKNMZ*, shisō-hen. Kobundō, 1942.

———. "Niimanabi." *NST 39*. Iwanami Shoten, 1972.

Kinsei bungei sōsho. Kokusho Kankōkai, 1912.

Kōhon Kamo no Mabuchi zenshū. Shisō-hen. 2 vols. Compiled by Yamamoto Yutaka. Kobundo, 1942.

Motoori Haruniwa. "Kotoba no kayoichi." In *Motoori Norinaga zenshū*, edited by Motoori Toyokai and Motoori Seizo. Yoshikawa Kobunkan, 1938.

———. "Isonokami no sasamegoto." In *Motoori Norinaga shū*, edited by Hino Tatsuo. Shinchōsha, 1983.

———. "Kuzubana." In *Motoori Norinaga zenshū*, vol. 8, edited by Ono Susumu and Okubo Tadashi. Chikuma Shobō, 1972.

Motoori Ohira. "Kogakuyō." In *Nihon kokusui zensho*, vol. 13, edited by Endō Takayoshi. Nihon Kokusui Kankōkai, 1916.

Motoori Norinaga. "First Steps into the Mountains." A translation of "Uiyamabumi" with an introduction by Sey Nishimura. *Monumenta Nipponica* 42, 4 (1987): 449–493.

———. "The Jeweled Comb-Box." A translation of "Tamakushige" with an introduction by John S. Brownlee. *Monumenta Nipponica* 43, 1 (1988): 35–61.

———. *Kojiki-den, Book 1*. Translated by Ann Wehmeyer. Cornell East Asia Series 87. Cornell University East Asia Program, 1997.

———. "Naobi no mitama." Translated with an introduction by Sey Nishimura. *Monumenta Nipponica* 46, 1 (1991): 21–41.

———. "Naobi no mitama." Translated by Harry Harootunian as "Spirit of

Renovation." In *Readings in Tokugawa Thought,* edited by Tetsuo Najita. Chicago: Center for East Asian Studies, University of Chicago, 1994.

Motoori Norinaga zenshū. Compiled by Motoori Toyokai and Motoori Seizo. 13 vols. Yoshikawa Kobunkan, 1937–1938.

Motoori Norinaga zenshū. Compiled by Ono Susumu and Okubo Tadashi. 20 vols. Chikuma Shobō, 1968–1975.

Okuni Takamasa. "Bankoku kōhō." *NST* 50. Iwanami Shoten, 1973.

———. "Hongaku kyoyō." *NST* 50. Iwanami Shoten, 1973.

Shinshū Hirata Atsutane zenshū. 21 vols. Meicho Shuppan, 1978.

Secondary Sources

Abe Akio. "Keichu, Azumamaro, Mabuchi." In *Kinsei shintoron zenki kokugaku,* edited by Taira Shigemichi and Abe Akio. *NST* 39. Iwanami Shoten, 1972.

Amino Yoshihiko and Miyata Noboru, eds. *Rekishi to Minzokugaku. Nihon rekishi minzoku ronshū,* vol. 1. Yoshikawa kōbunkan, 1994.

Anesaki Masaharu. *History of Japanese Religion.* Rutland, Vt.: Charles E. Tuttle, 1963.

Aramata Hiroshi. *Hirata Atsutane ga toku Inou mononokeroku.* Kadokawa Shoten, 2003.

Aramata Hiroshi and Maita Katsuyasu. *Yomigaeru karisuma Hirata Atsutane.* Ronsōsha, 2000.

———, eds. *Chi no nettowaaku no senkakusha, Hirata Atsutane.* Heibonsha, 2004.

Aston, William G. *A History of Japanese Literature.* New York: Appleton-Century, 1937.

———. *Nihongi: Chronicles of Japan from the Earliest Times to A.D. 697.* Rutland, Vt.: Charles E. Tuttle, 1972.

———. "Russian Descents in Saghalien and Itorup in the Years 1806 and 1807," *TASJ* I (1874), 79–84.

———. *Shinto, The Way of the Gods.* London: Longmans Green. 1905.

Backus, Robert. "The Kansei Prohibition of Heterodoxy and Its Effects on Education." *Harvard Journal of Asiatic Studies* 39, 1 (1979): 55–106.

———. "The Motivation of Confucian Orthodoxy in Tokugawa Japan." *Harvard Journal of Asiatic Studies* 39, 2 (1979): 275–338.

———. "The Relationship of Confucianism to the Tokugawa Bakufu as Revealed in the Kansei Educational Reform." *Harvard Journal of Asiatic Studies* 34 (1974): 97–162.

Beasley, W. G., and Carmen Blacker. "Japanese Historical Writing in the Tokugawa Period (1603–1868)." In *Historians of China and Japan,* edited by W. G. Beasley and E. G. Pulleyblank. London: Oxford University Press, 1961.

Bellah, Robert N. *Tokugawa Religion*. New York: Free Press, 1957.

Berry, Mary Elizabeth. *Japan in Print: Information and Nation in the Early Modern Period*. Berkeley: University of California Press, 2006.

Bielefeldt, Carl. "Disarming the Superpowers: The abhijñâ in Eisai and Dōgen." In *Dōgen zenji kenkyū ronshū*, edited by Daihonzan Eiheiji Daionki Kyoku. Fukui-ken: Eiheiji, 2002.

Blacker, Carmen. *The Catalpa Bow: A Study of Shamanistic Practices in Japan*. London: George Allen and Unwin, 1975.

———. "Supernatural Abductions in Japanese Folklore." *Asian Folklore Studies* vol. XXVI-2 (1967): 111–147.

Bock, Felicia G. *Engi-Shiki. Procedures of the Engi Era*. 2 vols. Tokyo: Sophia University, 1970–1972.

Bokenkamp, Stephen. *Early Daoist Scriptures*. Berkeley: University of California Press, 1997.

Bolitho, Harold. "Metempsychosis Hijacked: The Curious Case of Katsugoro." *Harvard Journal of Asiatic Studies* 62, 2 (2002): 389–414.

———."Tidings from the Twilight Zone." In Susanne Formanek and William R. LaFleur, eds. *Practicing the Afterlife: Perspectives from Japan*. Vienna: Austrian Academy of Sciences, 2004.

Bourdieu, Pierre. *The Logic of Practice*. Stanford, Calif.: Stanford University Press, 1980.

Boxer, C. R. *Jan Compagnie in Japan 1600–1850: An Essay on the Cultural, Artistic, and Scientific Influence Exercised by the Hollanders in Japan from the Seventeenth to the Nineteenth Centuries*. Second revised edition. The Hague: Martinus Nijhoff, 1950.

Breen, John, and Mark Teeuwen, eds. *Shinto in History: Ways of the Kami*. Honolulu: University of Hawai'i Press, 2000.

Burns, Susan L. *Before the Nation: Kokugaku and the Imagining of Community in Early Modern Japan*. Durham, N.C.: Duke University Press, 2003.

Campany, Robert Ford. *To Live as Long as Heaven and Earth: A Translation and Study of Ge Hong's Traditions of Divine Transcendents*. Berkeley: University of California Press, 2002.

Campbell, William. *Formosa under the Dutch; Described from Contemporary Records, with Explanatory Notes and a Bibliography of the Island*. London: Kegan Paul, Trench, Trubner, 1903.

Castaneda, Carlos. *The Teachings of Don Juan; a Yaqui Way of Knowledge*. New York: Ballantine Books, 1969.

Chamberlain, Basil Hall, trans. *Kojiki, Records of Ancient Matters*. *TASJ* Supplement Vol. X (1906).

Chartier, Roger. *On the Edge of the Cliff: History, Language, and Practices.* Translated by Lydia G. Cochrane. Baltimore: The Johns Hopkins University Press, 1997.

Chigiri Kōsai. *Sennin no kenkyū.* Tairiku Shobō, 1976.

———. *Tengu no kenkyū.* Hara Shobō, 1975.

Clifford, James. "Introduction: Partial Truths." In *Writing Culture, The Poetics and Politics of Ethnography,* edited by James Clifford and George E. Marcus, 23--24. London: University of California Press, 1986.

———. *On the Edges of Anthropology (Interviews).* Chicago: Prickly Paradigm Press, 2003.

———. *The Predicament of Culture: Twentieth-Century Ethnography, Literature, and Art.* Cambridge, Mass.: Harvard University Press, 1988.

Clifford, James, and George Marcus, eds. *Writing Culture: The Poetics and Politics of Ethnography.* Berkeley: University of California Press, 1986.

Conze, Edward, trans. *Buddhist Scriptures.* New York: Penguin Books, 1959.

Crapanzano, Vincent. "Hermes' Dilemma: The Masking of Subversion in Ethnographic Description." In Clifford and Marcus, *Writing Culture,* 51–76.

———. "The Writing of Ethnography." *Dialectical Anthropology* 2: 69–73.

———. *Tuhami: Portrait of a Moroccan.* Chicago: University of Chicago Press, 1980.

Davis, Edward L. *Society and the Supernatural in Song China.* Honolulu: University of Hawai'i Press, 2001.

De Mille, Richard. *Castaneda's Journey: The Power and the Allegory.* Santa Barbara, Calif.: Capra Press, 1976.

Devine, Richard. "Hirata Atsutane and Christian Sources." *Monumenta Nipponica* 36, 1 (1981): 37–54.

Dumoulin, Heinrich. "Die Entwicklung der Kokugaku." *Monumenta Nipponica* 2, 1 (1939): 140–160.

———. "Kamo Mabuchis Kommenatar zum Norito des Toshi-goi-no-Matsuri." *Monumenta Nipponica* 12, 1(1956): 123–156.

———. "Kokuiko (Gendanken über den Sinn des Landes)." *Monumenta Nipponica* 2, 1 (1939): 165–192.

———. "Sō-gakkō-kei (Gesuch um die Einrichtung einer Kokugakuschule)." An annotated translation. *Monumenta Nipponica* 3, 2 (1940): 230–249.

———. "Motoori Norinaga." *Nippon* 4 (Berlin, 1939): 193–196.

Earl, David Magaray. *Emperor and Nation in Japan: Political Thinkers of the Tokugawa Period.* Seattle: University of Washington Press, 1964.

Ebersole, Gary L. *Ritual Poetry and the Politics of Death in Early Japan,* Princeton, N.J.: Princeton University Press, 1989.

Endō Jun. "Hirata Atsutane no takairon saikō – *Tama no mihashira* o chūshin ni." *Shūkyō kenkyū* (1995): 305.

———. "Hirata Atsutane to Yoshidake – jūkyū seiki no nihon shakai ni okeru Kokugaku no ichi o megutte." *Nihon bunka to shintō* (2005): 1.

Faure, Bernard. *The Power of Denial: Buddhism, Purity, and Gender.* Princeton, N.J., and Oxford: Princeton University Press, 2003

———. *The Red Thread: Buddhist Approaches to Sexuality.* Princeton, N.J.: Princeton University Press, 1998.

Figal, Gerald. *Civilization and Monsters: Spirits of Modernity in Meiji Japan.* Durham, N.C.: Duke University Press, 1999.

Formanek, Susanne, and William R. LaFleur, eds. *Practicing the Afterlife: Perspectives from Japan.* Vienna: Austrian Academy of Sciences, 2004.

Foster, Michael Dylan. "Morphologies of Mystery: Yōkai and Discourses of the Supernatural in Japan, 1666–1999." Ph.D. dissertation, Stanford University, 2003.

Frazer, James George. *The Golden Bough: A Study in Magic and Religion.* Oxford; New York: Oxford University Press, 1994.

Fujii Sadafumi. *Kokugaku tenseishi no kenkyū.* Yoshikawa Kobunkan, 1987.

Fujita Tokutarō. *Hirata Atsutane no kokugaku.* Iwakabechō, 1943.

Fung, Yu-lan. *A Short History of Chinese Philosophy.* Edited by Derek Bodde. New York: Macmillan, 1959.

Genette, Gérard. *Narrative Discourse: An Essay in Method.* Translated by Jane E. Lewin. Ithaca, N.Y.: Cornell University Press, 1980.

Graham, A. C., trans. *The Book of Lieh-tzu.* London: John Murray, 1960.

Greenblatt, Stephen. "Towards a Poetics of Culture." In *The New Historicism,* edited by H. Aram Veeser. New York: Routledge, 1989.

Haga Noboru. "Bakumatsu henkaku-ki ni okeru kokugakusha no undō to ronri." In *NST* 51. Iwanami Shoten, 1971.

———. *Bakumatsu kokugaku no kenkyū.* Kyōiku Shuppan Sentā, 1980.

———. *Bakumatsu kokugaku no tenkai.* Hanawa Shobō, 1963.

———. "Edo ni okeru Edo kabun-ha to Hirata Atsutane." In *Edo no geino to bunka,* edited by Nishiyama Matsunosuke. Yoshikawa Kobunkan, 1985.

———. *Hirata Atsutane no gakumon to shisō, Haga Noboru chosaku senshū 5.* Ōsankaku Shuppan, 2002.

———. "Kaisetsu (2)" In *SHAZ geppō* 2, vol. 9, 9.

———. *Kokugaku no hitobito: sono kōdō to shisō.* Nihonjin no kōdō to shisō, no. 42. Hyōronsha, 1975.

———. "Motoori Norinaga no shisō keisei: Kyoto yūgaku jidai wo chūshin to shite." *Kikan Nihon shisōshi* 8 (1978): 69–88.

———. "Suzuki Shigetane to Hirata-tō: Suzuki Shigetane ansatsu jiken no haikai." *Rekishi jinrui* 5 (March 1978): 45–86.

———. *Yanagita Kunio to Hirata Atsutane.* Kōseisha, 1997.

Haga Yaichi. "Hirata Atsutane okina ni tsuite." *Zenkoku shinshokukai kaihō* (1912): 167.

Hammitzsch, Horst. "Hirata Atsutane; ein geistiger Kämpfer Japans." *Mitteilungen der deutschen Gesellschaft für Natur und Völkerkunde Ostasiens,* vol. XXVIII, pt. E (5), (1936): 1–27.

———. "Kangaku und Kokugaku: Ein Beitrag zur Geistesgeschichte der Tokugawa Zeit." *Monumenta Nipponica* 2, 1 (1939): 1–23.

Hardacre, Helen. *Religion and Society in Nineteenth-Century Japan: A Study of the Southern Kantō Region, Using Late Edo and Early Meiji Gazetteers.* Ann Arbor: Center for Japanese Studies, The University of Michigan, 2002.

———. *Shinto and the State, 1868–1988.* Princeton, N.J.: Princeton University Press, 1989.

Harootunian, H. D. *Things Seen and Unseen.* Chicago: University of Chicago Press, 1988.

Hattori, Unokichi. *Kambun taikei.* Fuzambe, 1910–1916.

Havens, Norman, and Inoue Nobutaka, eds. *Encyclopedia of Shinto,* vol. 1, *Kami.* Tokyo: Kokugakuin University, 2001.

———, eds. *Encyclopedia of Shinto,* vol. 2, *Jinja.* Tokyo: Kokugakuin University, 2004.

Higuchi Kōzo. "Watarai Nobuyoshi to kinsei shintō no seiritsu." *Edo no shisō* 1 (1996): 118–135.

Hisamatsu Sen'ichi. "Bunkengaku-teki kenkyū to kōshōgaku: Ban Nobutomo o chūshin to shite." In *Ban Nobutomo zenshū,* bekkan, edited by Kawase Kazuma. Perikansha, 1979.

———. *Keichū.* Jinbutsu Sōsho no. 110. Yoshikawa Kobunkan, 1963.

———. "Man'yō daishoki no seikaku to ichi," in *Keichū zenshū,* vol. 1. Iwanami Shoten, 1973.

Holtom, Daniel C. *The Japanese Enthronement Ceremonies With an Account of the Imperial Regalia.* Tokyo: Kyobunkan, 1928.

———. *The National Faith of Japan.* New York: E. P. Dutton, 1938.

Hori Ichirō. *Folk Religion: Continuity and Change.* Edited by Joseph Kitagawa and Alan L. Miller. Chicago: University of Chicago Press, 1968.

Hostetler, Laura. *Qing Colonial Enterprise: Ethnography and Cartography in Early Modern China.* Chicago: University of Chicago Press, 2001.

Hymes, Robert. *Way and Byway: Taoism, Local Religion, and Models of Divinity in Sung and Modern China.* Berkeley: University of California Press, 2002.

Ikegami, Eiko. *Bonds of Civility: Aesthetic Networks and the Political Origins of Japanese Culture.* Cambridge, UK; New York: Cambridge University Press, 2005.

Inoue Nobutaka, ed. *Shinto – A Short History*. Translated by Mark Teeuwen
    and John Breen. London: RoutledgeCurzon, 2003.

Itō Hiroshi. *Taigaku Hirata Atsutane den*. Kinshōsha, 1973.

Ito Tasaburo. *Kokugakusha no michi*. Shintaiyōsha, 1944.

———. *Sōmō no kokugaku*. Masago Shobō, 1966.

Jansen, Marius B. *The Making of Modern Japan*. Cambridge, Mass., and Lon-
    don: The Belknap Press of Harvard University, 2000.

Kada no Azumamaro. "Petition for the Establishment of a School of National
    Learning." *Sources of Japanese Tradition*, vol. 2.

Kaempfer, Englebert. *The History of Japan together with a Description of the
    Kingdom of Siam*. Translated by J. G. Scheuchzer. Glasgow: James Mac-
    Lehose and Sons, 1906.

Kajiyama Yoshio. "Mitogaku to kokugaku no kankei: Hirata Atsutane no Mito-
    han shikan undō o megutte." *Geirin* 39, 3 (1990): 35–55.

———. "Mito-han wo meguru Oyamada Tomokiyo to Hirata Atsutane no
    kōyū." *Geirin* 44, 1 (1995): 55–71.

Kamata Tōji. *Basho no kioku – Nihon to iu shintai*. Iwanami Shoten, 1990.

———. "The Disfiguring of Nativism: Hirata Atsutane and Orikuchi Shinobu."
    In Breen and Teeuwen, *Shinto in History: Ways of the Kami*.

———. *Hirata Atsutane no shinkai fiirudowāku*. Sakuhinsha, 2002.

Kamo no mabuchi. "Kokuikō." Translated by Harry Harootunian. In *Readings
    in Tokugawa Thought*, edited by Tetsuo Najita. Chicago: Center for East
    Asian Studies, University of Chicago, 1994.

Katō Genchi and Hoshino Hikoshiro, trans. *Kogoshūi: Gleanings from Ancient
    Stories*. Tokyo: Meiji Japan Society, 1924.

———. "The Ancient Shinto Deity Ame-no-Mi-naka Nushi no Kami." *TASJ*
    XXXVI, 1 (1908): 137–162.

Katō Genchi, Karl Reitz, and Wilhelm Schiffer, comps. *A Bibliography of Shinto
    In Western Languages from the Oldest Times till 1952*. Tokyo: Meiji Jingū
    Shamusho, 1953.

Katsurajima Nobuhiro. *Bakumatsu minshū shisō no kenkyū: bakumatsu koku-
    gaku to minshū shūkyō*. Bunrikaku, 1992.

Keene, Donald. "Hirata Atsutane and Western Learning." *T'oung Pao* 42
    (1954).

———. *The Japanese Discovery of Europe, 1720–1830*. Stanford, Calif.: Stan-
    ford University Press, 1952 and 1969.

———. *Some Japanese Portraits*. Tokyo: Kodansha International, 1978.

Keichū zenshū. 16 vols. Edited by Hisamatsu Sen'ichi et al. Iwanami Shoten,
    1973.

Ketelaar, James E. *Of Heretics and Martyrs in Meiji Japan: Buddhism and its
    Persecution*. Princeton, N.J.: Princeton University Press, 1990.

Kirihara Yoshio. *Hirata Atsutane to Akita no monjin.* Bungeisha, 2001.

Kiyohara Sadao. *Kokugaku hattatsushi.* Kokusho Kankōkai, 1981.

Kloetzli, W. Randolph. *Buddhist Cosmology: Science and Theology in the Images of Motion and Light.* Delhi: Motilal Banarsidass Publishers, 1989.

Kobayashi Kenzo. *Hirata Shinto no kenkyū.* Osaka: Koshinto Senpyōkyō Honchō, 1975.

Kohn, Livia, ed. *Daoism Handbook.* Leiden: E. J. Brill, 2000.

Komatsu Kazuhiko, ed. *Tengu to yamamba in Kaii no minzokugaku* 5, Kawade Shobō Shinsha, 2000.

Koyasu Nobukuni. *Hirata Atsutane no sekai.* Perikansha, 2001.

———. "Hirata Atsutane no sekai." In *Hirata Atsutane,* edited by Sagara Akira, 25–80. Nihon no meicho, 24. Chūōkōronsha, 1984.

———. *Motoori Norinaga.* Iwanami Shoten, 1992.

———. *Motoori Norinaga mondai to wa nani ka.* Seibonsha, 1995.

———. *Norinaga to Atsutane no sekai.* Chukosōsho, 1977.

Krieger, Carol Coenraad. *The Infiltration of European Civilization in Japan during the 18th Century.* Leiden: Brill, 1940.

Kubo Noritada. *Dōkyōshi, Sekai shūkyōshi sōsho* 9. Yamakawa Shuppansha, 1977.

Kudo Shinjirō. *Fujii Takanao to Matsunoya-ha.* Kazama Shobō, 1986.

Kurodo Toshio. "Shinto in the History of Japanese Religion." Translated by James C. Dobbins and Suzanne Gray. *The Journal of Japanese Studies* 7, 1 (1981): 1–21.

Lacoste-Dujardin, Camille. *Dialogue des femmes en ethnologie.* Paris: Maspero, 1977.

Legge, James, trans. *The Four Books.* Shanghai: Chinese Book Co., 1933.

Leiris, Michel. *L'Afrique fantôme.* Paris: Gallimard, 1981.

Lin, Irene Hong-Hong. "Traversing Boundaries: The Demonic Child in the Medieval Japanese Religious Imaginaire." Ph.D. dissertation, Stanford University, 2001.

Maita Katsuyasu. "Yomigaeru karisuma, Hirata Atsutane." Interview by Aramata Hiroshi. *Shōsetsu subaru* 11, 1 (1997): 432–441.

Maita Katsuyasu and Aratamata Hiroshi, eds. *Chi no nettowaaku no senkakusha Hirata Atsutane.* Heibonsha, 2004.

Marcus, George, and Dick Cushman. "Ethnographies as Text." *Annual Review of Anthropology* 11 (1982): 25–69.

Martin, Wallace. *Recent Theories of Narrative.* Ithaca, N.Y., and London: Cornell University Press, 1986.

Maruyama Masao. *Nihon no shisō.* Iwanami Shoten, 1961.

———. "Orthodoxy and Legitimacy in the Kimon School." Part One. *Sino-Japanese Studies* 8, 2 (1996): 6–49.

———. *Studies in the Intellectual History of Tokugawa Japan*. Translated by Mikiso Hane. Princeton, N.J.: Princeton University Press, 1974.

Matsunami Kōdō. *Essentials of Buddhist Images*. Translated by Wilburn Hansen. Tokyo: Omega-Com, Inc., 2004.

McLuhan, Marshall. *The Extensions of Man*. New York: McGraw Hill, 1964.

———. *The Medium Is the Massage*. New York: Bantam Books, 1967.

McNally, Mark. "Phantom History: Hirata Atsutane and Tokugawa Nativism." Ph.D. dissertation, University of California, Los Angeles, 1998.

———. *Proving the Way, Conflict and Practice in the History of Japanese Nativism*. Cambridge, Mass.: Harvard University Press, 2005.

Mernissi, Fatima. *Le Maroc raconté par ses femmes*. Rabat: Société marocaine des éditeurs réunis, 1984.

Miki Shotaro. *Hirata Atsutane no kenkyū*. Kyoto: Shintoshi Gakkai, 1969.

———. "Hirata Atsutane no tenchi kaibyaku-setsu: toku ni Norinaga, Nakatsune to no kankei ni oite." *Kōgakkan daigaku kiyo* 2 (March 1964): 133–165.

Miki Yasutaka. "Shinkokugaku to sensō sekinin no mondai." *Nihon bungaku* 7, 1 (1958): 63–72.

Minami Kenji. *Kinsei kokugaku to sono shūhen*. Miyai Shoten, 1992.

Miyake Kiyoshi. *Kada no Azumamaro*. Unebi Shobo, 1932.

———. *Kada no Azumamaro no kotengaku*. Urawa-shi: Miyake Kiyoshi, 1981.

Montaigne, Michel de. *The Complete Essays of Montaigne*. Translated by Donald Frame. Stanford, Calif.: Stanford University Press, 1958.

Montesquieu, Charles de Secondat. *Persian Letters*. Translated by C. J. Betts. New York: Penguin Books, 1993.

Morita Yasunosuke. *Ban Nobutomo no shiso*. Perikansha, 1979.

Muraoka Tsunetsugu. "Hirata Atsutane no shingaku ni okeru yasukyō no eikyō." In *Zōtei nihon shisōshi kenkyū*. Iwanami Shoten, 1940.

———. *Motoori Norinaga*. Iwanami Shoten, 1928.

———. *Nihon shisōshi kenkyū*. Oka Shoten, 1930.

———. *Nihon shisōshi kenkyū*. 4 vols. Iwanami Shoten, 1930–1939.

———. *Norinaga to Atsutane*. Kobunsha, 1958.

———. *Studies in Shinto Thought*. Translated by Delmer Brown and James Araki. Japanese National Conference for UNESCO, 1964.

———. *Zōtei nihon shisōshi kenkyū*. Iwanami Shoten, 1940.

Murata Harumi. "Utagatari." *Nihon kagaku zensho*, vol. 12. Hakubunkan, 1911.

Najita, Tetsuo, ed. *Readings in Tokugawa Thought*, Select Papers, vol. 9. Chicago: The Center for East Asian Studies, The University of Chicago, 1994.

Nakamura Kazumoto. *Motoori-ha kokugaku no tenkai*. Osankaku, 1993.

Nishikawa Junshi. "Sandaikō no seiritsu ni tsuite." *Kogakkan daigaku kiyo* 10 (January 1972): 193–211.

Nosco, Peter. "Keichu (1640–1701): Forerunner of National Learning." *Asian Thought and Society* 5, 1 (1980): 237–252.

———. "Man'yōshū Studies in Tokugawa Japan." *TASJ*, 4th series 1 (1986): 109–146.

———. "Nature, Invention, and National Learning: The Kokka hachiron Controversy, 1742–46." *Harvard Journal of Asiatic Studies* 41, 1 (1981): 75–91.

———. *Remembering Paradise: Nativism and Nostalgia in Eighteenth-Century Japan.* Cambridge, Mass.: Council of East Asian Studies, Harvard University, 1990.

Odronic, Walter John. "Kodo taii (An Outline of the Ancient Way)." Ph.D. dissertation, University of Pennsylvania, 1967.

Ogawa, Shigeo, ed. *Kokugakusha denki shusei.* Kunimoto, 1934.

Okada Masahiko. "Vision and Reality: Buddhist Cosmographic Discourse in Nineteenth-Century Japan." Ph.D. dissertation, Stanford University, 1997.

Okino Iwasaburo. *Hirata Atsutane to sono jidai.* Koseikaku, 1943.

Omote Tomoyuki. "Chi no denpa to shōgeki: Hirata Atsutane to Kiyosōhansho." *Edo no shisō* 5 (1996): 134–149.

———. "Hito no kangaete shirubeki wa tada me no mae no oyobu kagiri: kokugaku-teki tenchi seiseizu to kindai." *Nihon gakuho* 15 (March 1996): 1–16.

———. "Katareru 'kamiyo' to 'utsushi': Sandaikō ni okeru 'katari' no kōzō tenkan." *Nihon gakuho* 12 (March 1993): 69–83.

Ooms, Herman. *Tokugawa Ideology: Early Constructs, 1570–1680.* Princeton, N.J.: Princeton University Press, 1985.

Origuchi Shinobu. "Hirata kokugaku no dentō." *OSZ*, vol. 20.

———. "Kokugaku no kōfuku." *OSZ*, vol. 20.

Origuchi Shinobu zenshū. Chūōkōronsha, 1976.

Ozawa Masao. "'Sandaikō' wo meguru ronsō." *Kokugo to kokubungaku* 20, 5 (1943): 465–476.

Philippi, Donald L., trans. *Kojiki. Translated with an Introduction and Notes.* Tokyo: University of Tokyo Press, 1968.

Pincus, Leslie. *Authenticating Culture in Japan.* Berkeley: University of California Press, 1996.

Pregadio, Fabrizio. "The Elixirs of Immortality." In *Daoism Handbook*, edited by Livia Kohn. Leiden: E. J. Brill, 2000.

Robertson, Jennifer. "Sexy Rice: Plant Gender, Farm Manuals, and Grass-Roots Nativism." *Monumenta Nipponica* 39, 3 (1984): 233–260.

Robinet, Isabelle. *Taoism: Growth of a Religion*. Translated by Phyllis Brooks. Stanford, Calif.: Stanford University Press, 1997.

Rubinger, Richard. *Private Academies of Tokugawa Japan*. Princeton, N.J.: Princeton University Press, 1982.

Said, Edward. *Orientalism*. New York: Pantheon, 1978.

Saigusa Yasutaka. *Kamo no Mabuchi*. Jinbutsu sōsho no. 93. Yoshikawa Kobunkan, 1962.

Sakamoto Koremaru. *Meiji ishin to kokugakusha*. Omeidō, 1993.

Sanford, James. "The Abominable Tachikawa Skull Ritual." *Monumenta Nipponica* 46, 4 (1991): 1–20.

Sansom, George B. *A History of Japan 1615–1867*. Stanford, Calif.: Stanford University Press, 1963.

———. *Japan: A Short Cultural History*. New York: Appleton-Century Crofts, 1943.

———. *The Western World and Japan: A Study in the Interaction of European and Asiatic Cultures*. New York: Knopf, 1958.

Satow, E. M. "Ancient Japanese Rituals," *TASJ*, Reprints II, 1927.

———. "The Revival of Pure Shintō." *TASJ*, III, Pt. L. Yokohama, 1875.

Schiffer, Wilhelm, trans. "Taidō wakumon (Es fragte einer nach dem Grossen Weg)." *Monumenta Nipponica* 2, 1 (1939): 212–236.

Shintō jiten. Edited by Kokugakuin daigaku nihon bunka kenkyūjo. Kōbundō, 1999.

Shostak, Marjorie. *Nisa: The Life and Words of a !Kung Woman*. Cambridge, Mass.: Harvard University Press, 1981.

Smith, Jonathan Z. *Imagining Religion: From Babylon to Jonestown*. Chicago: The University of Chicago Press, 1982.

Sources of Japanese Tradition, vol. II. Compiled by Ryusaku Tsunoda, Wm. Theodore de Bary, and Donald Keene. New York: Columbia University Press, 1958.

Stein, Rolf A. *The World in Miniature*. Stanford, Calif.: Stanford University Press, 1990.

Strickmann, Michel. *Chinese Magical Medicine*. Edited by Bernard Faure. Stanford, Calif.: Stanford University Press, 2002.

———. *Chinese Poetry and Prophecy*. Edited by Bernard Faure. Stanford, Calif.: Stanford University Press, 2005.

———. *Mantras et Mandarins: Le bouddhisme tantrique en Chine*. Paris: Gallimard, 1996.

Suzuki Akira. *Sandaikō Suzuki Akira setsu*. Microform copy. Nihon Bungaku Kenkyū Shiryōkan.

Tahara Tsuguo. *Hirata Atsutane*. Jinbutsu sōsho, no. 111. Yoshikawa Kobunkan, 1963.

Tahara Tsuguo et al., eds. *Hirata Atsutane, Ban Nobutomo, Okuni Takamasa.* NST 50. Iwanami Shoten, 1973.

Taira Shigemichi. "Kinsei no shintō shisō." In *Kinsei shintōron zenki kokugaku.* NST 39. Iwanami Shoten, 1972.

Taishō shinshū daizōkyō. Edited by Takakusu Junjirō and Watanabe Kaigyoku. 100 vols. Taishō issaikyō kankōkai, 1924–1932.

Taishō shinshū daizōkyō zuzōbu. Edited by Takakusu Junjirō and Watanabe Kaigyoku. 12 vols. *T.* 86–97. Taishō issaikyō kankōkai, 1924–1932.

Tamamura Sadayoshi. *Motoori Ohira no shōgai.* Kinki bunka-shi sōsho no. 2. Osaka: Kinki Bunka-shi Kankōkai, 1988.

Tanaka Yoshito. *Hirata Atsutane no tetsugaku.* Meiji Shoin, 1944.

———."Ijin Hirata Atsutane." *Tōa no hikari* (1922): 17-1.

Teeuwen, Mark. *Watarai Shinto: An Intellectual History of the Outer Shrine in Ise.* Leiden: CNWS Publications, the Research School CNWS, Leiden University, the Netherlands, 1996.

Teeuwen, Mark, and Fabio Rambelli, eds. *Buddhas and Kami in Japan: Honji Suijaku as a Combinatory Paradigm,* London: RoutledgeCurzon, 2003.

Terada Yasumasa. *Kamo no Mabuchi: shōgai to gyōseki.* Hamamatsu: Hamamatsu Shiseki Chōsa Kenshokai, 1979.

Thal, Sarah. *Rearranging the Landscape of the Gods: The Politics of a Pilgrimage Site in Japan, 1573–1912.* Chicago and London: The University of Chicago Press, 2005.

Togawa Yoshio, Hachiya Kunio, and Mizoguchi Yūzō. *Jukyōshi, Sekai shūkyōshi sōsho 10.* Yamakawa Shuppansha, 1987.

Tsunoda, Ryusaku, Wm. Theodore de Bary, and Donald Keene, comps. *Sources of Japanese Traditon,* vol. 2. New York: Columbia University Press, 1964.

Uchino Gorō. *Edo-ha kokugaku ronkō.* Sōrinsha, 1979.

———. "Hirata-ha to Edo-ha no gakushi-teki tei-i: Atsutane no 'Tamadasuki' wo chūshin ni." *Kokugakuin zasshi* 24, 11 (1973): 12–24.

———. "Norinaga to Atsutane: sono shisō kankei wo meguru mondai." *Kokugakuin zasshi* 66, 12 (1965): 1–17.

Ueda Kenji. "Kada no Azumamaro no shingaku." *Kokugakuin zasshi* 80, 12 (1979): 1–12; 81, 1 (1980): 131–147; 81, 2 (1980): 54–67.

Wakabayashi Haruko. "Tengu zōshi ni miru Kamakura bukkyō no ma to tengu." In *Emaki ni chūsei o yomu,* edited by Gomi Fumihiko and Fujiwara Yoshiaki. Yoshikawa Kobunkan, 1995.

Waley, Arthur. *The Analects of Confucius.* New York: Random House, 1938.

———. *The Way and Its Power: A Study of the Tao Te Ching and Its Place in Chinese Thought.* New York: Houghton Mifflin, 1935.

Walthall, Anne. "Off With Their Heads! The Hirata Disciples and the Ashikaga Shoguns." *Monumenta Nipponica* 50, 2 (1995): 137–170.

————. *The Weak Body of a Useless Woman: Matsuo Taseko and the Meiji Restoration.* Chicago: University of Chicago Press, 1998.

Ware, James R., trans. *Alchemy, Medicine, Religion in the China of A.D. 320: The Nei P'ien of Ko Hung (Pao-p'u tzu)* Cambridge, Mass.: The M.I.T. Press, 1966.

Watanabe Hiroshi. "Michi to miyabi – Norinagagaku to kagakuha kokugaku no seiji shisōshiteki kenkyū." *Kokka Gakkai Zasshi* 87 (1974): 477–561, 647–721; 88 (1975): 238–268, 295–366.

Watanabe Kinzō. *Hirata Atsutane kenkyū.* Rokko Shobo, 1942.

Watanabe Shōichi. "Motoori Norinaga no 'kami no michi' to 'hito no michi': sono kōzō to seikaku ni tsuite." *Kikan Nihon shisōshi* 8 (1978): 89–105.

Watson, Burton, trans. *The Lotus Sutra.* New York: Columbia University Press, 1993.

————. *Ssu-ma Ch'ien Grand Historian of China.* New York: Columbia University Press, 1958.

White, Hayden. *The Content of the Form: Narrative Discourse and Historical Representation.* Baltimore: Johns Hopkins University Press, 1987.

————. *Metahistory: The Historical Imagination in Nineteenth-Century Europe.* Baltimore: Johns Hopkins University Press, 1973.

————. *Tropics of Discourse: Essays in Cultural Criticism.* Baltimore: Johns Hopkins University Press, 1978.

Wigen, Kären. *The Making of a Japanese Periphery, 1750–1920.* Berkeley: University of California Press, 1995.

Winkler, John J. *Auctor & Actor: A Narratological Reading of Apuleius's Golden Ass.* Berkeley and Los Angeles: University of California Press, 1985.

Yamada Kanzo. *Motoori Haruniwa.* Matsusaka: Motoori Norinaga Kinenkan, 1983.

Yamada Yoshio. *Hirata Atsutane.* Hobunkan, 1940.

Yanagita Kunio. "Sanmin no seikatsu." In *Teihon Yanagita Kunio shu,* vol. 4. Chikuma Shobō, 1969.

————. *Teihon Yanagita Kunio shu,* vol. 4. Chikuma Shobō, 1969.

————. "Tōno monogatari." In *Teihon Yanagita Kunio shu,* vol. 4. Chikuma Shobō, 1969.

————. "Yama no jinsei." In *Teihon Yanagita Kunio shu,* vol. 4. Chikuma Shobō, 1969.

————. *Yanagita Kunio zenshū,* vol. 4. Chikuma Shobō, 1989.

————. "Yūmeidan." In *Yanagita Kunio zenshū,* vol. 31. Chikuma Shobō, 1991.

Yasunishi Katsu. *Oyamada Tomokiyo no sōken.* Yokohama: Sometani, 1990.

Yoshida Asako. "Hirata Atsutane no Hitachi · Shimosa hōmon – Bunka 13 nen *Kagushima nikki* to Bunsei 2 nen *Nido no Kashimadachi* o chūshin ni." *Kinsei bungei* (Nihon kinsei bungaku kai) 56, 1999.

————. "Honkoku Hirata Atsutane jishitsu Bunka 13 nen *Kagushima Nikki.*" *Kinsei bungei kenkyū to hyōron* 57, 1999.

————. "Ibukinoya no chojutsu shuppan – shinshutsu *Ibukinoya nikki* o chū-shin ni," *Kinsei bungei* (Nihon kinsei bungaku kai) 75, 2002.

————. "*Inō mononokeroku* no shohon to Hirata Atsutane *Inō mononokeroku* no seiritsu." *Kinsei bungei kenkyū to hyōron* 54, 1998.

Yoshikawa Kojiro et al., eds. *Motoori Norinaga. NST* 40. Iwanami Shoten, 1975.

————, ed. *Motoori Norinaga shū. Nihon no shisō,* 15. Chikuma Shobō, 1969.

Yoshino Hiroko. Yama no kami: Eki, gogyō to nihon genshi hebi shinkō. Jin-bun Shoin, 1989.

Index

About the Author

Wilburn Hansen received his Ph.D. from Stanford University. He has taught at the University of California, Santa Barbara, Western Kentucky University, and is currently assistant professor of Japanese religions at San Diego State University. He has published on ethnography, folklore, and healing. *When Tengu Talk* is his first book.